DATE			

Public Broadcasting

George H. Gibson

Public Broadcasting

The Role of the Federal
Government, 1912-76

Praeger Publishers   New York   London

Library of Congress Cataloging in Publication Data

Gibson, George H   1932–
    Public broadcasting.

    (Praeger special studies in U.S. economic, social,
and political issues)
    Includes index.
    1. Radio programs, Public service. 2. Television
programs, Public service. 3. Broadcasting policy—
United States. I. Title.
HE8689.8.G5   1977   384.54'53   77-24422
ISBN 0-03-022831-X

PRAEGER SPECIAL STUDIES
200 Park Avenue, New York, N.Y., 10017, U.S.A.

Published in the United States of America in 1977
by Praeger Publishers,
A Division of Holt, Rinehart and Winston, CBS, Inc.

789   038   987654321

© 1977 by Praeger Publishers

Printed in the United States of America

For Judy and our two sons, Hank and Peter

CONTENTS

LIST OF ACRONYMS

ABC	American Broadcasting Company
ACER	Advisory Committee on Education by Radio
ACNO	Advisory Committee of National Organizations
ACUBS	Association of College and University Broadcasting Stations
AM	Amplitude Modulation
AT&T	American Telephone and Telegraph Company
CBS	Columbia Broadcasting System
COMSAT	Communications Satellite Corporation
CPB	Corporation for Public Broadcasting
CPT	Corporation for Public Television
ERP	Educational Radio Project
ETS	Educational Television Stations
FCC	Federal Communications Commission
FM	Frequency Modulation
FRC	Federal Radio Commission
FREC	Federal Radio Education Committee
ICC	Interstate Commerce Commission
IER	Institute for Education by Radio
IERT	Institute for Education by Radio and Television
ITFS	Instructional Television Fixed Service
JCET	Joint Committee on Educational Television
JRP	Joint Radio Project
NAB	National Association of Broadcasters
NACRE	National Advisory Council for Radio in Education
NAEB	National Association of Educational Broadcasters
NBC	National Broadcasting Company
NCER	National Committee on Education by Radio
NEA	National Endowment for the Arts
NEH	National Endowment for the Humanities
NET	National Educational Television
NPACT	National Public Affairs Broadcasting Center for Public Television
NPR	National Public Radio
OE	Office of Education
OMB	Office of Management and Budget
OTM	Office of Telecommunications Management
OTP	Office of Telecommunications Policy
PBL	Public Broadcasting Laboratory
PBS	Public Broadcasting Service
RCA	Radio Corporation of America
RMA	Radio Manufacturers Association
TASO	Television Allocations Study Organization

UHF   Ultra High Frequency
VHF   Very High Frequency

Federal policies toward noncommercial or public broadcasting were developed after intensive study and probing debate. They are the result of a gradual and evolutionary process begun about 1912. Individual educators and groups of educational broadcasters have profoundly influenced and significantly reinforced government action. Yet it is the federal government—through its appointed, elected, and employed officials—that created the public broadcasting industry out of a largely nonpartisan commitment to education and concern for the general welfare of the American people.

The secretary of commerce in the 1920s tried to establish order in the radio spectrum and to protect the interests of weak stations, including those of educators. Herbert Hoover brought broadcasters together in a series of conferences in an attempt to marshal support for the idea that broadcasters regulate themselves and, in so doing, prevent educators with poor equipment, low power, and inadequate personnel and financing from being driven from the airwaves.

The Federal Communications Commission in 1938, 1940, 1945, and 1952 reserved portions of the spectrum for the exclusive use of noncommercial educational broadcasters. On its own initiative, it reserved AM radio channels; with little initial enthusiasm or interest on the part of educators, it reserved FM radio channels; and after counseling noncommercial broadcasters in the art of influencing regulatory agencies, it reserved television channels for educational purposes. Commissioners fostered cooperation between commercial and educational interests, advised on the importance of establishing educational FM stations, dogged broadcasters into creating educational television, and sponsored Instructional Television Fixed Service.

Commissioners of education provided influential leadership and much needed services to educational radio and television. They testified on behalf of reserving channels and brought in educators to do likewise. They used federal funds to produce programs, established a script and transcription exchange, and provided technical assistance to help new stations get on the air.

Congress granted funds for research and dissemination of information regarding educational broadcasting through the National Defense Education Act, established a multitude of educational assistance programs with broadcasting components during the Kennedy and Johnson eras, and appropriated $1 million to each state to construct and equip educational radio and television stations (and then extended the legislation to provide additional millions). Congressional committees guarded the interest of educators from commercial and government foes.

The Department of Health, Education and Welfare skillfully administered the programs that Congress had established for educational broadcasting and spent millions of dollars in discretionary funds to create radio and television broadcasts for children and adults.

Presidents supported this activity, and in 1967, Lyndon B. Johnson proposed legislation to found the quasi-governmental Corporation for Public Broadcasting. Building on studies and suggestions made by the prestigious Ford Foundation and Carnegie Commission on Educational Television, the proposal initiated a new era in the management of public broadcasting and annual funding for national program production and local station operating expenses.

Congress rode out Richard M. Nixon's attempt to choke public affairs broadcasting thought to be inimical to the administration and to establish the corporation as an extension of the White House. After Nixon's resignation, the House and Senate provided funding for public broadcasting three years in advance so as to insulate it from further governmental interference.

Opportunities and concerns still confront the industry, but the federal government has shown that it is firmly committed to what it has created and that it will continue to work to meet these challenges with imagination.

This book, then, chronicles the expansion of the role of the federal government in noncommercial educational broadcasting since about 1912 and describes in detail the work that presidents, members of Congress and the Federal Communications Commission, commissioners of education, the Department of Health, Education and Welfare, foundations, and educational broadcasters have done at the federal level to make public radio and television broadcasting a fundamental institution in American culture.

The author has based this study on an extensive examination of public documents: reports of conferences; annual and special reports of the Federal Radio Commission, the Federal Communications Commission, the Commissioner of Education, and the Department of Health, Education and Welfare; the Congressional Record; Senate and House of Representatives hearings and reports; and published papers of the presidents. He has also made thorough use of that great newspaper of public record, the New York Times, from 1912 to 1977. In completing the study, he read widely among the books and periodicals pertinent to the field and conducted several personal interviews.

The study was begun as a doctoral dissertation in history under the direction of Fletcher M. Green at the University of North Carolina at Chapel Hill. It was completed during a sabbatical leave granted by the University of Delaware in 1976.

Public Broadcasting

1

THE SECRETARY OF COMMERCE AND THE FEDERAL RADIO COMMISSION

DEVELOPMENT OF RADIO AS AN EDUCATIONAL TOOL

The Italian inventor Guglielmo Marconi built a crude induction coil in 1895 by which he produced signals that were received without wires about 1,200 feet from the coil. He traveled to England the next year and obtained the first patent for a radio device. News of Marconi's feat spread quickly through scientific channels to the United States.

In 1896, W. M. White, a Tulane University student, repeated the Marconi experiments. During the same year, experimenters at Wittenberg College in Ohio transmitted in code across their physics laboratory and into other rooms. Ohio State, and the universities of Arkansas, Nebraska, Minnesota and Wisconsin, as well as other universities, established radio laboratories. Experimental work in radio spread rapidly to college physics and electricity laboratories throughout the United States. Radio became a subject of research for faculty and students alike. For the application of principles of physics, radio became an important teaching device. Transmitters were available in science laboratories, and because transmitter operators were science students, their transmissions were the coded jargon, gibberish, and esoteric jokes of laboratory periods. In 1906, Cornell University offered credit courses in communications engineering and radio code.[1] Not until 1920, following the advent of voice transmission, did it occur to educators that the phenomenon of radio might be usable by the entire school for the benefit of the whole community.

GOVERNMENT REGULATION OF RADIO
COMMUNICATIONS

Any group or individual could participate in the novelty of code broadcasting. There were no rules or regulations with which to comply. The Wireless Ship Act, the first law dealing with radio, was passed in the summer of 1910. Congressional interest was only in the safety of ship passengers at sea. The law required all ships of U.S. registry carrying 50 or more passengers and crew to be equipped with a radio apparatus capable of transmitting and receiving code for 100 miles. The secretary of commerce and labor (secretary of commerce after 1913) was responsible for administering the law.[2]

In 1912, the Senate began hearings on a bill concerning interstate radio communications. From the start, it was recognized that all radio transmissions were interstate broadcasts. The legislators viewed radio as an "unfulfilled promise" of some years' standing and framed a law dealing with radio as it had developed in 1912. They intended to make adjustments in the law as radio developed.[3] The Radio Act, passed by Congress in 1912, was the first act regarding interstate communication by radio. It required that all transmitters and transmitter operators be licensed by the secretary of commerce and labor. So that there would be no interference with government ship-to-shore stations, the act required interstate broadcasters to operate on channels unassigned to government stations.[4] Whereas the Radio Act of 1912 contained all the rules for broadcasting, laws were later enacted establishing agencies to make discretionary rulings.

GOVERNMENT LICENSING POWER

The secretary of commerce and labor asked the attorney general for an interpretation of the licensing power. Attorney General George W. Wickersham ruled that the issuance of a license was mandatory if the applicant were a citizen of the United States and if he agreed to broadcast in the channels provided by Congress.[5] In essence, Congress established an office for the perfunctory issuance and registration of licenses. In addition, Congress reserved to itself the right to assign radio channels.

The secretary of commerce and labor issued the first experimental license to St. Joseph's College in Philadelphia in 1912 and issued the first code-broadcasting license to the Philadelphia School of Wireless Telegraphy in the same year. Having been among the first experimenters with radio, college physics and electricity laboratories were among the first licensed stations. College stations experimented with radio transmissions in signals other than code. The University of Wisconsin originated the first music broadcast in 1917 and received an experimental license, 9XM, in 1919.[6]

During World War I, important technical improvements made in radio communications bode well for the rapid development of broadcasting after the war. C. M. Jansky, a radio inventor and college teacher, felt that in the postwar expansion of broadcasting, educational institutions would continue to play a very important part.[7]

EARLY BROADCASTING STATIONS

One of the stations to begin operations after the war was KDKA in Pittsburgh. On October 27, 1920, KDKA received a commercial license for a code transmitter and authority to experiment with voice transmission for one year. On November 2, 1920, KDKA broadcast the Harding–Cox election returns. This use of voice radio transmission for informational purposes received widespread publicity. Radio as an educational, informational, and entertainment device caught the imagination of the public. Radio was about to leave the laboratory to enter the home.

WBZ, in Springfield, Massachusetts, received the first regular broadcast license on September 15, 1921, and KDKA got a regular broadcast license later in the year. The Latter Day Saints University, in Salt Lake City, Utah, acquired a broadcast license for KFOO in 1921 also, but the exact date does not appear in the records. On January 13, 1922, the universities of Wisconsin and Minnesota had their licenses changed from experimental to regular broadcast. A total of 72 other educational institutions received broadcast licenses in 1922. The next year, 39 colleges and universities were licensed, and 34 were licensed in 1924.[8]

KDKA's performance awakened some educators to the potentialities of radio as a means of broadening their educational services. No longer was radio only an instrument in the physics laboratory. In the educator's dreams, radio became an instrument for the dissemination of knowledge. Educational institutions, as the storehouses of knowledge, were obviously well equipped to render an important service through radio. Some thought radio would surpass the printing press as a transmitter of educational matter.

To bring their dreams to fruition, colleges broadcast from stadiums, auditoriums, and lecture halls. They offered sporting events for public relations and publicity, dramas and concerts for adult entertainment and education, and complete courses for college credit. In many institutions, however, only a few teachers and

administrators realized the capabilities of radio for education and
were enthusiastic about its use. Some teachers feared technological
unemployment, while most damned radio with their indifference.

NEED FOR GOVERNMENT TO REGULATE
BROADCASTING

Hundreds of new stations were licensed and began broadcasting
in 1922. Secretary of Commerce Herbert Hoover was doubtful of
his power under the Radio Act of 1912 to control this unprecedented
growth. Sensing the potential problems of unregulated broadcasting,
Hoover took the initiative and called a public conference to study the
problems of unrestricted broadcasting, to make recommendations
for the extension of the regulatory powers of the government, and
to draft technical provisions for model legislation to be submitted
to Congress.[9]

Hoover realized that the then current federal policy of perfunctory licensing and registration would be inadequate as radio broadcasting reached boom proportions. He acted to make it relatively
easy for Congress to redeem its pledge to adopt a new policy when
radio developed new applications.

The First National Radio Conference met in Washington, D.C.,
in February 1922. Hoover asked the members of the conference to
discover broad areas of general agreement among themselves and
to establish fundamental principles of broadcasting that might be
useful to Congress in framing new legislation to cope with the bur-
geoning conditions in radio. Accordingly, the conference enunciated
three fundamental tenets of American broadcasting: that the radio
channels belonged to the public; that licensed privately owned transmitters could use the channels in the public interest; and that the
federal government should regulate the licensees to prevent interference.[10]

The conferees believed that broadcasting would develop four
classes of broadcasters: government, public, private, and toll.
Government stations were already in existence for the protection of
life at sea and were beyond the scope of prospective regulation.
Public stations would be licensed to public and educational institutions for the dissemination of informational and educational programs.
Private broadcasters would use radio for commercial point-to-point
communication. Although commercially sponsored broadcasts did
not begin until September 1922, the conferees foresaw this development in what they called toll broadcasts.[11]

No one at the conference knew where radio was going or how far
Congress would let it go, but there was general agreement that educa-

tional institutions would be there wherever it went. During this conference and others to follow, Herbert Hoover stressed the importance of radio as an educational medium and the necessity of providing for stations whose primary objective was education.[12] Having established fundamental principles and directions for broadcasting, the conference adjourned, confidently expecting Congress to establish a new federal policy for broadcasting, but Congress took no positive action.[13]

In the summer of 1922, when the department of commerce refused to license a radio station because its apparatus would interfere with an existing station, the rejected licensee took its case to court. By its decision in 1923, a federal court ruled that under the Radio Act of 1912, the secretary of commerce had no authority to refuse a broadcasting license to a citizen of the United States for any reason whatsoever.[14] New stations continued to go on the air, and the problem of interference became critical.

Hoover anxiously waited for Congress to act. A mildly regulatory bill was passed by the House of Representatives, but the bill was not reported out of the Senate committee.[15] As even more stations began to broadcast and conditions became chaotic, Secretary Hoover called another conference to meet in March 1923.

Because the courts declared that the secretary of commerce had no authority to limit the number of radio licensees and because Congress had provided no regulatory legislation, Hoover simply asked broadcasters at the Second National Radio Conference to regulate themselves. The conference members expected Congress to pass legislation that might possibly upset any of their efforts to regulate themselves, but they nevertheless accepted the responsibility of self-regulation and attacked the problem of radio interference. When the number of stations and the amount of transmission power were small, the secretary of commerce had assigned two channels for broadcasters, but interference was too great with only two channels as the number of stations and amount of power increased. The conference devised the scheme of assigning one channel to each station, but before implementing the plan, it decided to wait for congressional action and adjourned.[16]

Radio companies having enough power to drown out less powerful stations feared that government regulation might deprive them of their favorable position in the radio industry. They were able to bring enough political pressure to bear to prevent passage of a radio law before Congress adjourned in June 1924.[17]

GOVERNMENT REGULATION OF BROADCASTING

Hoover convened the Third National Radio Conference on October 6, 1924, and the group took immediate steps to implement the

plan devised at the previous conference. It established radio broadcasting on 96 channels between 550 and 1,550 kilocycles. Six channels
were allotted to Canadian stations. The conference asked Herbert
Hoover to assign the channels and then adjourned.[18]

In response to the request of the self-regulated broadcasters,
Hoover assigned a particular channel to each station. Since there
were more stations than channels, Hoover attempted to accommodate
all of them by requiring power restrictions and time division, so
that more than one station could operate on the same channel.[19]
When Congress bogged down in its radio hearings, Hoover withdrew
his support from the bills before Congress and waited one year to
evaluate the effectiveness of self-regulation.[20]

The Fourth National Radio Conference met in Washington, D.C.,
November 9-11, 1925. Among the 400 persons attending the conference were many educational broadcasters. Educational institutions
held 129 broadcasting licenses in 1925, more than in any previous
or subsequent year. The idea of using radio to supplement the school
curriculum and augment the service of education to the community
had spread rapidly. Educational broadcasters had a great vision,
but they often lacked the talent or the technique to develop interesting
programs. Many stations lacked sufficient financial support to offer
a regular schedule of programs or to replace outmoded equipment.
Competition from commercial stations cut deeply into their audiences.
Educational broadcasting was not living up to its great expectations.
Educational broadcasters felt frustrated and cheated somehow of
what they thought was their birthright to radio, and they wanted something done about it.

Those demanding the most positive action were broadcasters
from midwestern agricultural colleges. More than $100 million was
spent annually on agricultural research, and these broadcasters had
pinned great hopes on radio as a means of disseminating information
to farmers. They were losing their audiences to commercial stations,
and their stations were being restricted in power and broadcast time
to make room for new commercial stations. They demanded full
recognition by the Department of Commerce of the needs of their
services, and they demanded that adequate, definite, and specific
provisions be made for these services in the broadcasting band.[21]

A group of educational broadcasters, mainly from the agricultural
colleges, met separately during the conference and organized the
Association of College and University Broadcasting Stations (ACUBS).[22]
Their initial effort was to present their demands to the conference
in the form of a resolution and to put pressure on the Department of
Commerce to get the special consideration they desired.

The most pressing problem for all the radio broadcasters at the
conference was the number of stations on the air. There were 578

stations licensed, and there were 175 applications pending. The only way to accommodate these stations was to increase the number of channels or to restrict further time and power. The number of channels could not be increased without disturbing old services, and new channels could not be received on standard radios. The only solution was to restrict broadcasting, an action that would result in more limited service from each station. Since neither proposal satisfied the broadcasters and since the self-regulators were unwilling to make a decisive move, they appealed to Congress to settle their dilemma through legislation.[23] Only in desperate situations do businessmen ask the federal government to regulate their activities. The situation soon became even more desperate.

In consonance with the 1924 request of the self-regulators, the Department of Commerce limited the Zenith Radio Corporation to two hours of broadcast time from its Chicago station. When the station ignored the limitation and began broadcasting on a Canadian channel, the Department of Commerce brought criminal action against Zenith. A federal court dismissed the case on a technicality but added that the department's action to restrict channels and hours of operation might be unconstitutional, since the action had no basis in law.[24]

The court rendered its decision in April 1926, and Hoover asked the attorney general for an opinion. Acting Attorney General William J. Donovan replied that the secretary of commerce had no authority to determine or restrict channels, time, or power.[25]

On July 9, 1926, the day after Donovan's decision, all self-imposed restraints were cast aside as the self-regulators engaged in an orgy of broadcasting with unlimited time, unlimited power, unlimited channel shifts, and unlimited interference. The Department of Commerce once again became only a license registration bureau. Self-regulation had ceased. All radio regulation was abandoned, and the public was abandoning radio. The sale of radio receivers dropped significantly as the public showed its disgust with the confusion in the radio industry and the interference on the radio band.

Secretary of Commerce Hoover had so thoroughly convinced President Calvin Coolidge of the necessity for congressional action to regulate radio that in his annual message delivered in December 1926, Coolidge urgently recommended that Congress speedily enact radio regulation.[26] Congressmen also knew from the large number of irate letters from their radio-listening constituents that they must take action.

Congressional action was slow; however, it was not from a lack of desire but from a lack of understanding of radio terminology and technological advances. It was the final realization of their inability

to cope with the details of regulating a multifaceted industry that
persuaded them to establish an independent agency to regulate radio
on general instructions laid down by Congress.

The decision to delegate authority did not come easily for Congress. The House radio bill retained the secretary of commerce as
the licensing authority and established a Federal Radio Commission
(FRC) to review his decisions. The Senate bill provided for a permanent radio commission to regulate the medium entirely. The final
decision was a compromise. The conference bill instituted a temporary commission to establish order in the radio industry. After one
year, the regulatory authority was to revert to the secretary of
commerce, and the commission was to be retained as an appellate
body. During the first year, the FRC was charged to reduce interference by assigning channels, time, and power.[27]

It was more difficult for Congress to establish a commission
than to lay down instructions for the commission's actions. Congress
simply borrowed an amorphous phrase from nineteenth-century state
public utility laws and from the Transportation Act of 1920. Congress
instructed the FRC to regulate radio "in the public interest, convenience, and necessity."[28]

While the legislators were hammering out the details of the law,
educational broadcasters sought to have their special interests safe-
guarded. The ACUBS and the land grant colleges had some farm
bloc support for two proposals. The association suggested that the
FRC be instructed to give due regard to the needs of college stations
when it assigned channels, hours, and power. ACUBS Secretary
J. C. Jensen explained that channels assigned to college stations
were so crowded that satisfactory broadcasting was hopeless. Since
educational stations had neither the time nor the money to challenge
the commercial stations that were crowding them off the air, they
asked for special consideration from the FRC.[29] Congress refused
to make this proposal part of its instructions to the FRC. Those
congressmen interested in educational broadcasting thought the proposal had already been covered in the phrase "public interest, convenience, and necessity."

The land grant colleges proposed that Congress assign a block
of channels to the states so that the state universities might broadcast farm information without the threat of interference from commercial stations.[30] The House radio bill allotted one channel to each
state to be used by the land grant colleges under the control of the
secretary of commerce, and the Senate bill provided for one channel
for each state under the control of the FRC. The Senate and House
conferees were responsive to the aims of noncommercial educational
agricultural broadcasters, but they feared what the precedent might
mean.[31] Dozens of special interest groups were ready to press their

claims if the land grant colleges were successful; therefore, the conferees instructed the FRC only in general terms.[32]

Congress passed the Radio Act of 1927 on February 23.[33] President Coolidge appointed William H. G. Bullard, retired naval officer; Orestes H. Caldwell, editor of a radio publication; Henry A. Bellows, director of a radio station; Eugene O. Sykes, Mississippi supreme court justice; and John F. Dillon, radio engineer, to serve on the FRC.[34]

The FRC received less than the wholehearted support of Congress. The Senate confirmed only three of the five commissioners before adjournment. By November 1927, two commissioners had died and one had resigned. The House failed to make an appropriation for the FRC, and only through the generous support of the Department of Commerce was the FRC able to pay salaries and assemble a staff.[35] In this atmosphere of uncertainty, the FRC began the Herculean task of creating order in radio broadcasting.

There were 725 existing licensees, but the FRC believed there was room for only 240 stations. The obvious solution was to reduce the number of stations; however, without an adequate staff and with only one year in which to accomplish its task, the FRC feared that such action would involve it in endless litigation and that nothing would be accomplished. Effective June 15, 1927, the FRC adopted an allocation plan accommodating all 725 licensees by increasing the number of channels and restricting time and power. The commission then began hearings to revoke the licenses of the weakest stations.[36]

PLIGHT OF EDUCATIONAL STATIONS

To accomplish its mission, the FRC needed the cooperation of the powerful radio interests, and it acquired this cooperation by assigning favorable channels and hours to the large stations. Educational stations, with old equipment, poor programs, and uncertain schedules, received little consideration in the allocation of channels, time, and power. Since 1925, the number of educational institutions holding licenses had dropped more than 20 percent, and educational broadcasters feared FRC weeding-out procedures would annihilate noncommercial educational broadcasting altogether. To survive, educational broadcasters felt that their service needed protection, and they appealed to the FRC and to Congress.

Charles A. Culver, president of the ACUBS, addressed an appeal to the FRC. He urged the commission to give special consideration to college stations and suggested that this be done by placing six or eight college stations on one channel and by letting the colleges work

out their own schedule for broadcasting farm extension and general
educational material. He reminded the FRC that the college stations
had no revenue from advertising and broadcast only programs of
special value to the public.[37]

Secretary of Agriculture William M. Jardine, former president
of Kansas State Agricultural College, wrote to the FRC toward the
end of 1927. He cited the splendid and valuable services of college
stations, particularly to the farm community, and asked, once again,
for protection and special consideration for these stations. He suggested that to provide this protection, the FRC should refuse the use
of channels or the increase of power to stations interfering with farm
programs from agricultural colleges.[38]

Representatives of the Association of Land Grant Colleges met
informally with the FRC in January 1928. When asked to make power,
time, and channel assignments favorable to land grant college stations,
the FRC replied that it was sympathetic with the objectives of educational stations and would be glad to make all possible adjustments in
the case of specific complaints of interference with educational stations. But the broadcasters had neither the time nor the money to
appear at the hearings required to make the adjustment. When asked
to reserve at least one channel in each state for education, the FRC
replied that such action was beyond the power of the FRC and that
the educational broadcasters should properly make such a request
to Congress.[39]

In 1928, Congress debated extending the authority of the FRC
for another year. Many congressmen thought the FRC was creating
a radio monopoly by catering to the powerful radio stations. Some
congressmen thought the FRC was destroying noncommercial educational broadcasting. Representative Ewin L. Davis felt that the
commission had misinterpreted the public interest clause, and he
attempted to redefine the clause by amending the bill to continue the
authority of the FRC. The Davis amendment directed the FRC to
equalize geographically the assignment of channels, time, and power.
But reducing the large number of powerful stations in metropolitan
areas and by increasing the time and power of small stations throughout the United States, Davis said his amendment would make available
more local addresses and entertainment and end discrimination
against nonprofit stations and noncommercial educational stations.[40]
Educational broadcasters gave their wholehearted support to the
amendment and gave thanks when Congress passed the amended bill.[41]

Knowing that the Davis amendment required them to perform a
hopeless, thankless task, the FRC paid only lip service to the law.
The FRC felt that geographical redistribution would destroy the radio
industry, not equalize it. Still, uncertainty of tenure and complete
dependence on Congress for its existence made the FRC a timid

agency, sensitive to congressional criticism and appeals. Aware of congressional interests in educational broadcasting, the FRC decided to reevaluate its policy toward that interest.

In its second annual report, the commission stated that there was no room in the broadcast band for every school of religious, political, social and economic thought to have its separate broadcasting station, for if the license to broadcast were extended to every group with a specialized audience, there would be no room for licensees of general public service stations.[42] Although it did not feel any obligation to give special consideration to educational stations, the FRC did feel the responsibility to encourage more educational programming on the general public interest stations.

Commissioner Bullard, in a speech to the National Association of Broadcasters (NAB), urged commercial broadcasters to increase the number of educational and instructional programs emanating from their stations. Observing that educational programs did not receive the attention they deserved, Bullard appealed to commercial broadcasters to develop educational programs that would arouse the general public interest and to produce programs usable in the public schools.[43]

The National Broadcasting Company (NBC) and the Columbia Broadcasting System (CBS) were amenable to Bullard's suggestion. The NBC Advisory Council, composed of leaders in the fields of education, music, agriculture, religion, and labor, increased its efforts to stimulate educational and cultural programs. CBS initiated the National Radio Assembly in cooperation with the National Education Association (NEA) to present programs of high quality concerning history, civics, music, art, drama, and health for school audiences.[44]

Educators, who had been cooperating with local stations and national networks in the production of educational programs on a limited basis over a period of years, were pleased with the FRC attempts to stimulate the broader use of their services. Educators associated with college broadcasting stations were incensed at being denied special consideration and special channels and for being snubbed by the FRC. A smoldering mutual distrust between educators who cooperated with commercial stations and educators who associated with college stations was soon to break out in the open.

Secretary of the Interior Ray Lyman Wilbur, on leave of absence from his responsibilities as president of Stanford University, called a conference, to meet in his office in May 1929, to discuss the potentialities of radio education and the role of the federal government in developing these potentialities. In a preconference interview, Wilbur attempted to establish a conciliatory atmosphere for conflicting interests when he declared that just what percentage of the radio band should be devoted to education was beyond the ken of man but that a proportion of it should be used for education was self-evident.[45]

Opening the conference, Wilbur noted the general interest of educators, broadcasters, manufacturers, and the public at large in the possibilities of radio as an educational tool. Educators cooperating with commercial stations approved when he observed that radio was being used for entertainment and amusement and wanted to know what could be done for education and culture. He was applauded by college broadcasters when he asked whether true educational principles could be adopted when the expense of radio transmission was borne by advertisers.[46]

FRC Commissioner Ira Robinson disapproved of network commercialism. A former law school lecturer, he personally favored a radio university operating over a number of channels specifically reserved for education. H. Robinson Shiperd, of the NEA radio committee, supported the radio university proposal. Commissioner Sykes expressed the view that the networks had done promising work in education and would do more if educators would assist them. Sykes declared that purely educational programs were not practical because they could not hold the audience; he added that it was impractical to disassociate educational broadcasting from commercial stations. Representatives of NBC and CBS seconded Sykes's position and reviewed their contributions to education. Everett Case, secretary of the NBC Advisory Council, said the networks would provide the facilities if the educators would supply the programs.[47]

The conference did little more than state the existing conflicting opinions but before adjournment voted unanimously to ask Secretary Wilbur to appoint a fact-finding committee to investigate further the possibilities of radio education. Consequently, on June 6, Wilbur appointed the Advisory Committee on Education by Radio (ACER).

The ACER held an organizational meeting in Chicago in June 1929 and divided into four subcommittees. The fact-finding subcommittee was asked to investigate educational programs, methods, and costs and to prepare a report. The research subcommittee was asked to perform research in the possibilities for further utilization of radio for education, measure the accomplishments of past performances, study broadcasting techniques, and seek the cooperation of authorities broadcasting educational programs. The finance subcommittee was responsible for getting $25,000 to finance the committee's work, and the executive subcommittee was to correlate the reports and recommendations for the whole committee.

On November 6, the fact-finding subcommittee met and reported the results of its investigations. It found widespread interest in radio education and noted considerable progress, especially in Ohio and California. It had gathered much factual information on programs from questionnaires returned from the 77 educational stations on the air and from many colleges that broadcast over commercial stations.

The subcommittee recommended that channels be reserved for education, and, specifically, for a radio university, which would combine the talents and finances of the nation's colleges in one program service.

The full committee met in December and heard all the reports and recommendations. The subcommittees had gathered a large amount of information on radio education by college stations and through commercial facilities. Armstrong Perry concluded his report to the full committee by stating that educators must arrive at a consensus, formulate a plan of action, and seek federal assistance or else broadcasting facilities and educational broadcasting would fall under the control of businessmen rather than professional educators.

The subcommittees recommended that channels for educational broadcasting be reserved, a radio university established, congressional appropriations for radio education work by the U.S. Office of Education (OE), a permanent advisory committee on radio education in the OE, private foundation support for educational programs, and that letters be written to the FRC, urging the importance of radio education, and to the president of the United States, outlining the need for members of the FRC who were sympathetic to radio education. The presidents of CBS and NBC rejected the recommendations, and a long hassle followed. The ACER finally agreed to appoint a subcommittee to prepare a final report without recommendations.

On February 15, 1930, the ACER presented its final report to Secretary Wilbur. The report was only a list of advantages and disadvantages of educational broadcasting.[48]

As a result of this series of meetings and reports, the OE, in 1930, appointed Perry and, in 1931, Cline M. Koon as specialists in radio education. They were instructed to initiate and conduct research studies of radio as an educational agency, to organize and maintain an informational and advisory service to schools and other agencies interested in education by radio, to become familiar with college and university extension work, to evaluate radio as an educational tool, and to prepare for publication material on various phases of education by radio.[49]

A committee of the American Association for Adult Education met in New York on November 18, 1929, to discuss the action of the subcommittee of the ACER on November 6. Most efforts at adult education by radio had been made through commercial stations, and the committee was concerned that the attitude of some ACER members might alienate the commercial broadcasters. The committee expressed its appreciation to the networks for their cooperation in furthering the cause of education by radio. It declared that the commercial broadcasters and educators had the same principles and that further cooperation between the two groups would bring steady and continuous improvement in the quality of radio.

The committee met again in January 1930, after the explosive December 30 meeting of the ACER, and reaffirmed its dedication to cooperation with commercial broadcasters. The committee authorized Levering Tyson to make a study of the need for a national organization to promote cooperation between commercial broadcasters and educators. Tyson's report affirmed the need for such an organization. Consequently, in May, a 50-member National Advisory Council for Radio in Education (NACRE) was appointed. Provision was made for regional and local councils throughout the United States. An advisory and informational service was established at the New York headquarters of the organization, with Tyson as director. The Rockefeller Foundation and the Carnegie Corporation financed the NACRE.[50]

Tyson announced three primary objectives for the organization: to develop programs and bring them to the microphone; to secure broadcasting facilities from educational and commercial stations; and to measure the effectiveness of the program. The NACRE appointed committees in every major field of learning to develop program material and planned to cooperate with colleges, schools, and networks, stations, governments, and civic organizations in getting the programs on the air. The NACRE appointed an analyst in each state to examine and report on broadcasting in his area. It also planned to conduct research and act as a clearinghouse for information and statistics. The NACRE wanted to make known by conference, publication, and lecture the educational opportunities in radio.[51]

The NACRE held five annual assemblies. Five hundred persons attended the first assembly, which met in New York, May 21-23, 1931. Among other speakers, the conferees heard the president of the United States and the secretary of the interior. Each assembly attracted notables among educators who used commercial facilities, executives of networks, and a small number of educators who had their own facilities.[52]

Ohio used radio extensively in school classrooms. Leaders in educational broadcasting in Ohio observed the growing division among educators over the means of broadcasting but felt that common ground existed among all educational broadcasters, whether they used commercial facilities or operated their own stations. They founded the Institute for Education by Radio (IER) and called a conference of this organization in Columbus, Ohio, in 1930.[53]

This conference failed to pass any resolutions nor did it count noses on controversial issues. E. L. Bushnell recalled presiding over groups viewing each other with suspicion and distaste. He

asked educators and broadcasters to quit bickering among themselves
and join together in their larger objectives. He felt that broadcasters,
educators, and the public would benefit from such dedication. The
1930 conference, as well as each succeeding conference, concentrated
on techniques and objectives of educational broadcasting. The exchange of ideas through technical reports and program demonstrations
and the sharing of goals and dreams through formal addresses and
informal conversation at least kept the warring factions on speaking
terms.[54]

William J. Cooper, U.S. commissioner of education, called a
meeting of former ACER members actively interested in institutionally
owned and operated stations and committed to the proposition that a
percentage of radio channels be reserved for education. The meeting
was held in Chicago in 1930. Since 1925, the number of licenses
held by educational institutions had been cut in half, and the group
decided that a national organization was necessary to protect educational stations from extinction. This group organized the National
Committee on Education by Radio (NCER), which held its first meeting in Washington, D.C., in December 1930. Members included
directors of educational broadcasting stations, presidents of state
universities, representatives of state departments of education, and
officers of national education associations. Among the strongest
supporters of the NCER were representatives of agricultural colleges,
who for some years had sought legislation from Congress or rulings
from the FRC to obtain assignment of definite channels to educational
institutions, and, especially, land grant colleges, for educational
broadcasting. Now the proposal had wider support. The conferees
decided to seek 15 percent of all channels for the exclusive use of
educational institutions. To this end, the NCER obtained a five-year
foundation grant to conduct research and experimentation, establish
an information service, institute a service bureau to advise and
protect educational stations, and publish a bulletin.[55]

Joy Elmer Morgan, director of the NCER and editor of the
Journal of the National Education Association, used his wide contacts
to warn educators of the threat to educational stations and to spread
the idea that a reservation of 15 percent of radio channels would
effectively turn back the threat. He took advantage of a wave of
indignation at the rise of commercialism in broadcasting and sought
to merge the two forces of protest. The National Congress of Parents
and Teachers, however, went far beyond Morgan's suggestion and
passed a resolution favoring public ownership and control of radio
broadcasting to eliminate commercial advertising in radio operations.[56]

Charles Saltzman, FRC chairman, urged college broadcasters
to appeal to Congress for help. In an address to the American

Association of Agricultural College Editors, Saltzman said the FRC
was sympathetic with the aims of educational broadcasters and wanted
to aid in the development of radio education. Under existing law,
however, the FRC was required to treat all stations alike and could
give no special consideration to college stations in allocating channels.
If educators wanted 15 percent of the radio channels, they should get
them from Congress.[57]

The NCER addressed an open letter to Congress, appealing for
independence and freedom for education on the air. The letter claimed
that the control of broadcasting by commercial interests had trans-
formed the air waves into "the dollar sign's mightiest megaphone."
It described the Radio Corporation of America (RCA) as a selfish
organization that would exclude all others from the field of broadcasting. It described the FRC as generally ineffective and urged
Congress to pass legislation to preserve a percentage of radio channels for educational broadcasting.[58]

NOTES

1. S. E. Frost, Jr., Is American Radio Democratic? (Chicago:
University of Chicago Press, 1937), pp. 212-14 (hereafter cited as
Frost, American Radio).

2. Public Law 61-262.

3. Senate, Report 62-698.

4. Public Law 62-264.

5. Opinions of the Attorneys General, XXIX, 579.

6. Frank Ernest Hill, Listen and Learn (New York: American
Association for Adult Education, 1937), pp. 16, 17; House of Representatives, Report 94-245, part I.

7. C. M. Jansky, The Problem of the Institutionally Owned
Station (1933), p. 214 (hereafter cited as Jansky, Institutionally
Owned Station).

8. Frost, American Radio, pp. 215, 216.

9. Department of Commerce, Annual Report of the Secretary
of Commerce, vol. 11 (Washington, D.C.: U.S. Government Printing Office, 1923), pp. 13, 14.

10. Department of Commerce, Minutes of the Open Meeting of
the Department of Commerce Conference on Radio Telephony,
mimeographed (1922).

11. Jansky, Institutionally Owned Station , pp. 216, 217.

12. C. M. Jansky, "Contributions of Herbert Hoover to Broadcasting," Journal of Broadcasting 1 (1957): 242.

13. Congressional Record, LXVIII, 2571.

14. Hoover v. Intercity Radio Company, 286 Fed 1003 (1922),
266 U.S. 636 (1923).

15. Congressional Record, LXVIII, 2572.

16. Department of Commerce, Annual Report of the Secretary of Commerce, vol. 12 (Washington, D.C.: U.S. Government Printing Office, 1924), pp. 17, 18.

17. Congressional Record, LXVIII, 2573, 2574.

18. Department of Commerce, Third National Radio Conference, Recommendations for the Regulation of Radio (Washington, D.C.: U.S. Government Printing Office, 1924).

19. Department of Commerce, Annual Report of the Secretary of Commerce, vol. 13 (Washington, D.C.: U.S. Government Printing Office, 1925), pp. 23, 24.

20. Congressional Record, LXVIII, 2575.

21. Department of Commerce, Fourth National Radio Conference, Proceedings and Recommendations for the Regulation of Radio (Washington, D.C.: U.S. Government Printing Office, 1926).

22. Harold Ernest Hill, The National Association of Educational Broadcasters: A History (Urbana: National Association of Educational Broadcasters, 1954), p. 4.

23. James M. Herring and Gerald C. Gross, Telecommunications (New York: McGraw-Hill Book Company, 1936), p. 243.

24. United States v. Zenith Radio Corporation, 12 Fed (2d) 614 (1926).

25. Opinions of the Attorneys General, XXXV, 126.

26. Congressional Record, LXVIII, 32.

27. House of Representatives, Bill 69-9971; Senate, Bill 69-1754; House of Representatives, Report 69-1886.

28. Senate, Committee on Interstate and Foreign Commerce, Hearing on S1 and S1754, 69 Cong., 2 Sess.; Murray Edelman, The Licensing of Radio Service in the United States, 1927-1947 (Urbana: University of Illinois Press, 1950), p. 9.

29. Congressional Record, LXIX, 3989.

30. Ibid., LXVIII, 2568; New York Times, June 13, 1926.

31. House of Representatives, Report 69-464; Senate, Report 69-772; Congressional Record, LXXVIII, 8845.

32. Senate, Committee on Interstate and Foreign Commerce, Hearing on S2920, 73 Cong., 2 Sess.; Senate, Document 69-200.

33. Public Law 69-632.

34. New York Times, March 6, 1927.

35. Congressional Record, LXIX, 3980, 3981.

36. Ibid., 1791-1793; Federal Radio Commission, Annual Report, vol. 1 (Washington, D.C.: U.S. Government Printing Office, 1928), pp. 7, 8.

37. New York Times, April 10, 1927.

38. Congressional Record, LXIX, 3986; New York Times, November 13, 1927.

39. Armstrong Perry, Radio in Education (New York: Payne Fund, 1929), pp. 83, 84.

40. Congressional Record, LXIX, 3599, 3985.

41. Public Law 70-195.

42. Federal Radio Commission, Annual Report, vol. 2 (Washington, D.C.: U.S. Government Printing Office, 1929), p. 34.

43. New York Times, September 22, 1928.

44. National Broadcasting Company, Broadcasting in the Public Interest (New York: NBC: 1938), 25; New York Times, March 9, 1929.

45. New York Times, May 22, 1929.

46. Department of the Interior, Report of the Advisory Committee on Education by Radio (Columbus, Ohio: Heer Printing Company, 1930) (hereafter cited as ACER Report).

47. New York Times, May 25, 1929.

48. ACER Report; Department of the Interior, Report of Armstrong Perry to the Advisory Committee on Education by Radio, mimeographed (1929); Congressional Record, LXXII, 11291, 11292; New York Times, November 7, 1929, December 31, 1929, February 28, 1930.

49. New York Times, September 27, 1931.

50. Levering Tyson, National Advisory Council for Radio in Education (New York: National Advisory Council for Radio in Education, 1936), pp. 1, 2.

51. New York Times, April 3, 1931.

52. Levering Tyson, ed., Radio and Education 1931, 1932, 1933, 1934: Proceedings of the First, Second, Third, Fourth Annual Assembly of the National Advisory Council on Education by Radio (Chicago: University of Chicago Press, 1931-34).

53. New York Times, June 29, 1930.

54. Josephine H. MacLatchy, ed., Education on the Air: First-Thirtieth Yearbook of the Institute for Education by Radio (Columbus: Ohio State University, 1930-59), vol. 19, p. 378; vol. 15, p. 65, and passim.

55. Frank Ernest Hill, Tune in for Education (New York: National Committee for Education by Radio, 1942), pp. 14-19.

56. New York Times, May 17, 1931, June 30, 1931, July 3, 1931.

57. Ibid., September 14, 1930.

58. Ibid., December 6, 1931.

2

THE FEDERAL COMMUNICATIONS COMMISSION AND THE OFFICE OF EDUCATION—AM RADIO

EFFORTS TO GET PROTECTION FOR SPECIAL CLASSES OF BROADCASTERS

Hearings before the Committee on Interstate Commerce of the U.S. Senate on a proposal, ultimately unsuccessful, to establish a federal commission to regulate transmissions by wire and wireless lasted off and on from May 1929 to February 1930. The senators heard testimony from scores of manufacturers, technicians, inventors, broadcasters, telegraphers, and special interest groups.

At this hearing, educational broadcasters joined a loose federation of nonprofit organizations seeking to obtain a congressional allocation of a definite portion of radio channels for their exclusive use. The testimony of Edward N. Nockels, secretary of the Chicago Federation of Labor and manager of broadcasting station WCFL, in January typified efforts during the next four years to get protection and consideration from Congress for special classes of broadcasters. Nockels averred that broadcasting had been prostituted to its lowest use—that of amusing the multitudes in order to sell merchandise. The radio trust that had the best channels, time, and power claimed that this was what the public wanted. Nockels maintained that noisy public acclaim was not the best criterion; if it were so, prize fights would overwhelm the universities and the cheapest sex novels would put to shame the greatest classical literature. Nockels believed that it was in the public interest to license stations that would provide wholesome entertainment, increase knowledge, arouse individual thinking, break down hatreds, and encourage respect for law.[1]

A resolution was introduced in the House of Representatives in May 1930 and in the Senate the following December to take three channels away from commercial broadcasters and assign them to

the Departments of Labor, Agriculture, and the Interior. Each
department would have one channel to which it would assign those
stations most representative of the work of the department. The
OE, under the Department of the Interior, was to assign educational
stations to the department's channel.[2]

Labor stations supported this proposal, because one channel
was about all they could use. Their proposal also included stations
primarily concerned with agriculture and education in order to gain
wider support among the nonprofit stations. Educators appreciated
this demonstration of mutual concern, but they had a plan of their
own.

At the urging of the National Committee on Education by Radio,
Simeon Fess, former president of Antioch College, introduced a bill
in the Senate in January 1931 to reserve not less than 15 percent of
all radio broadcasting channels for educational broadcasting by
educational agencies of the federal or state governments and to
educational institutions chartered by the United States or by the
respective states and territories.[3]

Neither educators, the public, nor the Congress were prepared
for such drastic legislation, and the NCER began an information
program in February 1931 to obtain support for the proposal. Commercial broadcasters knew that the NCER did not have a chance of
pushing this bill through Congress; indeed, no hearings were held
nor did the bill get out of committee, but they took the precaution to
bring pressure of their own through the National Advisory Council
for Radio in Education to prevent a united front of educators.

The battle raged through the first annual assembly of the NACRE,
which met in May 1931. Joy Elmer Morgan, representing the 15
percenters and the NCER, charged the federal government had bar-
tered away the rights of the people in allocating radio channels to
private companies and had failed to take due cognizance of the interests of the states, localities, and educational institutions. He felt
that an agency for good had been seized by agents of profit. Commercial sponsors of educational programs had refused certain material,
deleted portions of texts, and interrupted transmissions with commercial drivel. He accused networks of providing time for educational
broadcasts only when commercial sponsors were unavailable and of
canceling educational programs when a sponsor was willing to pay
for the time. He condemned the Federal Radio Commission for
requiring college stations to meet the same standards for expensive
equipment as commercial stations. Morgan urged all educators to
support the NCER's efforts to obtain channels for education.

Henry Adams Bellows, vice president of CBS and former FRC
commissioner, answered Morgan's charges. Bellows stated that
as a whole educational broadcasting was depressingly low in quality

and that educational stations were willing to turn over their unsold time to educators, with the generally vain hope that educators would make sensible use of it, but that educational institutions were neither equipped nor willing to take the opportunity. He rejected the Fess bill and exclaimed that there could be no greater disaster for education than the legal divorce of education and commercial broadcasting. Educators had free access to vast audiences built up by commercial stations, with the only provision being that they not bore audiences too much. "Segregate the teachers," he concluded, "in the limbo of special wave lengths, and we condemn them to remain unheard and disregarded."

Harold Lafount, member of the FRC, said more and more time was being given to educational programs by commercial broadcasters and suggested that businessmen be allowed to operate the plant. Charles Saltzman, FRC chairman, explained once again that in the commission's view, they could not give special consideration to one applicant over another and that only Congress could take channels from one and give to another.[4]

With the support of educators divided, with the opposition of commercial broadcasters unshaken, and with the indifference of the FRC unaltered, the NCER returned to Congress for help. In the discussion on the floor of the Senate on a bill to make minor technical changes in the Radio Act of 1927, Senator Fess inquired whether consideration had been given to his proposal to allot a percentage of channels to education. He was told that the committee had considered the proposal but did not recommend it.[5]

By 1931, the number of educational institutions holding licenses had dropped by 60 percent since the high mark of 129 in 1925. Only 51 stations were on the air. Lafount explained to the Institute for Education by Radio that the reduction in the number of educational stations occurred by virtue of the voluntary surrender by educational stations of their licenses, either because they were unable for financial reasons to maintain them or because they did not have sufficient program material to continue operations.[6]

THE FRC AND ITS ATTITUDE TOWARD EDUCATIONAL BROADCASTING

Public concern over the increase of blatant commercialism in radio broadcasting received expression in a resolution introduced in the Senate by James Couzens in January 1932. Couzens resolved to ask the FRC to make a survey to determine to what extent stations were used for advertising and what might be done to eliminate advertising. There was a general feeling that the answer to "bad" commercial practices was more educational stations. Senator Clarence Dill, who had once taught school for three years, reflected this attitude when he amended Couzens's resolution by adding to the FRC survey questions concerning facilities offered educational stations.[7] Most of the questions required statistical answers.

The resolution passed on January 12, and the FRC answered on June 9. Advertising appeared in a favorable light in the FRC report. To the question, "Since education is a public service paid for by taxes of the people, and therefore the people have a right to have complete control of all the facilities of public education, what recognition has the commission given to the applications of public educational institutions?," the FRC answered that from February 23, 1927, to January 1, 1932, it had licensed 95 stations, of which 44 were still in operation, 23 had voluntarily assigned their channels to commercial stations, 18 had voluntarily abandoned their licenses, and 10 had been deleted for cause. The FRC did not say why these stations had given up their licenses. Some college broadcasters blamed the FRC because it had assigned them poor hours and low power and because it had required them to purchase improved studio and transmitter equipment, which they could not afford. Other college broadcasters blamed disinterested administrators and the inability to compete with the money, talent, and technical proficiency of commercial stations. To the question, "Does the commission believe that educational programs can be safely left to the voluntary gift of the use of facilities by commercial stations?," the FRC replied that the attitude of broadcasters justified such belief. Of 533 stations replying to the survey, 521 said they offered facilities to educational institutions; of 525 stations answering, 496 said the educators did not use all the time available.[8] Once again, the FRC did not explain why. Educational broadcasters claimed that stations repeatedly changed the available time, forced them to delete material, and offered no advice or assistance in preparing interesting programs.

Senator Jesse Metcalf was not convinced that the FRC was doing all that it could to foster educational broadcasting, and in the summer of 1932, he offered a bill suggesting that $10,000 be expended by the FRC for the purpose of cooperating with the states in the development and promotion of education by radio, providing for cooperation by the states, and requiring every applicant for a broadcasting license to file an agreement to set aside not less than five percent of its hours of operation for the purpose of broadcasting educational programs under regulations prescribed by the states and approved by the FRC.[9]

This was not the solution, however. Congress was concerned about advertising abuses; the NCER wanted channels; and the NACRE, which wanted better and more permanent commercial facilities, was loath to antagonize commercial broadcasters by seeking federal intervention on their behalf. The Metcalf proposal got little support and was never reported out of committee.

EFFORTS TO ESTABLISH ONE
COMMUNICATIONS AGENCY

For the next two years, the people of the United States were too busy electing Franklin D. Roosevelt, and the Congress was too busy dealing with the Great Depression to hear the appeals of special interest groups for the allocation of radio channels for their exclusive use. But when Roosevelt proposed the regulation of all communications through one agency, the pitchmen of nonprofit organizations descended on Congress in hopes of favorable legislation.

Prior to 1934, there was a general feeling that federal regulation of telephone and telegraph communications had been ineffective, because of a division of authority among several agencies, lack of adequate regulatory power, and preoccupation of the Interstate Commerce Commission (ICC) with other duties. Consequently, there was a growing perception of the problem and a feeling that one federal agency was necessary to regulate telephone, telegraph, cable, and radio. Shortly after taking office, President Roosevelt directed Secretary of Commerce Daniel C. Roper to organize an interdepartmental committee to investigate the problem and to present recommendations for appropriate legislation.[10]

The interdepartmental committee report suggested three alternatives. It first recommended government ownership and operation of communications services. Second, it suggested substantial revision of the existing system of regulation. Third, it recommended continued regulation as it existed.[11]

The report was leaked to the press. After surveying public reaction and gauging the relative chances of passage of each alternative, Roosevelt forwarded the report without comment to the appropriate congressional committees in January 1934. After a round of conversations with congressional leaders, the president decided that a bill most likely to pass would be one consolidating the regulatory powers in one agency and letting the agency study the need for merging communications into giant monopolies under strict government control.[12] This decision to leave a controversial subject for later study had significance for another problem soon to arise.

Roosevelt sent a special message to Congress in February urging the immediate creation of a Federal Communications Commission (FCC). Noting that the ICC regulated the transportation industry, he further noted that there was no central agency to regulate communications. He suggested that the regulatory powers in the ICC

and FRC in regard to communications be merged and that this new
agency be granted authority to study outstanding problems. Roosevelt
excluded radio from his recommendations and suggested that a special
study and report on it be made later.[13]

On February 27, Sam Rayburn, chairman of the House Committee
on Interstate and Foreign Commerce, introduced a bill providing for
all the president asked and went further by transferring all the functions of the FRC to the FCC. The same day, Dill, chairman of the
Senate Committee on Interstate and Foreign Commerce, introduced
a bill following the president's recommendations. In addition, it
would repeal the Radio Act of 1927 and place control of radio broadcasting in the FCC.[14]

On five days in March, the Senate held hearings on the Dill bill.
Representatives of the networks and commercial stations urged the
senators to return to the recommendations of President Roosevelt
and leave broadcasting out of the proposed legislation. Bellows
opposed repealing the Radio Act, which had stood court tests and
brought stability to commercial broadcasting. David Sarnoff, president of the Radio Corporation of America, believed that the Senate
should follow Roosevelt's lead and leave the regulation of radio with
the FRC. On the last day of the Senate hearings, May 15, Father
John B. Harney, Superior of the Missionary Society of St. Paul the
Apostle, testified before the Senate committee. Harney approved
the Senate bill and suggested an amendment that he claimed would
forestall monopoly in broadcasting and secure channels for nonprofit
religious, educational, cultural, and social service organizations.
His amendment provided for the revocation of all licenses 90 days
after the law was enacted, reallocation of all channels, and reservation of 25 percent of all broadcasting channels to nonprofit organizations.[15]

A meeting was held in the office of Congressman William P.
Connery, chairman of the House Committee on Labor, attended by
several congressmen and representatives of education, labor, and
religion. The principal speaker was Father Harney, who dealt at
length with the problems nonprofit organizations had in acquiring
desirable channels, time, and power authorizations from the FRC,
and particularly with the difficulties of the station in New York of
which he was director. Harney described how his station had been
required to change channels repeatedly, each change resulting in
poorer reception. He also stated that broadcasting time had been
reduced and allotted in the least desirable portion of the day. Authorized power had been reduced several times. Representatives of
educational and labor stations buttressed Harney's story with their
own experiences. They also backed Harney's request for congressional legislation to reserve channels for nonprofit organizations.[16]

Congressmen were impressed by the stories of the plight of educational broadcasters and appointed a committee to draft an amendment to the communications bill pending in the House. On April 5, Representative Stephen Rudd introduced a resolution in the House. It was an amendment to the communications bill and provided for the revocation of all licenses in 90 days and the reservation and allocation of 25 percent of the broadcasting channels within the jurisdiction of the FCC. Channels equally as desirable as those allocated to commercial stations were to be assigned to educational, religious, agricultural, labor, cooperative, and similar nonprofit organizations.[17]

At the conclusion of its public hearings, the Senate committee began making technical changes in the bill, as the result of testimony at the hearings and meetings with attorneys for the ICC, FRC, and State Department. A new bill encompassing all the technical changes was introduced in the Senate by Dill on March 28. The new bill contained a provision directing the FCC to investigate the desirability of having Congress allocate by law a fixed percentage of radio channels for educational, charitable, religious, labor, and other nonprofit organizations. The bill was reported out of the Senate committee without hearings on April 19. On April 27, Senator Robert Wagner introduced an amendment to his bill to allocate 25 percent of all channels for nonprofit-making organizations.[18]

The trade magazine Variety reported on May 8 that the networks and commercial stations were making frantic efforts through their lobbyists to mobilize strength to defeat this amendment. The stations threatened as a last resort to ask their listeners to write their senators demanding that the amendment be defeated.[19]

Educational broadcasters were not without resources, however. The NCER held a conference in Washington, D.C., on May 7-8. The conference, on the "Use of Radio as a Cultural Agency in a Democracy," was attended by leaders in education, recreation, government, and civic affairs. The conference concluded that commercial radio was not a genuine expression of the listener's choice; that responsible groups, including minorities, should not be debarred from broadcast privileges; and that wholesome broadcasting for youth at home and at school should be provided.[20] While in Washington, educators made the rounds of congressional offices to request radio channels for education.

The House Committee on Interstate and Foreign Commerce held hearings on the Rayburn communications bill from April 10 to May 17. On May 9, the day after the NCER conference ended, Father Harney testified before the committee. He related the difficulties that station WLWL, owned and operated by the Paulist fathers, had had at the hands of the FRC and charged unjustifiable discrimination against

high-quality nonprofit radio stations. Harney asked the committee
to make provisions in its bill to allot 25 percent of the radio channels
to nonprofit organizations. Twenty-five representatives appeared
with him in support of his proposal. Gross W. Alexander, representing the Federal Council of Churches of Christ in America, and
the NCER reported three recommendations passed at the NCER
conference on the "Use of Radio as a Cultural Agency in a Democracy."
The conference recommended that an independent study be made of
the radio situation by an agency other than the proposed FCC. It
suggested that each state have channels to be used in the public interest, that the federal government aid these stations financially, and
that the stations pay back the federal government by giving a percentage of their time to reporting the activities of the government. It
proposed that there be three classes of stations, government, educational and eleemosynary, and commercial, and that each class be
allotted one-third of the available channels. Alexander concluded
by attacking the NACRE as a commercial front organization.[21] Noncommercial educational broadcasters probably had made a serious
tactical error. Rather than propose an alternate plan, they might
have agreed with other nonprofit organizations on one plan and worked
with them for its adoption.

In the Senate, the revised communications bill[22] was debated on
May 15. Senator Wagner, in support of his amendment, stated that
commercial stations, enjoying the free use of the air, had captured
98 percent of broadcasting, while nonprofit-making stations, devoted
to education, religion, culture, labor, and agriculture, had secured
only 2 percent. "Let's not be too solicitous," he said, "over the
large stations who through the favor of government have secured a
practical monopoly." Senator Henry Hatfield, cosponsor of the
amendment, listed a score of national organizations supporting the
proposal. Senator Fess recalled his bill of 1931 to allot 15 percent
of radio channels to education and stated that pressure from commercial stations prevented favorable action on the bill. Senator Royal
Copeland stated that educational stations had tried to get concessions
from the FRC with no results and believed that legislative action was
necessary. He said that the trials of station WLWL brought into
focus the whole problem facing nonprofit broadcasters. Senator Dill
then spoke for the Committee on Interstate and Foreign Commerce
and explained why the proposal had been rejected. He explained
that nonprofit did not mean noncommercial, that a nonprofit licensee
might sell such part of his allotted time as would make the station
self-supporting, and that considering the high cost of broadcasting
and the fact that many commercial stations lost money, a nonprofit-
making station might be as commercial as a profit-making station.

Dill also said that the provision to end all allocations and make new assignments within six months was technically impossible. He further explained that the amendment was impractical because it provided for no basis upon which to divide 25 percent of the channels between labor and education, North and South, and Protestants, Catholics, and Jews. Dill urged the Senate to pass the committee bill, which instructed the FCC to study the proposal that Congress allot a percentage of channels to nonprofit broadcasting. The Senate defeated the amendment 42 to 23 and then went on to pass the committee bill. Broader support of a single, practical proposal by educators might have led to its passage.23

On June 2, the House of Representatives passed by voice vote its communications bill, which abolished the FRC but reenacted the Radio Act of 1927 as Title III of the law. The bill neither allotted a percentage of channels for nonprofit organizations nor required the FCC to study the proposition. The Senate and House conference committee compromised the differences in the two bills,24 and the two houses passed the new law on June 9. The president signed the act on June 20, and the Communications Act of 1934 became effective on July 1.25

The act abolished the FRC, repealed the Radio Act of 1927, and established the FCC. It provided for seven commissioners to serve staggered terms of seven years each. The law reenacted much of the Radio Act, by giving the FCC authority to issue licenses in the public interest, convenience, and necessity; classify stations; assign channels; determine locations; and inspect apparatus. In Section 307(c), Congress required the FCC to study the proposal that Congress by statute allocate fixed percentages of radio broadcasting channels to particular kinds of nonprofit radio programs or to persons identified with particular kinds of nonprofit activities and report to Congress not later than February 15, 1935, its recommendations and reasons for these recommendations.

President Roosevelt appointed to the FCC Eugene O. Sykes, chairman of the FRC; Thad Brown, member of the FRC; Paul Walker, Oklahoma expert on telephone and telegraph; Everett Case, former governor of Rhode Island; Irwin Stuart, State Department expert on radio; George Henry Payne, author, playwright, and journalist; and Hampson Gary, Washington lawyer. A New York Times survey of opinion regarding the FCC and the Communications Act revealed that the law made no important changes in broadcasting and that regulation under the new law would be as good or bad as the personnel. Any changes would be due to changes in agency policy and not changes in the law.26

EDUCATIONAL BROADCASTERS AND THE FCC

The FCC announced a public conference to be held before its broadcasting division, in October and November 1934, to gather information and opinions upon which to base a recommendation to Congress in accordance with Section 307(c) of the Communications Act.27 Educational broadcasters had tried from 1930 to 1934 to effect a federal policy favorable to them through congressional action. They massed for another assault at the FCC conference. Educators felt that if they could not convince the FCC of a need for legislative protection, at least they could show the FCC their need for administrative protection from the commission itself.

Gary was chairman of the FCC broadcast committee that would hear public testimony and render an impartial recommendation to Congress on the proposition that Congress allot a fixed percentage of the broadcast channels to nonprofit organizations. In a speech entitled "The Spirit of Broadcasting under the New Deal," delivered to the National Association of Broadcasters and broadcast to a nationwide audience on August 18, 1934, Gary offered a clue to his possible predisposition on the question. He stated that if any changes were to be made in broadcasting, they would be evolutionary rather than revolutionary. The FCC, he declared, would build on what had already been done by the FRC. He promised there would be no radical shifting of channels. "We have one of the finest systems in the world. We do not want to exercise bureaucratic control and we do not want to dictate what manner of entertainment or discussion shall go on the air. It is not desirable or even necessary." He made his position quite clear when he stated, "What we do will be a minimum of breaking down the present allocation and assignments thereunder."28

There seems little room for doubt that Gary was predisposed to accept broadcasting as it existed. Educational broadcasters would have to build a strong, unified case before they could convince Gary of the worthiness of their cause. Commercial broadcasters apparently thought they had more to fear from Congress than from the FCC.

In a speech to the legislative committee of the NAB, Bellows declared: "Don't for one moment forget that the only reason why we escaped special legislation in the last session of Congress was because such legislation was expressly reserved for the session which begins next January. The President," he continued, "has told the FCC to make recommendations to Congress, and unquestionably the Commission will do so. Even if, as we expect, its recommendations call for no radical changes, we are still facing the certainty of legislative attacks in the next session of Congress."29

The NACRE, usually the wholehearted supporter of commercial broadcasters, met in Washington during the first days of the FCC

conference. Its delegates had a wide variety of opinions. There
were traditional defenders of the alliance between commercial broadcasters and educators, who believed that the quality of radio broadcasting was improving and urged that radio not be opened to pressure
groups and propagandists. But Robert M. Hutchins of the University
of Chicago believed that unless radio became more effective in education and more satisfactory to the public, it would find itself in danger
of more drastic regulation or in competition with publicly owned
stations. Bruce Bliven, magazine editor, condemned "the moronic
drivel and oral garbage" on the radio and said nothing from government-
owned stations could be as bad as what they had. Robert M. Sproul
of the University of California advocated independence and proper
time allowance for educational broadcasting. He thought that might
be done by setting aside definite useful hours on commercial stations
or withdrawing channels from commercial use and handing them over
to educational broadcasters. George Zook, director of the American
Council on Education, suggested that new areas in the radio spectrum
be assigned for educational stations.[30]

The Association of College and University Broadcasting Stations,
which was organized at the Fourth National Radio Conference in 1925
and which had always supported the reservation of channels for
educators, and particularly for agricultural broadcasters, decided
to reorganize in 1934. It changed its constitution, enlarged its membership; and changed its name to the National Association of Educational Broadcasters (NAEB). Meeting in Kansas City, Kansas, it
vowed to rally support for college stations at the FCC conference.[31]

The FCC order calling for the conference invited any person or
licensee to attend. The broadcast division listened to testimony
from October 1 to 20 and from November 7 to 12, 1934. During the
conference, 135 witnesses were heard, 14,000 pages of testimony
were recorded, and several thousand pages of exhibits and several
hundred letters were put in the record.[32]

Testimony came from four general sources: private nonprofit
organizations, government agencies, commercial broadcasters, and
FRC-FCC files. The FCC heard testimony by private nonprofit
organizations—the NCER, the NACRE, and unaffiliated persons
representing education; by religious organizations—the Watch Tower
Bible and Tract Society, the Missionary Society of St. Paul the
Apostle, and the Christian Science Church; and from labor unions,
the American Red Cross, and the American Civil Liberties Union.
Among the government agencies offering testimony were the Federal
Trade Commission, Office of Education, Department of Agriculture,
Veterans Administration, and the Tennessee Valley Authority. In
support of commercial broadcasters, there was testimony from
broadcasters and nonbroadcasters, representing the National Association of Broadcasters, NBC, and CBS.

Spokesmen for private nonprofit organizations made contradictory statements about their situations and offered a dozen different solutions to their problems. Apparently, no effort was made to coordinate their appeal or build a unified case for their position.

Representatives of education made the following requests or statements in regard to a percentage of channels: a reasonable share, a reasonable number, an adequate percentage, an adequate number for day and night broadcasting, 15 percent, 15 percent is more than is needed, impossible to arrive at a fixed percentage, no attitude toward a percentage, opposed to a percentage. Others requested the federal government to establish a National Radio Institute to produce programs, to build a network of educational stations, and to levy a 25 cent tax on each radio receiver to finance educational programs. One spokesman asked for a channel for each state, and others wanted protection for existing assignments. In regard to commercial stations, educators said the stations tried to crowd educators off the air, promoted a happy relationship between educators and commercial broadcasters, and cooperated fully with educational stations. It hardly needs to be said that educators were woefully divided. Indeed, there was no agreement on a single point.

No more discordant testimony was given than by representatives of religious broadcasting. Joseph Rutherford, of the Watch Tower Bible and Tract Society, alleged that NBC practiced censorship by not letting him broadcast and then made a vehement attack on the Roman Catholic Church. Father Harney, of the Missionary Society of St. Paul the Apostle, described RCA as a monopoly. A representative of the National Council of Catholic Men criticized Rutherford's attack on the Catholic Church. The Christian Science spokesman thanked commercial stations for their wholehearted support. Father Wagner, of the Roman Catholic-owned station WHBY, thought the allocation of a percentage of channels to religious groups would be unworkable. Clearly, there was no accord among the spokesmen for religion.

Nor was there agreement among the representatives of government agencies. John W. Studebaker, U.S. commissioner of education, declared that educators were not yet prepared to use a percentage of channels. Floyd W. Reeves, personnel director for the Tennessee Valley Authority, presented a packaged proposal. He advocated government ownership and operation of a national system of radio stations that would give full coverage over the country through a suitable allocation of facilities. These facilities were to be allotted with as little disruption of existing communications facilities as possible. Technical operation of the system was to be financed by the federal government. Control of programs was to be under the direction of a committee from the foremost nonprofit national educa-

tional and cultural agencies, as designated by the president. These
facilities would then be available to nonprofit organizations, including
government departments for educational-cultural programs.

In contrast with the discordant, disorganized testimony of the
nonprofit organizations, the networks and commercial stations staged
a performance so polished as to rival any radio production. They
made two points. First, the commercial broadcasters established
that they were providing their audiences with educational programs
on their own initiative and in cooperation with educational and religious
organizations. To support this, they introduced into evidence 269
sworn statements from station directors listing educational programs
on their schedules. From January 1934 to June 1934, these stations
broadcast in cooperation with, or on behalf of, educational institutions
77,542 hours of educational material, or 11.3 percent of their total
operating time. Including station-initiated educational programming,
these stations broadcast 114,159 hours of educational material, or
16.7 percent of their total operating time. To support further this
contention, they paraded a number of prominent educators, who
testified that commercial stations were most cooperative in the
preparation and presentation of educational programs and, except
for editorial selection, exercised no censorship of contents. They
also entered into the record numerous letters from nationally known
Americans, including Nicholas Murray Butler, Walter Damrosch,
H. L. Mencken, George Jean Nathan, and Alexander Woollcott,
which supported their position. Second, the network presidents
expressed their complete willingness to continue to extend the facilities of their networks to all responsible groups that had a message
of real interest for a representative public and pledged their wholehearted cooperation with educational broadcasters.

The results of this conference might have been forecast by anyone who followed its proceedings. Nonprofit broadcasters destroyed
their statement of the problem by conflicting and contradictory testimony. They precluded any legislative solution to whatever problems
existed by offering a bewildering number of possible answers. In
fact, a bulk of the representatives of nonprofit organizations opposed
a congressional allocation of a fixed percentage of broadcasting channels. By stating and restating the beneficial results already accrued
to cooperation between commercial and noncommercial broadcasting,
the networks and commercial stations could be assured that their
voices were the ones that made an impression. Even if the chairman
of the hearing had not been predisposed to support the commercial
interests, he could hardly have been impressed by the cacophonous
testimony of the nonprofit interests.

The FCC reported to Congress in January 1935 and recommended
that at that time, no fixed percentage of radio broadcast channels be

allocated by statute to particular kinds of nonprofit radio programs
or to persons identified with particular kinds of nonprofit activities.
The FCC reasoned that there was no need for change in existing law
to accomplish the purpose of the proposal and that flexibility in the
law was essential to regulation if the growth of broadcasting was to
be encouraged and regulated for the best interests of the public. It
stated that insufficient broadcast channels were available to provide
for specialized broadcasting service. The FCC explained that neither
a feasible allocation plan nor a demand on the part of a large number
of nonprofit organizations or the general public had been expressed
to the commission. It appeared that the interests of nonprofit broadcasters would be served best by the use of existing network and
commercial facilities. To obtain the maximum service possible,
cooperation in good faith by all broadcasters was required.[33]

The FCC recommended no congressional action, and Congress
took none. For four years, some educators, in cooperation with
nonprofit organizations, had tried to effect a positive federal policy
toward noncommercial educational broadcasting through congressional
action. When they finally had an opportunity to make a case for themselves at the FCC conference, they made a shambles of it. Education
got a new policy, however, from an unexpected source—the FCC.

Although in its report to Congress, the FCC did not recommend
that Congress allocate a fixed percentage of channels for nonprofit
broadcasting, it did declare that it intended to foster cooperation
between commercial and noncommercial broadcasters. To encourage
this cooperation, the FCC proposed holding a national conference in
Washington to plan mutual assistance by combining education's experience with technical experience, so that better service in the public
interest would result, and to consider complaints against commercial
broadcasters, so that any necessary remedial action might be taken.
It planned to promote better educational broadcasting techniques in
cooperation with the OE. The FCC also declared that it was its firm
intention to assist nonprofit organizations to obtain the fullest opportunity for expression.

The FCC's declaration of intent to foster cooperation was a major
shift in policy. A federal regulatory agency had assumed a positive
role in radio education by acknowledging the importance of educational
broadcasting and its problems and by expressing its willingness to
make special efforts to foster its growth. The National Committee
on Education by Radio should have been pleased that the FCC recognized the importance of the problem to which it had so often called
attention. The National Advisory Council on Radio in Education
should have been pleased, because the FCC gave impulse to a movement for cooperation that it had advocated. Commercial interests
should have been pleased, because their property rights were pre-

served and because they were to be given an opportunity to continue the educational program service they professed to be eager to render.34

Gary resigned from the FCC effective January 1, 1935. President Roosevelt appointed Anning S. Prall to replace Gary as head of the broadcast committee. He had been president of the New York City Board of Education and member of Congress for 12 years. On March 1, he became chairman of the FCC, and Sykes became head of the broadcast division.35 The presence on the commission of a man once actively engaged in educational work heartened educators.

In a radio address delivered in late May, Prall stated, "The fullest possible use of radio as an educational medium has not yet been found." After studying the record, he had come to believe that commercial and educational broadcasters had not cooperated to the fullest extent and that they must get together. As promised in the FCC report to Congress, Prall announced a conference to be held for commercial and noncommercial educational broadcasters in Washington, D.C., on May 15.36

In a speech to educational broadcasters in Columbus, Ohio, Prall declared: "You have my assurance that we are ready to cooperate fully with you and to contribute as far as possible to the final and complete development of a definite, practical, and workable plan for the extension, expansion, and modernization of education by means of radio broadcasting." Educators, communicators, and regulators working together could not fail to offer a real demonstration of education by radio, he said.37

Payne, FCC commissioner and a former editor, music and drama critic, playwright, and political writer, spoke highly of the work of educational broadcasters in a speech at Harvard University. He cited stations in Ohio, Illinois, South Dakota, North Dakota, and Kansas as doing good work but limited in transmitter power. He felt that an increase in the number of educational programs and stations would rejuvenate radio broadcasting.38

THE FEDERAL RADIO EDUCATION COMMITTEE

The FCC seemed genuinely anxious to be of aid to persons using radio for educational purposes. The conference to work out a plan of cooperation among broadcasters opened in May 1935. Invitations to the meeting had been sent to broadcast licensees, the NAB, networks, education, religious, and eleemosynary institutions, individuals, groups, and associations interested in noncommercial broadcasting, and government agencies.39

Commissioner Sykes began the conference by saying, "We cannot get anywhere by criticizing and fault-finding with each other." He

applauded commercial broadcasters for giving interesting and diversified programs and urged that they make even stronger efforts to
provide more educational features. He cited the need for national
cooperation and suggested that the conference work out a plan for
mutual cooperation. J. Truman Ward, president of the NAB, said
commercial stations would willingly work toward an equitable distribution of time and recommended the formation of a committee to coordinate commercial and educational programs. Other representatives
spoke of their needs and their willingness to work together. The FCC
announced at the conclusion of the two-day meeting that it would
appoint a Federal Radio Education Committee (FREC), composed of
commercial and educational broadcasters under the chairmanship of
U.S. Commissioner of Education Studebaker to study plans to obtain
more time for purely educational programs.[40]

A preliminary planning committee met in November 1935 to
survey the possibilities of collecting and correlating data on which
the FREC, when appointed, might base its deliberations. The planning committee discovered that there was an almost total lack of
factual material and realized that information was needed. It proposed that the FREC undertake a program of research investigations
and outlined a number of proposed studies for discussion by the
general committee.[41] Although it was true that there was need for
information, the main purpose of the FREC was to promote cooperation between broadcasters. To turn the committee into a study group
would have been to divert it from its planned purpose.

At the end of 1935, the FCC announced the appointment of 40
educators and broadcasters to work out a plan to end controversy
and misunderstanding between the radio industry and educators and
to promote cooperative arrangements for broadcasting of educational
and religious programs. Two members of the FCC served on the
committee under the chairmanship of Studebaker.[42]

The FREC held its first general meeting early in 1936. The
FCC announced once again that the object was to eliminate controversy and misunderstanding between groups of educators (for example,
the NCER and the NACRE) and between the industry and educators
and to promote actual cooperative arrangements between educators
and broadcasters on national, regional, and local bases. Nevertheless, the FREC decided to inaugurate a study program before suggesting or taking any other action. The general committee agreed to the
study outlines developed by the planning committee, and each member
was invited to submit additional topics. The FREC then appointed
three subcommittees. The conflicts and cooperation subcommittee
was to review existing study outlines and prepare new outlines for
additional topics. The technical subcommittee was to review these
outlines, estimate their cost, and make recommendations to the

executive subcommittee that was responsible for carrying out the
investigation. The conflicts and cooperation subcommittee and the
technical subcommittee met in April and May and recommended 17
studies, with an estimated cost of $257,800. The executive sub-
committee had difficulty raising the money, and Commissioner Sykes
called a meeting of representatives of networks, the NAB, philan-
thropic organizations, and the NACRE. At this meeting, held in
January 1937, the conferees agreed to reduce the amount of money
needed by restudying the project outlines. They appointed a committee
of six, three educators and three broadcasters, to make the reduction.
At a meeting on March 12, the committee of six, by elimination and
combination, reduced the cost of the projects by less than $8,000.
The studies were to last over a period of two years. The committee
of six resolved to canvass potential financial sources and agreed that
two-thirds of the money should come from educational foundations
and one-third from the broadcast industry.43

In June 1937, the first project got underway when the Rockefeller
Foundation agreed to underwrite a study of the influence of radio on
children and adults. The project was completed in May 1940. The
General Education Board agreed to sponsor a two-year evaluation of
radio broadcasts for in-school listening and later extended the program
to five years. Smaller projects financed by the NACRE and NAB
lasted until 1940. The FREC had difficulty in getting money from
the broadcasting industry, yet a total of $500,000 was expended for
research on behalf of the committee.44

Because Studebaker continued as chairman, the FREC gradually
slipped into the orbit of the OE. In 1939, the OE began publishing
monthly a four-page FREC Service Bulletin to disseminate research
results to leaders in radio and education. In cooperation with the
FREC, the Office of Education prepared a list of college courses in
broadcasting education (which has been repeatedly revised). World
War II interrupted most of the projects and plans, but the FREC
issued seven reports in 1944, looking toward the future of educational
broadcasting in the postwar period. Among the authors were James
Lawrence Fly, chairman of the FCC, and George P. Adair, chief
engineer of the FCC. In 1945, the commissioner of education
attempted to revive the FREC with the new members, who recommended continuance of the committee's activities, but the FREC
never survived World War II. The OE continued to publish the FREC
Service Bulletin irregularly until 1950.45

Appointed in 1935 to promote cooperation between educational
and commercial broadcasters, the FREC never got around to its
task. The FREC experience disappointed educational broadcasters
and disillusioned the FCC, the OE, and the NACRE as to the efficacy
of attempts to foster cooperation among all groups of broadcasters.46

THE JOINT RADIO PROJECT

In its 1935 report to Congress, the FCC announced that in cooperation with the OE, it would promote better educational broadcasting techniques. Commissioner of Education Studebaker, as
chairman of the FREC, had heard the statement repeated again and
again in FREC meetings of the planning committee, general committee,
and subcommittees that local radio station managers offered free
time to educators but that educators were unprepared for it. After
consultations with the FCC, Studebaker decided to institute an experimental project to produce educational radio programs for commercial
stations and thereby demonstrate to educators how they could produce
programs of their own. Studebaker conferred with President Roosevelt concerning the project, and in December, the president announced
that he had allotted $75,000 from emergency relief funds to get a
project underway.[47]

Cosponsored by the FCC and OE, the Joint Radio Project (JRP)
was established immediately. Because the project was financed by
funds appropriated for the president's use in fighting the Great
Depression by getting people back to work, the JRP recruited 60
writers, researchers, announcers, actors, directors, and producers
from the Works Progress Administration and began planning, writing,
producing, and distributing radio programs.

William D. Boutwell, chairman of the project, took over "Education in the News," a three-year-old series of weekly programs, using
personnel of the OE, and began planning five new experimental weekly
radio programs to be broadcast through national facilities and independent stations by transcription. The first new series, directing
unemployed adults to sources of vocational training, began in March
1936. The JRP quickly followed with "Answer Me This," a program
that featured questions for which listeners looked up answers, and
"Have You Heard," a program that related unusual facts regarding
science, history, literature, art, and nature. By October, the JRP
was broadcasting five series of programs each week over network
facilities and was receiving 1,000 letters a day. Although ostensibly
a project to put people to work, the JRP's main objectives were to
demonstrate to educational broadcasters effective use of program
material and broadcasting techniques and to foster cooperation between
education and commercial broadcasters.[48]

The JRP enjoyed such success that President Roosevelt allocated
$113,000 from Federal Emergency Relief Funds to continue the pro-
ject through the fiscal year. With the increase in funds, Studebaker
said the project would discover not only successful methods by which
education could take to the airways but also methods of organizing
and financing educational broadcasting that agencies of education could
follow.[49]

The project employed additional talent, and the networks contributed enough time, personnel, studio facilities, and counsel to allow the JRP to increase the number of weekly programs to seven. In late spring of 1937, the JRP sponsored the first National School Assembly, in which thousands of school children all across the continent gathered in school auditoriums to hear a commencement address by Secretary of the Interior Harold L. Ickes.50

In October 1936, Studebaker announced the creation of the Educational Radio Script Exchange to collect, edit, and reproduce radio scripts for distribution to local educational groups for delivery at the request of local commercial stations. In six months, the exchange distributed 40,000 copies of 100 radio scripts tested for their effectiveness and still had a backlog of 1,600 other scripts on file to be edited and reproduced for distribution. The JRP distributed 10,000 copies of a radio manual for educational broadcasters and nearly as many copies of a glossary of technical radio terms.51

The JRP sponsored a six-week radio workshop in educational broadcasting in cooperation with New York University. Courses in producing, directing, writing, and acting in educational broadcasts lasted from April 5 to May 15, 1937.52

At the end of the 1936/37 fiscal year, Studebaker reported to President Roosevelt on the activities of the JRP and said, "This project killed for all time a dangerous radio myth, that people do not want radio education." He believed that the audience for radio education was probably as large as the audience for radio entertainment. "The law says that radio frequencies shall be used for the public interest, convenience, and necessity," he continued. "Education is certainly in the public interest, but there has been far too little of it on the air. This has been because educational and commercial broadcasters have not found ways to make educational programs interesting to large numbers of listeners."53

THE EDUCATIONAL RADIO PROJECT

Although still encouraged by the FCC, the JRP became a program of the OE in name as well as in fact. The Office of Education established the Radio Division as a part of its organization and made the JRP, renamed the Educational Radio Project (ERP), the chief function of the new division. The president allotted relief funds to the ERP for the next three years, and the ERP performed additional service for educational broadcasters.

The ERP employed 245 writers, producers, actors, and other trained persons from the Works Progress Administration in producing national educational radio programs. In addition to its own weekly

programs, the project cooperated with national associations, such
as the American Red Cross, and other government agencies, such
as the Department of Commerce and the Smithsonian Institution, in
producing programs. A 16-page weekly newspaper published by the
Columbia University Press supplemented the series "The World is
Yours," produced by the ERP for the Smithsonian. Teachers and
other listeners purchased 109,553 copies. The project allocated
funds to school systems and college centers for radio program demonstration and for studies to promote education by radio. It undertook
a program of technical assistance to schools, colleges, civic organizations, and local stations by consultation and publication. The ERP
conducted research for the FREC and coordinated FREC research
in study centers in New York, Chicago, Detroit, and California. In
1939, it began publishing the FREC Service Bulletin.[54]

The Educational Radio Script Exchange increased its activities
by inaugurating an Educational Transcription Exchange, to provide
complete recorded programs for broadcast groups. A teacher's
manual and a source booklet of up to 120 pages accompanied most
of the transcriptions. By 1940, more than 1,200 school groups were
using scripts and transcriptions from the OE to produce programs
in classrooms and over local stations. The Radio Division became
a major center for national information on education by radio. The
division received 1,000 letters a month asking for information and
advice. The OE established an Information and Idea Section in the
Radio Division to collect books, pamphlets, bibliographies, articles,
and newspaper clippings and to share these with the public.[55]

In 1940, Congress struck out a section of the Relief Appropriation
Act that would have permitted the use of relief funds for theater, films,
and radio projects and thus ended abruptly the ERP. Studebaker sought
an appropriation in the Federal Security Bill to authorize the project
on a permanent basis. Congress objected to the fact that the project
had never been authorized by Congress and refused. In this way,
200 persons employed by the ERP were put out of work, and five
years of cooperation with schools and colleges in radio research and
demonstration ended.[56]

First jointly sponsored by the FCC and OE and then entirely by
the OE, the ERP had produced national educational radio programs
on networks, instituted a script exchange, founded a transcription
exchange, cooperated with research projects in universities, provided
an information service, and sponsored radio workshops. It was a
useful service to educational broadcasters and should not have been
ended.

With a few thousand dollars a year from regularly appropriated
funds, the OE managed to salvage a few of the activities of the ERP.
During and after World War II, the Radio Division (renamed Uses of

Educational Radio Unit in 1945) continued to lend scripts and transcriptions, to maintain a file of printed reference material, and to
provide information and advice to questions regarding education by
radio. In 1953, the OE discontinued the Educational Radio Script
and Transcription Exchange and broke up the file of reference material.
It retained a representative sampling of the collection in a Reference
Resource Material Library in the OE.57

FCC-SPONSORED NATIONAL CONFERENCES
ON EDUCATIONAL BROADCASTING

In consonance with its policy to foster cooperation between educational and commercial broadcasters, the FCC sponsored two national
conferences on educational broadcasting. Levering Tyson, in dis-
cussing plans for the conference, stated: "The Conference will be
devoted to an exposition and discussion of what has already been
accomplished in the field of educational broadcasting. It will be
purely an experience meeting," he continued, "with the view of applying the lessons of the past and the fruits of this experience to a general
improvement of educational programs; a forum in which all such
controversial subjects as the allocation of wave lengths will be
scrupulously avoided."58

The first conference, sponsored by the FCC and in cooperation
with 18 national organizations, met in Washington, D.C., in December
1936. More than 1,000 persons from 17 countries, representing a
wide variety of people and organizations actively interested in educational broadcasting, attended the meetings. Seven general sessions
featured such speakers as Secretary of the Interior Ickes, Commissioner of Education Studebaker, and FCC Chairman Prall. The latter
said: "The FCC is sincerely interested and wholeheartedly supports
the movement looking toward the development of a comprehensive
plan for education by radio." He hoped that the FREC, formed by
the FCC as an arm of the federal government, would submit "an all-
embracing plan for broadcasting education." In sectional meetings,
representatives focused their attention on such topics as broadcasting
stations as community enterprises, educational broadcasting in other
countries, radio in the life of the child, classroom broadcasting,
psychological problems in broadcasting, polling and measuring audiences, effects of broadcasting on rural life, state plans for radio,
music in broadcasting, religious broadcasting, and research problems
in radio education.59

A second national conference on educational broadcasting, sponsored by the FCC and 28 national organizations, met in Chicago from
November 29 to December 1, 1937. Its objectives were to act as a

national forum for the exchange of ideas and experiences, to examine
present and potential resources of education by radio, to examine
the interests of organized education in broadcasting, and to bring
together the findings of research.[60]

FCC Commissioner Payne declared that the studies proposed by
the FREC were important but that the vital problem was to create
machinery to put good programs on the air. He praised the FCC
cosponsored JRP for showing educators the way to develop such programs. James R. Angell, former president of Yale and then education
counselor for NBC, seconded Payne's remarks and declared, "I think
the time has come when the great radio organizations may be asked
and expected to accept once and for all the responsibility for a definite
policy of creating the finest programs which can be devised in the
general interest of the cultural development of our people."[61]

NBC and CBS both made concerted efforts to accept the responsibility Angell said was theirs. NBC, through its education counselor
and division of radio education, cooperated with school officials and
supplemented classroom instruction with special programs on music,
literature, social science, and health. The CBS Education Board,
composed of educators and publicists, coordinated network plans
and broadened its programs for school children and instituted programs
during evening hours for adult education.[62]

STATUS OF COOPERATION BETWEEN
COMMERCIAL AND EDUCATIONAL
BROADCASTERS

Fostering cooperation between commercial and educational
broadcasters was a significant step in the development of a federal
interest in noncommercial educational broadcasting, but there was
a growing realization during 1936 and 1937 that this was not enough.
There was a growing perception that the role of education's own
stations was being denigrated by an illusory dependence on commercial stations to provide educational programs.

The FCC's Federal Radio Education Committee was diverted
from its objective to establish a working agreement among all classes
of broadcasters and was bogged down in planning expensive studies
of educational broadcasting. Much interest in educational broadcasting was shown at the FCC conferences, but little was done as a
result of the conferences. The JRP demonstrated how educational
broadcasting could be done and relieved some of the programming
burden of educational stations and of educators using commercial
stations by means of its script and transcription exchanges. Still,
there was dissatisfaction.

The NACRE, long the champion of cooperation with commercial stations, issued a pamphlet in 1937 summarizing its experiences with the networks. Programs were repeatedly changed from one time period in the day to another and from one network to another, resulting in an inability to build up an audience for the programs. The NACRE found that the networks did not always keep stated agreements. The organization was disillusioned with network cooperation and became practically inactive after the resignation of Tyson, its director, in January 1937.63

Senator Wallace White introduced a resolution in the Senate in mid-1937 to investigate broadcasting "and the extent to which, basis upon which, and times at which broadcasting stations carry educational programs."64 The resolution did not pass but not from a lack of congressional concern with educational broadcasts.

Commissioner Payne articulated the concern of some members of the FCC in an address to the Columbia University School of Journalism, when he said: "If commercial stations do not increase the educational and cultural value of programs and reform advertising methods, indignation, unspoken except by educators and publicists, will spread."65

The allocation of channels to education was seemingly a dead issue, and the beneficial effects of cooperation between broadcasters were seemingly a vain hope. What were educators to do? Was there anything further the federal government would do?

NOTES

1. Senate, Committee on Interstate and Foreign Commerce, Hearing on S6, 71 Cong., 1 Sess.

2. House of Representatives, Joint Resolution 71-334; Senate, Joint Resolution 71-220.

3. Senate, Bill 71-5589.

4. New York Times, May 23, 1931, May 24, 1931.

5. Congressional Record, LXXIV, 5206.

6. Josephine H. MacLatchy, ed., Education on the Air: Second Yearbook of the Institute for Education by Radio (Columbus: Ohio State University, 1931), p. 107.

7. Senate, Resolution 72-129.

8. Senate, Document 72-136.

9. Senate Bill 72-4933.

10. New York Times, December 14, 1933.

11. Senate, Committee on Interstate and Foreign Commerce, Study of Communications by an Interdepartmental Committee, 73 Cong.

12. New York Times, December 14, 1933, December 27, 1933, January 24, 1934, January 27, 1934.

13. Senate, Document 73-144.

14. House of Representatives, Bill 73-8301; Senate, Bill 73-2910.

15. Senate, Committee on Interstate and Foreign Commerce, Hearing on S2910, 73 Cong., 2 Sess.

16. Congressional Record, LXXVIII, 6939.

17. House of Representatives, Bill 73-8977.

18. Senate, Bill 73-3285; Bill 73-3660.

19. Variety, May 8, 1934, quoted in Carl J. Friedrich, Radio-broadcasting and Higher Education, Studies in the Control of Radio no. 4 (Cambridge, Mass.: Harvard University Press, 1942), p. 37.

20. Tracy Tyler, ed., Radio as a Cultural Agency (Washington, D.C.: National Committee for Education by Radio, 1934); Frank Ernest Hill, Tune in for Education (New York: National Committee for Education by Radio, 1942), pp. 64-65.

21. House of Representatives, Committee on Interstate and Foreign Commerce, Hearing on H8301.

22. Senate, Report 73-781.

23. Congressional Record, LXXVII, 8828-8844.

24. House of Representatives, Report 73-1850, Report 73-1918.

25. Public Law 73-416.

26. New York Times, July 1, 1934.

27. Ibid., August 1, 1934.

28. Ibid., August 19, 1934.

29. Ibid., September 30, 1934.

30. Ibid., October 9, 10, 1934.

31. Harold Ernest Hill, The National Association of Educational Broadcasters: A History (Urbana: National Association of Educational Broadcasters, 1954), p. 20.

32. Federal Communications Commission, Record of the Hearing Before the Federal Communications Commission Pursuant to Section 307(c) of the Communications Act of 1934, mimeographed (1934).

33. Federal Communications Commission, Report of the Federal Communications Commission to Congress Pursuant to Section 307(c) of the Communications Act of 1934, mimeographed (1935).

34. Frank Ernest Hill, Listen and Learn (New York: American Association for Adult Education, 1937), p. 53.

35. New York Times, January 4, 1935, March 9, 1935.

36. Congressional Record, LXXIX, 4945-4946.

37. Ibid., 7792-7793.

38. Ibid., 8181-8186.

39. Federal Communications Commission, Annual Report, vol. 3 (Washington, D.C.: U.S. Government Printing Office, 1937), p. 45 (hereafter cited as FCC, Annual Report, vol. 3).

40. New York Times, May 16, 1935, May 17, 1935.

41. FCC, Annual Report, vol. 3, p. 46; Secretary of the Interior, Annual Report, 1936 (Washington, D.C.: U.S. Government Printing Office, 1937), p. 241 (hereafter cited as Interior, Annual Report, 1936).

42. New York Times, December 20, 1935.

43. FCC, Annual Report, vol. 3, pp. 46-49.

44. Federal Communications Commission, Annual Report, vol. 4 (Washington, D.C.: U.S. Government Printing Office, 1938), p. 61, Federal Communications Commission, Annual Report, vol. 5 (Washington, D.C.: U.S. Government Printing Office, 1939), p. 50; Federal Communications Commission, Annual Report, vol. 6 (Washington, D.C.: U.S. Government Printing Office, 1940), p. 70; Secretary of the Interior, Annual Report, 1939 (Washington, D.C.: U.S. Government Printing Office, 1940), p. 82.

45. U.S. Commissioner of Education, Annual Report, 1941 (Washington, D.C.: U.S. Government Printing Office, 1941), p. 91; U.S. Office of Education, Annual Report, 1941-42, 1942-43 (Washington, D.C.: U.S. Government Printing Office, 1943), p. 83; U.S. Office of Education, Annual Report, 1944 (Washington, D.C.: U.S. Government Printing Office, 1945), p. 59; Federal Security Agency, U.S. Office of Education, Annual Report, 1946 (Washington, D.C.: U.S. Government Printing Office, 1947), p. 160 (hereafter cited as USCE, Annual Report, 1941; OE, Annual Report, 1941-42, 1942-43 and Annual Report, 1944; and FSA, OE, Annual Report, 1946).

46. Federal Security Agency, U.S. Office of Education, Annual Report, 1951 (Washington, D.C.: U.S. Government Printing Office, 1952), p. 31.

47. FCC, Annual Report, vol. 3, pp. 49, 50; Clarence S. Marsh, ed., Educational Broadcasting 1936: Proceedings of the First National Conference on Educational Broadcasting (Chicago: University of Chicago Press, 1937) (hereafter cited as Marsh, Educational Broadcasting 1936).

48. New York Times, January 5, 1936, March 22, 1936; Interior, Annual Report, 1936, p. 239.

49. New York Times, November 1, 1936; Secretary of the Interior, Annual Report, 1937 (Washington, D.C.: U.S. Government Printing Office, 1938), pp. 276-77 (hereafter cited as Interior, Annual Report, 1937).

50. Interior, Annual Report, 1937, pp. 278-79.

51. New York Times, July 4, 1937; Interior, Annual Report, 1937, p. 277.

52. New York Times, February 21, 1937.

53. New York Times, July 11, 1937; Congressional Record, LXXIV, A2653, A2654.

54. John W. Studebaker, "Promoting the Course of Education by Radio," Journal of Educational Sociology 14 (February 1941): 325-33; Secretary of the Interior, Annual Report, 1938 (Washington, D.C.: U.S. Government Printing Office, 1939), p. 306; Secretary of the Interior, Annual Report, 1939 (Washington, D.C.: U.S. Government Printing Office, 1940), pp. 81-82; U.S. Commissioner of Education, Annual Report, 1940 (Washington, D.C.: U.S. Government Printing Office, 1941), pp. 87-90 (hereafter cited as USCE, Annual Report, 1940).

55. USCE, Annual Report, 1940, pp. 88, 89.

56. New York Times, June 2, 1940.

57. USCE, Annual Report, 1941, p. 82; OE, Annual Report, 1941-42, 1942-43, p. 82; OE, Annual Report, 1944, p. 56; Federal Security Agency, U.S. Office of Education, Annual Report, 1945 (Washington, D.C.: U.S. Government Printing Office, 1946), p. 69; FSA, OE, Annual Report, 1946, p. 156; Federal Security Agency, U.S. Office of Education, Annual Report, 1947 (Washington, D.C.: U.S. Government Printing Office, 1948), p. 232; Federal Security Agency, U.S. Office of Education, Annual Report, 1948 (Washington, D.C.: U.S. Government Printing Office, 1949), p. 505; Department of Health, Education and Welfare, Annual Report, 1953 (Washington, D.C.: U.S. Government Printing Office, 1954), p. 178.

58. New York Times, December 6, 1936.

59. Marsh, Educational Broadcasting 1936, pp. i-iii; New York Times, December 11, 1936, November 22, 1936.

60. Clarence S. Marsh, ed., Educational Broadcasting 1937: Proceedings of the Second National Conference on Educational Broadcasting (Chicago: University of Chicago Press, 1938); New York Times, November 28, 1937.

61. Congressional Record, LXXXIII, A149, A150, LXXXII, A577, A578.

62. New York Times, July 4, 1937, September 26, 1937, January 10, 1938, January 23, 1938.

63. S. E. Frost, Jr., Four Years of Network Broadcasting (Chicago: University of Chicago Press, 1937).

64. Senate, Resolution 75-149.

65. New York Times, November 1, 1935.

3

THE FEDERAL COMMUNICATIONS COMMISSION—FM RADIO

THE STATE OF EDUCATIONAL STATIONS

The Federal Communications Commission was concerned about the state of educational stations, as well as determined to foster cooperation between commercial and educational broadcasters. When the FCC began to regulate radio, there were 42 educational radio stations. By 1936, there were 40. A comparison of 23 educational stations from 1931, when regulated by the Federal Radio Commission, to 1936, when regulated by the FCC, shows that 12 had greater power, 10 had more time, and 6 had better channels. A few stations had less time but at the request of the stations. None had less power or a less desirable channel.[1] A solicitous attitude on the part of the FCC had slowed the loss of educational licenses and had provided the remainder with better broadcasting opportunities.

But the number of educational stations was dwindling. Lack of finances, indifference of administrators, disillusion among educators, and constant pressure from commercial competition took their toll. Educational broadcasters had for many years looked longingly for a haven in the radio spectrum that would be all theirs, a group of channels on which they could broadcast at their convenience and develop techniques at their leisure. They had tried to obtain a portion of the standard amplitude modulation (AM) broadcast band, but they were unsuccessful because there was too much demand for the space, too little agreement among the educators on what was required, and no federal patron to understand their hopes and to help them achieve their dreams.

FCC INFORMAL ENGINEERING HEARINGS

By 1936, theoretical research and practical experimentation demonstrated that areas of the radio spectrum previously unused because of technical limitations might be utilized for the expansion of existing services. In order that it might be apprised of these technical developments and of present and future needs for spectrum space, the FCC held an informal engineering hearing on June 15.[2]

Testimony concerned four main topics: new radio channels for other than broadcast services; allocation of new channels for standard AM broadcasting; visual broadcasting; and aural broadcasting above the standard AM band. Approximately 1,907 frequencies would become available as a result of technical developments. Government spokesmen expressed a need for 1,012 of the frequencies for use by law enforcement and military agencies and for aviation, shipping, forest service, and weather reporting. Commercial stations complained of restricted time and power and asked that the standard broadcasting band be expanded. Experimenters with visual broadcasting asked that provision be made for continued experimentation with television but asked that it not be commercialized until fully perfected. Developers of broadcasting by frequency modulation (FM) explained the technical aspects of their experiments and asked that radio channels for FM broadcasting be reserved for their use when commercialization became practical in the future.

Remembering educators' unsuccessful attempts to obtain a reservation of standard AM radio broadcasting channels and wishing to give them a second chance in educational broadcasting, the FCC invited the U.S. Office of Education and various educational groups to appear at the hearing and testify regarding their possible use of channels outside the standard broadcasting band for educational purposes.[3] Such an invitation was unprecedented and unexpected. A federal agency was actually asking educators to request a reservation of radio channels for education.

John W. Studebaker, commissioner of education, reported this development in a letter to every school superintendent and college president in the United States and asked them what his position should be at the FCC hearings. Half of the recipients responded and were practically unanimous in urging Studebaker to request radio channels for education. Consequently, Commissioner Studebaker invited a group of leaders in education to a meeting in his Washington office to help him prepare a brief for presentation to the FCC. As a result of the meeting, the commissioner wrote a 75-page paper asking for channels above the standard AM band but assuring the FCC that educational FM channels would be acceptable.[4]

At the hearings, Studebaker presented his brief and declared
that educators could make good use of the channels; he urged the FCC
to give education a new opportunity to expand educational broadcasting
by reserving a band of radio frequencies for the exclusive use of
organized education. Harry Woodburn Chase, representing the
National Advisory Council for Radio in Education, did not appear at
the hearing, although he had accepted an invitation to testify. Albert
L. Colston, of the Board of Education of New York City, said such
channels would be useful for broadcasting to classrooms and would
afford an opportunity to supplement classroom instruction and to
communicate with classroom teachers. He urged the FCC to reserve
channels in the newly developing areas of the radio spectrum for
educational broadcasting.5

Educator response to the FCC invitation was adequate but cool.
Lack of financial support and administrative backing for broadcasting
were not the principal reasons for the coolness of their interest.
No one had ever broadcast outside the standard band of channels, and
no equipment existed for such broadcasting. Educators did not possess
the technical knowledge to comprehend how these channels might be
used. As yet unaware or unimpressed by experiments in FM and
visual broadcasting, education failed to appreciate the significance
that the precedent of reserving portions of the radio spectrum might
have for the future development of educational broadcasting.

The FCC called another hearing, to begin in October 1936, to
obtain complete information with respect to the broad topic of the
allocation of frequencies, "not only in its engineering, but also in
its corollary social and economic phases." The FCC also wanted
to consider further the "desirability of establishing new classes" of
broadcasting stations.6

Again, educators were specifically invited to attend the hearing.
During the two-week hearing, four educational broadcasters testified.
S. Howard Evans, director of the National Committee on Education
by Radio, spoke of the difficult time educators had in getting satisfactory time from networks and affiliated stations for educational
programs and of the unequal time, power, and channels of educational
stations compared with commercial stations. He realized that these
situations resulted from the limited number of channels available
and stated that it was the responsibility of the commission to correct
these inequalities in any future allocation of radio channels. A. G.
Crane, chairman of the NCER, asked the FCC to protect the privileges
of the few remaining education-owned stations and endorsed the request of Studebaker, on June 15, to reserve a group of channels for
noncommercial educational broadcasting. Edward Bennett and H. B.
McCarthy of the University of Wisconsin, representing the National

Association of Educational Broadcasters, requested the FCC to open up more of the radio band to broadcasting.[7]

The hearing was held by the engineering department of the broadcasting division of the FCC. In its report and recommendations to the broadcasting division, the engineering department summarized the educators' position by saying that technical limitations in the standard band prevented the FCC from granting the traditional demands of educational broadcasters and that educators then wanted a group of channels outside the standard band. The engineering department, after considering the limits of the regular AM band, the financial problems of educational broadcasters, and their unpreparedness for assuming a large role in broadcasting, recommended that a number of channels outside the standard band be reserved for the exclusive use of educational broadcasters.[8]

Alfred N. Goldsmith, pioneer researcher in ultrahigh frequency (UHF) broadcasting (above the standard broadcast band), offered some good advice to educators. "It would probably be good counsel to the educators of the United States to advise them to keep fully informed on the technical and industrial developments in ultra-high frequency broadcasting, and to study carefully in advance what may probably be accomplished by the use of the radio and visual services which can be established in this domain." He continued: "If education is to derive its full benefit from these new instrumentalities of science, it will involve much sober thought, cooperative effort, and systematic planning on the part of educators. The field is too complex and its problems too numerous," he said, "to make an unplanned success at all probable or to reward casual, meager efforts." Goldsmith said that he was "hopeful that the educators of America, fully awakened to the interesting civic possibilities which these media offer, will similarly avail themselves of their potentialities systematically and effectively."[9]

FCC Commissioner George Henry Payne, in a sharp attack on commercial practices and arrogant radio lobbies, warned educators that there would be a fierce behind-the-scenes struggle for control of the newly usable radio frequencies soon to be allocated. He urged educators to become acquainted with the importance these frequencies could have for education.[10]

In a speech to the National Education Association meeting in New Orleans, Commissioner Studebaker said, "I think we should reserve certain high-frequency wave lengths for the exclusive use of local educational agencies and for the free discussion of civic affairs." He urged educators to support his official request for this reservation.[11]

Frank E. Hill, in a book written for the American Association for Adult Education, scored the indifference on the part of educators to the use of radio, the lack of agreement on what was educational broadcasting, and the confusion and hesitancy on the part of the networks in handling educational programs. He accused the networks of giving the final responsibility for educational programs to educators, while keeping the final authority and blaming the educational experts for lack of action. Hill felt that the ultrahigh frequency field of broadcasting held the best potential for the expansion of educational broadcast activity. [12]

NONCOMMERCIAL EDUCATIONAL
BROADCASTING STATIONS

Unheralded, unexpected, and unprecedented was the FCC action of January 26, 1938. On that day, the commission adopted a set of rules governing a new class of stations called <u>noncommercial educational</u>. The term <u>noncommercial educational broadcasting station</u> meant "a high frequency broadcasting station licensed to an organized nonprofit educational agency for the advancement of its educational work and for the transmission of educational and entertainment programs to the general public." The FCC ruled that a noncommercial educational broadcasting station would be licensed only to an organized nonprofit educational agency and upon a showing that the station would be used for the advancement of its educational program. Each station might transmit programs directed to specific schools in the system for use in connection with the regular courses, as well as routine and administrative material pertaining to the school system, and might also transmit educational and entertainment programs to the general public. Each station was required to furnish a nonprofit and noncommercial broadcast service. The FCC allocated 25 channels between 41,000 and 42,000 kilocycles for the exclusive use of this class of stations. The commission required that AM be employed unless it could be shown that there was a need for FM, in which case FM would be authorized. [13]

There were no shouts of joy or glad hosannas sung by educators. Perhaps, they were stunned. After all, the FRC had said it had no power to allocate channels to a special class of broadcasters, and most people believed the FRC when it said such action was the responsibility of Congress. But the FCC had taken the initiative, invited educators to request a reservation of channels, and reserved 25 channels on the basis of a slim demonstration of interest on the part of a few educators, chiefly the commissioner of education. Probably, educators just did not know how to go about using the channels. No one had ever broadcast on those channels. Neither transmitters nor receivers were available. Equipment would have to be made to speci-

50   PUBLIC BROADCASTING

fications. Theoreticians said transmission power was limited to
from 100 to 1,000 watts and reception was limited to from 3 to 15
miles.[14]

The FCC was confident that eventually a substantial program of
educational broadcasts would be forthcoming after the reservation
of 25 channels for education's exclusive and independent use.[15]
Studebaker was highly optimistic and predicted results for education
"as revolutionary as those which followed the invention of the printing
press." It would be possible for educators to establish 1,250 stations
to stimulate the interest of students in new subjects, to conduct model
classes by experts to improve teaching, and to allow supervisors to
keep in touch with classes.[16]

Soon, educators recovered from their shock, and the FCC and
OE were besieged with requests for information. There was little
to offer except FCC rules and OE enthusiasm. Less than a month
after the FCC announcement, however, the Cleveland Board of Education applied for, and got, a license. No other group was willing to
gamble on the operation. After a year, the Cleveland station issued
a report on its activities and described how to plan, install, and
operate a UHF educational broadcasting system, and the OE published
a bulletin on how to establish a noncommercial educational station.
The bulletin announced that 1,500 stations could be operated by local
school authorities as an integral part of the school curriculum.
Stations were not suited for adult education because programs could
not be received on standard radio sets. The FCC clarified its rules
for noncommercial stations on April 17, 1939, and stated that no
fixed schedule or minimum hours of broadcasting would be required
on the new class of stations.[17]

The principle of broadcasting by FM was recognized and patented
in 1905. Edwin Howard Armstrong experimented extensively with
FM and patented improved techniques for broadcasting in 1933. He
conducted tests in New York City during 1934 and 1935 and made his
findings public in 1935. Armstrong received an experimental license
in 1936 to broadcast on frequencies above the standard AM radio
band and, in 1940, urged the FCC to issue commercial licenses for
FM broadcasting.[18]

In March 1940, the FCC held a hearing on FM broadcasting.
FM experimenters, manufacturers, and prospective broadcasters
had organized in January and presented a logical, coherent case for
the commercialization of FM radio. They explained the principles
of FM, demonstrated its capabilities, showed their agreement on
manufacturing standards, promised full production and promotion,
and urged the commission to set aside the frequencies from 40,000
to 50,000 kilocycles for FM broadcasting and to authorize its full
commercialization.[19]

In the two years following the FCC's gift to noncommercial educational broadcasting, many educators had become interested in the new frequencies, had kept up with developments in FM broadcasting, and were now anxious for the FCC to reserve channels for educational broadcasting using the frequency modulation method of broadcasting. In FM, they saw the solution to many of the problems inherent in the AM broadcasting service created for educators by the FCC in 1938. Rather than pay a high price for specially built high-frequency AM transmitters, educational broadcasters could buy standard competitively produced FM transmitters at a saving. Rather than buy custom-made receiving sets, educators could buy production line receivers for much less than custom AM models. If standard receivers were equipped to receive all FM channels, then educational stations could be used for adult education, as well as in-school instruction.

Those interested in the commercialization of FM did all the work for educators. Armstrong, long a professor of electrical engineering at Columbia University, spoke eloquently of FM's usefulness in education and urged that the FCC make provision for educational broadcasting in any assignment of channels to FM service. Conscious of a potential market for transmitting equipment and receivers, prospective FM manufacturers promised that if channels were reserved for noncommercial educational broadcasting, they would include these channels on standard receiving equipment. Conscious of the prestige educators would give to FM radio, prospective commercial broadcasters gave their full support to the reservation of channels for educators.

When two educators appeared at the last day of the hearing, FCC Chairman James Lawrence Fly mused, "As I view the opinions that have been expressed here regarding the educational assignment of the frequencies, I hardly think that the interests of the educational groups are in any way in jeopardy."[20] Studebaker made no statement, except to enter into the record the written comments of Willard Givens, secretary of the National Education Association; Sidney Hall, state superintendent of public instruction in Virginia, representing the National Council of Chief State School Officers; Mary T. Bannerman, National Congress of Parents and Teachers; and Keith Tyler, representing colleges and universities. S. Howard Evans spoke briefly in behalf of the National Association of Educational Broadcasters and the NCER in support of the reservation of FM channels for noncommercial educational broadcasting.

In its Report and Order 67, dated May 20, 1940, the FCC established FM broadcasting on a limited basis immediately and on a full basis as of January 1, 1941. The commission set aside 35 channels between 43,000 and 50,000 kilocycles for commercial broadcasting and reserved 5 channels between 42,000 and 43,000 kilocycles for noncommercial educational broadcasting. The FCC declared that FM was highly developed and "ready to move forward on a broad scale and full commercial basis."[21] Because of its restricted range and coverage, FM was not expected to supplant AM broadcasting, but Commissioner Fly said FM offered better service than AM, and he expected a great public demand for FM broadcasting.[22]

In August 1940, the Board of Education of San Francisco received a license to broadcast for the San Francisco Unified School District. The next month, the Cleveland Board of Education switched from AM to FM broadcasting, and the University of Kentucky requested a construction permit to build a station at Beattysville, Kentucky, to provide educational program service to 60 mountain schools. Within the next year, the boards of education of New York City, Chicago, and San Diego and the University of Illinois received educational FM broadcast licenses.[23]

Armstrong, in a letter to Studebaker, promised to license his patented equipment to educational institutions for the nominal sum of $1 per year and offered free technical assistance and advice to educational broadcasters.[24]

Educational broadcasting was once again off to a good start. It was unfortunate that the Educational Radio Project of the OE had been discontinued by congressional inaction, for the project could have rendered a vital service in getting educational FM broadcasting under-way. Even more unfortunate for nascent FM educational broadcasting was World War II. In a memorandum opinion of February 23, 1942, the FCC announced that it was not in the public interest to allow the further construction of commercial broadcasting facilities.[25] Al-though the FCC never formally applied this restriction to the construc-tion of educational facilities, wartime conditions virtually ended all construction of facilities and manufacture of receivers anyway.[26]

During the war, the FCC received several hundred applications for licenses for commercial FM stations. Probably thinking that there would be plenty of time after the war was over to make plans for educational broadcasting, educators did not make applications during the war for educational stations. On several occasions during 1943 and 1944, Commissioners Fly and Clifford J. Durr urged edu-cators to get busy and make plans.

In a September 17, 1943, speech before the Executive Committee of the FREC in Washington, D.C., Fly said, "Education now has what it has sought through bitter battle over more than a decade—a home of its own on the air. But—and this is the point I want chiefly to stress—those choice channels were not set aside for absentees. The ether," he continued, "is far too crowded, the pressures from other interests seeking to use radio far too great, to permit continued

reservation of those channels, unless educators actually get busy
and fill them with educational stations." Fly concluded, "If education
doesn't want and doesn't use these channels, and if it doesn't prove
its desires and needs by actually making intensive use of them, history
is going to repeat itself, and education will again find it is left with
memories of a lost opportunity."27

POSTWAR EDUCATIONAL BROADCASTING

The OE began a campaign to arouse concern for postwar educational broadcasting. Realizing that there would be a general reallocation of broadcasting channels after the war, Studebaker, on New
Year's Day, 1944, officially requested the FCC to reserve for education 15 FM channels adjacent to commercial FM channels and receivable on standard FM radios. He also requested the FCC to protect
existing plans for regional and statewide educational radio networks
and to furnish ten relay frequencies to link the network stations.
A few weeks later, on January 26, the OE sponsored in New York
the first of 16 regional meetings held during the year to explain to
educators the principles of station planning and to show that cooperation was necessary. The conferees asked the OE to act as their
official representation at FCC hearings, to continue to help them
develop plans for regional and statewide networks, to make consultation services available to them for station planning and construction,
and to keep them informed of developments in educational broadcasting. In a talk regarding problems of education after the war, Studebaker advised educators to use radio for vocational and technical
training of veterans with less than a college education. In 1944, the
Office of Education published a booklet, FM for Education, discuss-
ing educators' plans for the use of radio in the postwar period.28
In June, the OE held a conference in Cleveland of educational
broadcasters and radio equipment manufacturers to decide on standard
equipment for schools and colleges in the postwar period. Recommendations of the Joint Radio Manufacturers Association-Office of
Education School Radio Equipment Standards Study were reported to
a special committee of the Radio Manufacturer's Association (RMA),
which approved almost all the recommendations and provided wholehearted cooperation to serve the school market.29 The study of
radio equipment for education continued for three years and was
beneficial to educational broadcasters and equipment manufacturers.
On August 15, 1944, the FCC gave notice of a hearing to begin
on September 28 regarding the allocation of frequencies to nongovernment services from 10 to 30 million kilocycles. The FCC, the
Interdepartmental Radio Advisory Committee, and the radio industry,

represented by the Radio Technical Planning Board, had already
made studies, and the FCC wanted to make orderly plans for broadcasting before manpower, material, and manufacturing facilities
became available for civilian production of commercial equipment.[30]

The hearing lasted from late September to early November 1944.
Two hundred scientists, industrialists, and educators contributed
5,000 pages of testimony and 500 exhibits to the record.[31] There
was never any serious doubt that the commission would make some
provision for educational FM. The radio industry was acquiescent;
there seemed to be plenty of spectrum space; and an allocation would
not necessitate the destruction of any existing business.

The FCC made it a matter of record that at the time of the hearing, five noncommercial licensees were broadcasting, four construction permits had been issued, eight applications were pending, and
160 requests for information had been received. On October 13,
21 educational broadcasters told of their operations. Studebaker
and Ronald R. Lowdermilk, representing the OE, summarized the
plans of educational broadcasters. Educational groups in 28 states
were planning statewide networks, and 6 other states planned single
stations. Substantially all the witnesses agreed that educational
channels should be contiguous to commercial channels for broadcasting. Armstrong also supported the educational broadcasters. He
said: "An outstanding opportunity for peacetime service is just beginning to emerge in the field of educational broadcasting."[32]

On January 15, 1945, the FCC issued a proposed allocation of
all FM channels. The FCC said it had been committed to the principle
of allocating facilities for educational use since 1938, and it allocated
20 channels between 88,000 and 92,000 kilocycles for noncommercial
educational broadcasting.[33] These 20 channels, which were adjacent
to the 80 channels allocated to commercial FM broadcasting, would
be receivable on standard FM sets.

Oral arguments were held on the proposed allocation plan in
February and March. Lowdermilk appeared at the oral argument
in support of the proposed allocation. There was universal agreement to the educational allocation, and it was adopted by the FCC
in its report of allocations issued in June to become effective on
May 7, the following year.[34]

In March 1946, the commission proposed rules and regulations
for noncommercial educational FM broadcasting service. Because
26 states planned to establish statewide radio networks, the FCC
said that before making station assignments, it would consider
whether the assignment complemented or jeopardized statewide plans.
Licenses would be issued only to nonprofit educational organizations
furnishing a nonprofit and noncommercial service. Licensees could
broadcast regular courses and administrative material to classrooms

or education and entertainment programs to the general public.
Construction permits would be issued for eight months and licenses
for one year. Licensees could broadcast for an unlimited time each
day, but their applications had to show the minimum amount of time
they proposed to broadcast, and their compliance with this minimum
would be taken into account when they applied for renewal of their
licenses. Stations with transmitter power of 1,000 watts or more
were required to have one or more first-class operators on duty
while transmitting; stations with transmitter power of less than 1,000
watts were required to have one or more second-class operators on
duty while transmitting.[35]

Paul A. Walker, FCC commissioner, in a speech to the First
Educational FM-Station Workshop at Ohio State University exhorted
educators to use the 20 channels assigned to them. Four hundred
applications were on file for commercial FM stations, and Walker
warned that if educators did not use their channels, commercial
interests might legitimately demand that the channels be turned over
to those who would. He urged educators to take their second chance
at broadcasting to serve the specific needs of education and to provide high-quality programs for the public at large. Durr, also a
member of the FCC and a staunch advocate of educational broadcasting, asked a group of educators to be alert and aggressive in taking
advantage of FM as an educational tool, and he pleaded with them
not to give up in despair because of the difficulty of budgeting problems.[36]

For more than 10 years, educational broadcasters dogged the
federal government to grant them special considerations, protection,
and radio channels. In an ironic switch, the FCC gave them what
they asked for and dogged them to use what they had been given.

The FCC was not content merely to allocate channels for educational broadcasters. It listened to their complaints, anticipated their
needs, and, by modifying old rules and instituting new ones, made
it easier to establish and operate educational stations.

FM equipment was used extensively by the armed forces of the
United States during World War II. Immediately after the war, much
of this equipment was declared surplus government property. Under
the auspices of the FCC, school officials and representatives of the
OE and the Surplus Property Board met in Washington, D.C., to
discuss ways and means of using surplus military equipment for
educational broadcasting. Educational broadcasters were allowed
to purchase surplus equipment as soon as it became available, so
that they could modify their facilities and begin broadcasting.[37]
Twenty-four educational stations received FCC authorization within
a year after the 1945 allocation plan became effective.

Commissioner Durr, a Phi Beta Kappa at the University of
Alabama and also a graduate of Oxford University in jurisprudence,
was a strong advocate of educational broadcasting during his term
with the FCC, from 1941 to 1948. He was especially interested in
the promotion of educational FM radio and in the adoption of special
rules and conditions for educational broadcasters. The commissioner's
policy during this period reflected his special interest.

The FCC issued its proposed rules for educational FM stations
in March 1945 and allowed 60 days for comments before putting the
rules into effect. A month later, the National Association of Educational Broadcasters asked for a postponement of the effective date so
that it could study the rules, consult with its members, and make
recommendations for alterations. The FCC granted this request,
received the recommendations, and in February 1947 issued new
proposed rules, which became effective on April 1.[38]

Whereas the first proposed rules stated that in making channel
assignments, the FCC would take into consideration how the assignment fitted into statewide plans, the second set of plans "provided
that such plans afford fair treatment to public and private educational
institutions, urban and rural, at the primary, secondary, higher,
and adult education levels."[39] The first FCC proposal said only
that licenses would be issued to nonprofit educational organizations.
The second proposal clarified the point by adding that in determining
the eligibility of publicly controlled educational organizations, the
commission would take account of accreditation by state organizations
and that in determining the eligibility of privately controlled educational organizations, the commission would take account of accreditation by state departments of education and/or recognized regional
and national accreditation organizations.

The rules proposed in 1946 provided for eight-month construction
permits and one-year licenses. The rules proposed in 1947 authorized licenses for one year and construction permits for as long as
the permittees thought it would take them to build their stations.
The original plan allowed educational broadcasters unlimited broadcasting time but required licensees to file a statement indicating the
minimum number of hours they expected to broadcast. Performance
in accordance with the proposed minimum would be taken into account
when licensees asked for a renewal of their licenses. Educational
broadcasters did not like this rule, because educational AM broadcasters had often been temporarily unable to maintain a minimum
schedule, had had their time allowance reduced, and when they were
able to return to their old schedule had found that their time had been
granted to another station. The final plan stated that educational
broadcasters were not required to maintain a regular schedule or to
specify a minimum number of hours of operation. The commission

stated that it would consider the number of hours of broadcasting
when renewing a license only if the demand for educational channels
exceeded the supply. With the adoption of these rules, educational
broadcasters had the freest opportunity to develop educational broadcasting at their own pace that they had had since the beginning of the
regulation of broadcasting by a federal agency.

In a speech to the National Association of Broadcasters, the
organization's president, Justin Miller, made a statement that could
have been interpreted as critical of noncommercial educational FM
broadcasting. FCC Commissioner Durr wrote a letter to Miller and
requested him to clarify his remarks. Miller replied that he was
"definitely not opposed to the establishment and operation of educational broadcasting stations by state universities and colleges and
public school systems."[40] Durr's action was a subtle reminder to
the radio industry that noncommercial educational broadcasting had
the commission's support and sympathy.

Wayne B. Coy became chairman of the FCC in June 1948. In a
revised edition of FM for Education, published by the OE, Coy urged
educators to make full use of the 20 channels reserved for educational
broadcasting. Although the number of educational station authorizations had climbed to 46 in 1948, the number of commercial licenses
had skyrocketed to over 1,000. If this rate of increase continued,
the FCC was afraid that it would have to take some channels away
from education and grant them to commercial broadcasters.[41] The
number of educational FM stations increased slowly, but the number
of commercial FM stations reached a peak in 1948, and then rapidly
declined. Commercial stations gave up their licenses for many
reasons, but among the more important were that the stations were
unable to get network programs to suit their needs, the NAB's propaganda drove advertisers away from FM, and listeners were unable
to get sensitive receiving sets.[42] Because of the decrease in the
number of commercial FM stations, there was no immediate pressure
to take channels away from educational broadcasters.

Effective May 1, 1948, the FCC extended the normal licensing
period for noncommercial educational FM stations to three years.[43]
This was a saving in time and expense to educational broadcasters,
who had previously been required to renew their licenses annually.

At the direction of the FCC, Syracuse University conducted an
experiment in broadcasting with 2.5 watts of transmitter power.
The experiment successfully demonstrated over a one-year period
that a station could broadcast with low wattage over a distance of
three to five miles. It was estimated that if studio facilities were
available, a low-power station could be equipped for less than $2,000.
The FCC, in June, issued a notice of proposed rule making establishing 10-watt noncommercial educational FM broadcasting stations as

a new classification of educational stations. This action was a
deliberate effort to encourage educational FM broadcasting. The
commission reasoned that educational institutions could start broadcasting in a small way and then expand their operations after gaining
experience in broadcasting. Not only would low-power transmitting
equipment be less expensive than high-power equipment, but the FCC
specifically exempted low-watt stations from the commission's
Standards of Good Engineering Practice Concerning FM Broadcasting
Stations. The transmitter and associated transmitter equipment were
required to bear the Underwriter's Laboratory certificate for safety
but did not have to meet FCC standards. As proposed, low-watt
stations were required to provide "satisfactory service" in regard
to audio distortion, audio frequency range, carrier hum, and noise
level.[44] The commission purposely did not define "satisfactory
service."

To save educators time and money, the FCC held no hearing on
the proposals but invited written statements. The commission
received two statements in support of its suggestion and none in
opposition. A third statement, advocating the establishment of nonprofit commercial operation of low-watt stations, was found to be
beyond the purview of the proposal. The FCC apparently felt that
two supporters were sufficient and ordered the proposal to become
effective without change on September 27.[45]

At the International Telecommunications Convention held in
Atlantic City, New Jersey, in 1947, delegates instituted new minimum
requirements for radio operators and established a new class of permits. Holders of the new Radiotelephone Third Class Operator's
License were required to pass a simple, nontechnical examination
on radio. In 1949, the FCC proposed a rule that would allow 10-watt
FM transmitters on noncommercial educational broadcasting stations
to be operated by third-class operators. There being no statements
filed in opposition to the proposal, the FCC ordered the rule to become effective September 1, 1950.[46]

Further, to encourage the establishment of educational FM
stations, the FCC proposed in 1950 that the commission allow the
remote control operation of noncommercial educational FM broadcasting stations licensed for transmitter power output of 10 watts or
less. The proposal became effective January 25, 1951. This rule
permitted studio personnel having first- second- or third-class
licenses to operate the transmitter from the studio if there were an
on/off control switch and an aural monitoring device at the station.
Remote control of the transmitter from the studio permitted the
station to operate with a minimum number of personnel.[47]

In addition to the main carrier wave used for regular FM broadcasting, each frequency assigned to an FM radio station has a sub-

carrier wave, which cannot be received on standard FM receiving
sets. The subcarrier wave can be divided into four broadcasting
channels. Use of these channels in addition to the main broadcasting
channels is called <u>multiplexing</u>. In 1958 and 1959, the FCC held an
inquiry to determine whether commercial stations should be authorized to multiplex for such auxiliary services as broadcasting back-
ground music to specially attuned receiving sets in stores. The FCC
authorized commercial FM stations to engage in multiplex activities
in May 1960.[48]

Because the American Medical Association (AMA), the National
Association of Educational Broadcasters, and WGBH Educational
Foundation, Boston, Mass., petitioned the FCC to allow noncommercial stations to broadcast on a multiplex basis and because of comments made by Fordham University and the Pacifica Foundation
during the hearings regarding commercial multiplex activities, the
commission invited written comments in 1960 concerning proposed
rule making to permit noncommercial FM stations to engage in multiplex subsidiary operations for educational purposes. The FCC received favorable comments from the NAEB, AMA, four universities,
and two other noncommercial licensees and ruled on January 30,
1961, that noncommercial FM stations could engage in multiplex
operations.[49]

While multiplexing would not be used by all noncommercial FM
stations, it could serve several useful purposes. Stations could
multiplex broadcast special programs to classrooms and other
special audiences while continuing with their regular programming.
Multiplexing made it possible for listeners to "talk back" to network
lecturers and to participate in group discussions. It could be used
for the remote control of transmitters and to telemeter operations
back to the control point. Multiplex broadcasting could also be
utilized to relay programs between stations.[50]

After the FCC authorized commercial FM stations to broadcast
stereophonically on a multiplex basis on April 19, 1961, the commission received numerous letters requesting the same authorization
for noncommercial stations. Finding no reason to object, the FCC,
on November 8, 1961, without going through the formal rule-making
procedure, authorized noncommercial educational FM stations to
broadcast stereophonically.[51]

After the end of World War II, the number of FCC authorizations
for educational stations increased on an average of about 15 each
year, but the largest growth was in the 1960s. Starting with 24
authorizations one year after the war, the number increased to almost
300 by the end of 1965. Coincident with this growth, and contributing
significantly to it, were the deliberate efforts of the FCC to encourage
educational stations.

By allowing educational licensees to broadcast as little or as
much as they liked, the FCC solved the old complaint about having
time taken away from them. By calling for written statements rather
than oral hearings for proposed rule changes and by extending the
licensing period to three years, the FCC saved educators the time
and money involved in frequent appearances before the commission.
By establishing ten-watt stations operated by remote control by
third-class operators, the commission allowed educators to begin
broadcasting with minimum expense and minimum personnel. By
authorizing multiplex broadcasting, the FCC challenged educators
to make maximum use of their channels. Educational FM broadcasting did not prove as important to education as the printing press, but
educators had been given every opportunity to make of radio broadcasting what they would. The FCC demonstrated time and again that
it is the policy of the federal government to afford every encouragement and advantage to noncommercial educational FM broadcasting
stations.

NOTES

1. Frank Ernest Hill, Tune in for Education (New York:
National Committee on Education by Radio, 1942), p. 88 (hereafter
cited as Hill, Tune in for Education).
2. Federal Register, I, 537.
3. Federal Communications Commission, Official Report of
Proceedings; In the Matter of: The Allocation of Frequencies above
30,000 KC and the Review of Present Frequency Allocations, Docket
3929 (Washington, D.C.: Ward and Paul, 1936) (hereafter cited as
FCC, The Allocation of Frequencies above 30,000 KC).
4. U.S. Commissioner of Education, Annual Report, 1940
(Washington, D.C.: U.S. Government Printing Office, 1941), p. 92.
5. FCC, The Allocation of Frequencies above 30,000 KC.
6. Federal Register, I, 1149.
7. Federal Communications Commission, Official Report of
Proceedings, In the Matter of: Informal Hearings on Broadcasting,
Docket 4063 (Washington, D.C.: Ward and Paul, 1936).
8. Federal Communications Commission, Report on Social and
Economic Data Pursuant to the Informal Hearing on Broadcasting,
Docket 4063, Beginning October 5, 1936 (Washington, D.C.: U.S.
Government Printing Office, 1938).
9. New York Times, December 13, 1937.
10. Congressional Record, LXXXII, A35, A36.
11. New York Times, February 23, 1937.

12. Frank Ernest Hill, Listen and Learn (New York: American Association for Adult Education, 1937).

13. Federal Register, III, 364.

14. Hill, Tune in for Education, p. 91.

15. Congressional Record, LXXXIII, A1904–A1907.

16. New York Times, February 6, 1938.

17. New York Times, February 27, 1938; Cleveland Board of Education, Report on Radio Activities 1938–1939 (Cleveland, Ohio: Board of Education, 1939); Department of Interior, Office of Education, Ultra-High Frequency Educational Broadcasting Stations, mimeographed (1939); Federal Register, IV, 1670.

18. Sydney W. Head, Broadcasting in America (Boston: Houghton Mifflin Company, 1956), pp. 148, 149.

19. Federal Communications Commission, Official Report of Proceedings, In the Matter of: Aural Broadcasting on Frequencies above 25,000 KC, Docket 5805 (Washington, D.C.: Ward and Paul, 1940).

20. Ibid.

21. Federal Communications Commission, Annual Report, vol. 6 (Washington, D.C.: U.S. Government Printing Office, 1940), p. 65 (hereafter cited as FCC, Annual Report, vol. 6).

22. New York Times, November 3, 1940.

23. Federal Communications Commission, Annual Report, vol. 7 (Washington, D.C.: U.S. Government Printing Office, 1941), pp. 35, 36.

24. New York Times, June 29, 1941.

25. Federal Register, VII, 1702.

26. Murray Edelman, The Licensing of Radio Service in the United States, 1927–1947 (Urbana: University of Illinois Press, 1950), p. 128.

27. James Lawrence Fly, speech, in Federal Security Agency, Office of Education, FM for Education (Washington, D.C.: U.S. Government Printing Office, 1944) (hereafter cited as FSA, FM for Education).

28. Federal Communications Commission, Official Report of Proceedings, In the Matter of: Allocation of Frequencies to the Various Classes of Nongovernmental Services in the Radio Spectrum from 10 KC to 30,000,000 KC, Docket 6651 (Washington, D.C.: Ward and Paul, 1944), p. 1431 (hereafter referred to as FCC, Allocation of Frequencies from 10 KC to 30,000,000 KC); U.S. Office of Education, Annual Report, 1944 (Washington, D.C.: U.S. Government Printing Office, 1945), pp. 56, 57 (hereafter cited as OE, Annual Report, 1944); New York Times, February 2, 1944; FSA, FM for Education.

29. New York Times, June 25, 1944; OE, Annual Report, 1944, p. 58; Federal Security Agency, U.S. Office of Education, Annual Report, 1945 (Washington, D.C.: U.S. Government Printing Office, 1946), pp. 73-74.

30. Federal Register, IX, 10270.

31. Federal Communications Commission, Allocation of Frequencies from 10 KC to 30,000,000 KC.

32. Ibid.

33. Federal Communications Commission, Report of Proposed Allocations, January 15, 1945, mimeographed (1945).

34. Federal Communications Commission, Report of Allocations from 25,000 KC to 30,000,000 KC, May 25, 1945, mimeographed (1945); Federal Communications Commission, Report of Allocations from 44-108 MC, June 27, 1945, mimeographed (1945).

35. Federal Register, XI, 2839.

36. Congressional Record, XCI, A3547, A3548; New York Times, May 4, 1946.

37. Congressional Record, XCI, A3547, A3548.

38. Federal Register, XI, 2839, XII, 1369.

39. Ibid.

40. New York Times, September 30, 1947.

41. Federal Security Agency, Office of Education, FM for Education, rev. ed. (Washington, D.C.: U.S. Government Printing Office, 1948).

42. Congressional Record, XCV, A2206.

43. Federal Register, XIII, 1363.

44. Ibid., 3488.

45. Ibid., 4921.

46. Ibid., XIV, 5435, XV, 4374.

47. Ibid., XV, 6789, 9189.

48. Ibid., XXV, 4240-4243.

49. Ibid., 7405-7406, XXVI, 1027-1029.

50. Roger E. Peterson, "FM Multiplexing—A Tool for Educational Broadcasting," NAEB Journal, 21 (January-February, 1962): 73-78; Federal Communications Commission, Annual Report, 1961 (Washington, D.C.: U.S. Government Printing Office, 1962), p. 54.

51. Federal Register, XXVI, 10729.

4

THE FEDERAL COMMUNICATIONS COMMISSION—TELEVISION

EXPERIMENTATION WITH TELEVISION BROADCASTING

Whereas radio broadcasting burgeoned for seven years before it was regulated by the federal government, television broadcasting developed entirely under federal supervision. The first experiments with television began in 1874, when Paul Nipkow invested a mechanical system for transmitting views by direct wire. An electronic system to perform the same feat, an iconoscope, was patented by Vladimir Zworykin in 1923. That same year, a picture of President Warren Harding was transmitted from Washington, D.C., to Philadelphia by wire.[1] No license was needed to transmit pictures by wire, but Congress foresaw the use of radio waves for broadcasting pictures. In the Radio Act of 1927 Congress established the Federal Radio Commission to regulate all forms of interstate and foreign radio transmissions and communications within the United States. Radio communications were defined as "pictures or communications of any nature transferred by electrical energy."[2]

Congress established the FRC just in time to regulate television broadcasting, for, in 1927, the Bell Telephone Company demonstrated a new system in New York City by broadcasting the image of Herbert Hoover for newsmen. In a general order adopted in October 1928, the FRC provided for limited experimentation with television broadcasting on the radio band from 550 to 1,500 kilocycles under rigid conditions and at hours that would not interfere with radio broadcasting.[3] The FRC issued 16 experimental licenses. These licenses were truly experimental, for no one was allowed to broadcast for commercial speculation. The authority to regulate "transmissions by radio of pictures" was transferred to the Federal Communications Commission by the Communications Act of 1934.

Unlike the case of radio, colleges had nothing to do with the laboratory stages in the development of television. Some colleges were, however, among the first licensees for experimental television broadcasting and became immediately interested in the rise of television for education. Station W9XK, licensed to the electrical engineering department of the State University of Iowa, began broadcasting a series of educational programs in 1932. During the seven-year existence of this station, it broadcast 389 adult education programs in the evening hours. Kansas State University was telecasting in 1934 and Purdue University in 1935. In 1938, NBC arranged a demonstration of the use of television in college classrooms. C. C. Clark, associate professor of general science at New York University, lectured for 40 minutes to 200 students watching him on 15 receivers. Clark discussed the principles of television, and students asked him questions through microphones placed in the classrooms.[4]

The educational potentialities of television were noted by commercial interests, organizations of educational broadcasters, and agencies of the federal government. David Sarnoff, president of the Radio Corporation of America observed in 1930 that with television, educators could break the confining walls of masses of American people and bring into their homes forces that would stimulate higher standards. "There is little in the field of cultural education," he said, "that cannot be visioned for the home through television." In 1936, the National Advisory Council for Radio in Education noted experiments with educational television and said, "There is no question about the great possibilities of educational television development in the future." The organization published a pamphlet to keep educators abreast of technical developments in television broadcasting. At a hearing of the FCC in 1936 to determine the trends in broadcasting and the future requirements of broadcasters in the radio spectrum, John W. Studebaker, U.S. Commissioner of Education, speaking in behalf of educators, declared: "Television has infinite educational possibilities. I hope that in giving jurisdiction to licensees in television, the Federal Communications Commission will see to it that, as a matter of public interest, education is properly served." At the First National Conference on Educational Broadcasting, held in Washington, D.C., in 1936, FCC Chairman Anning S. Prall showed the commission's awareness of the tremendous possibilities of television for educational broadcasting when he stated: "In considering the potential expansion of education's use of radio, I assume you educators have in mind the possibilities of linking present broadcasting facilities with television. This is staggering to the imagination."[5]

GUIDING TELEVISION FROM EXPERIMENTATION
TO COMMERCIALIZATION

Equally staggering to the FCC was its total responsibility for
guiding television from experimentation to commercialization. The
commission encouraged the widest range of noncommercial experimentation, and by the end of the 1930s, a 441-line picture could be
used with reasonably good results. On April 30, 1939, NBC began
regular program service over its experimental station W2XBS by
televising Franklin D. Roosevelt as he opened the World's Fair in
New York City. Allen B. Dumont began manufacturing television
sets and sold about 1,000 of these in the New York area during the
first year.[6]

The FCC refused to be pushed into the commercialization of
television. It believed that television was still in the technical
research and experimental operations phase. It wanted the industry
to develop logically on a sound economic basis and warned against
premature commercialization or standards for television in view of
improvements necessary to establish television as a public service.
The commission feared that it would spawn a monopoly if it accepted
one set of standards and excluded all other experimental equipment.
It did not want the general public to buy expensive receivers that
would become obsolete as new discoveries were made.[7]

Pressure from the communications industry, however, was
very great. Experimenters had spent millions of dollars in research,
and they wanted some return for their money. On December 21,
1939, the FCC tentatively adopted a proposal of the Radio Manufacturers Association to allow television broadcasting by three different
systems. It proposed establishing two classes of stations: experimental for technical research and experimental for program research.
The latter research stations were to be authorized to broadcast five
hours a week under limited commercial sponsorship to cover production costs. In February 1940, the commission officially adopted the
plan, to become effective September 1.[8]

RCA began a large-scale advertising campaign in March to
promote the sale of its television receivers. The commission had
established no set of standards for television engineering practice
and would permit three different systems to experiment with program
production. The FCC feared that a large sale of RCA receivers
would tend to stop research, freeze technical development, and force
the commission to accept the RCA standards or bring down the wrath
of the public left holding obsolete receivers if the commission adopted
another system. Consequently, on March 22, the commission
rescinded its order allowing commercially sponsored experimental
programs to begin on September 1.[9]

In a nationwide radio broadcast explaining the commission's action, Chairman James Lawrence Fly warned that premature standardization and obsolescence of receivers would result from the kind of full-scale commercialization the RCA advertising campaign would tend to produce. Fly believed that television had a great potential for development into a permanent instrument of entertainment, of information, and of education, and he refused to permit this development to be jeopardized by commercial attempts to get a quick return on their investments in research.[10]

RCA was furious, but the rest of the industry breathed a sigh of relief. The RMA in cooperation with the FCC established a National Television Standards Committee to recommend a universally usable system.[11] In March 1941, the committee proposed a system using 525 lines; the FCC adopted the system on May 2 and ordered full commercial sponsorship of programs beginning July 1. The FCC allotted 18 channels for television broadcasting and required a minimum of 15 hours of broadcasting a week on each station.[12] WNBT, the NBC station in New York City, was the first station to broadcast sponsored programs. Ten construction permits were issued before World War II began. On April 27, 1942, the commission announced that because of the wartime restrictions on materials and labor, it would grant no new television licenses or construction permits during the war.[13] Six commercial stations operated during the war and broadcast about four hours a week.

World War II gave the FCC a respite. The commission was not wholly satisfied with technical developments in television in 1941, but pressure from the communications industry and the public made it necessary to compromise on the best system then available. Research developments in electronics during the war contributed significantly to the development of television, made 1941 television obsolete, and opened, once again, the question of television standards.

Eight years after he expressed the hope that the FCC would serve the purpose of education in television, Studebaker, in June 1944, formally requested the FCC to reserve two television channels for education. The use of television for educational purposes had been largely ignored by educators, but at a regional conference of the American Association of School Administrators, a delegate from New Jersey, Thomas Ray Jones, boosted the use of television for instructional purposes.[14] At an FCC hearing in 1944 regarding the postwar allocation of the radio spectrum to nongovernment services, the only voice requesting television channels for education was Studebaker's.[15]

The big battle at the hearing was among prospective television manufacturers. CBS had concentrated its research in the UHF range of the radio spectrum and requested the FCC to wait to set standards

after its research was completed. The Television Broadcasters
Association said that there was no guarantee that UHF could be
received with greater effectiveness. FCC Chairman Fly agreed
that the advantages of UHF broadcasting were unknown and thought
it would be foolish to commercialize television at its current standards.
The powerful Radio Technical Planning Board, representing the RMA
and the Institute for Radio Engineers, urged the FCC to accept the
current standards in the very high frequency (VHF) range, which
were good enough to satisfy the public. RCA favored VHF broadcasting because it could be started immediately, while color and
better black and white in the UHF range would require more research
and experimentation.

FCC TELEVISION ALLOCATION REPORTS

In a preliminary television allocation report in mid-January
1945, the FCC stated that educator interest in television did not
warrant an immediate reservation of channels for education. Indeed,
the only person showing any interest at all was Commissioner of
Education Studebaker; however, the FCC guaranteed that applications
of educational institutions for television licenses would be treated
"on an equal basis with applications from non-education applicants"
and promised that "if at any future date educational institutions
believe that there is sufficient educator interest in television and
sufficient probability of developing a useful educational television
service, the matter can be raised anew at that time."[16] The FCC
had just reserved 20 FM radio channels for education and was now
announcing its willingness to discuss the reservation of television
channels when educators showed a genuine interest in them.

In its final television allocation report of May 1945, the FCC
bowed to public clamor and pressure from commercial broadcasters
and manufacturers by making available 13 channels in the VHF range
for commercial television. The FCC intended that VHF television
should be a temporary expedient. The commission expected to foster
a nationwide, competitive system in the UHF realm of the radio
spectrum, where there was enough space for nearly 100 channels
and for the broadcasting of color and superior monochrome pictures.
The FCC expressed the hope "that all persons interested in the future
of television will undertake comprehensive and adequate experimentation in the upper portion of the spectrum." Because the FCC had
shown a concern for the special interests of educators for seven
years, it probably felt that by the time research had opened UHF
for broadcasting, educators would be interested in television and
that there would be plenty of space for educational stations. A

further indication of the crowded conditions in the VHF range and the
temporary nature of the television assignments there was the fact
that the FCC required television to share the channels with fixed
and mobile radio services.[17]

The television industry knew that the assignments were temporary
because it repeatedly asked the commission to guarantee that VHF
channels would be used for television for at least ten years. The
FCC rescinded its freeze order on October 7, 1945, and thereby
allowed commercial manufacturers to resume their activities.
Because materials were still in short supply and because manufacturers wanted some assurance before they started full-scale production that there would be no immediate shift to UHF, the manufacture
of television equipment began slowly.[18] CBS scared the VHF boosters
during the spring and summer of 1946 by publicly demonstrating a
UHF color system that could not be transmitted or received on VHF
equipment. CBS petitioned the FCC in September 1946 for full commercial authorization of its system. After hearings that lasted for
three months, the FCC regretfully denied the petition, because the
system was incompatible with monochrome receivers and because
the pictures were of poor quality.[19] This decision removed the threat
of UHF broadcasting, and a television "gold rush" began in the summer
and fall of 1947.

PROBLEMS WITH INTERFERENCE

The boom had hardly started before there were reports of interference on television channel 1 from fixed and mobile services and
other sources. A hearing in June 1947 established that no sharing
arrangements with other services were practicable on any television
channels. After another hearing, the FCC deleted channel 1 from
television service. The order assigned it to nongovernment fixed
and mobile radio services and eliminated the sharing of channels 2
through 13 by nontelevision services. The commission reiterated
at this time its contention that a "truly nationwide and competitive
television system must find its home higher in the spectrum."[20]

As more and more television stations began broadcasting,
reports of interference from new sources piled up in the offices of
the FCC. As each new station went on the air, it caused interference
with stations with which it was sharing the channel and with stations
using adjacent channels. In addition, engineers reported that the
troposphere was causing television interference. During the summer
of 1948, the FCC held a hearing to gather specific information on the
newly discovered sources of interference. The commission felt that
by reassigning each television station at a greater distance from

others, it would be able to reduce interference from cochannel and adjacent channel stations. It had no suggestions for the elimination of tropospheric interference.[21]

The commission announced an informal conference with representatives of the television industry for September 13 to discuss the best method of securing engineering data regarding tropospheric interference, the advisability of reassigning all television channels to reduce cochannel and adjacent channel interference before the engineering data was received, and the policy that should be adopted concerning pending applications for new stations.[22] Since this was to be an informal conference, there was no requirement that conferees file official notices of their intention to appear or that their testimony show a connection to the stated issues; consequently, Commissioner Wayne Coy issued two separate invitations to educators to appear at the conference and to request the FCC to set aside channels for education.[23] None appeared.

BEGINNINGS OF THE EDUCATIONAL
TELEVISION MOVEMENT

In 1945, the FCC said it would take up the matter of educational reservations when educator interest was aroused. The commission probably felt that there would be room in the UHF range when television moved to that area of the spectrum. UHF developments were slow, while VHF usage grew rapidly. The FCC, realizing that VHF was gaining a permanent foothold, had aided this development by attacking interference problems and clearing the waves for television. Little educator interest in television had developed by 1948, and some commissioners felt that educators would be prevented from having their own stations if they did not evince some interest before commercial stations had acquired all the channels. Coy's invitation to educators was an attempt at stimulating the interest of educators in requesting television channels.

Information received at the informal conferences raised serious objections to the basis upon which allocations were made, and the commission, in September 1948, announced that pending further consideration of the problems facing television, it would refuse all requests for television licenses. To consider the problems that had necessitated the television "freeze," the FCC instituted an ad hoc committee to investigate the effects of the troposphere and terrain on television reception and called a series of engineering conferences to study a wide range of ancillary problems.[24]

At a joint meeting of the Institute for Education by Radio (IER) and the National Association of Educational Broadcasters on October 12,

1948, a group of aggressive NAEB delegates called a special caucus
and succeeded in passing a resolution favoring the reservation of
UHF channels for the future use of educators. No school was actively
ready to undertake television broadcasting, but these delegates realized the danger of waiting too long, just as Cóy did. They pushed
the passage of the resolution in the hope that the channels would be
available when educators would be able to use them. Wilbur Schramm,
dean of the communications division of the University of Illinois,
brought 30 educational broadcasters to the Allerton House Seminar
in 1949 to develop a synthesis of purpose and working philosophy.
At this meeting were the leaders of the subsequent educational television movement.[25]

After the FCC assimilated the evidence presented by the ad hoc
committee and the engineering conferences, it announced, in July
1949, a new round of hearings encompassing all the problems facing
the industry and, especially, the nationwide allocation of television
channels. As a basis of discussion, the FCC offered to add 42 UHF
channels to the 12 VHF channels and proposed a revision of the table
allocating stations to the available channels. The invitation to the
hearing included all previous persons who had appeared before the
commission regarding television and all persons who had indicated
by petition, letter, or application their interest in the allocation of
television channels to specific areas. The FCC had heard about the
resolution passed at the meeting of educators in October the previous
year, and on the basis of this slim evidence of educational interest
in television, it specifically invited educators to appear and make a
case for the reservation of television channels for education.[26]

Commissioner Frieda B. Hennock, who before her appointment
to the FCC on May 24, 1948, had been associated with a law firm in
New York City and a leader in the liberal wing of the Democratic
Party, dissented from the commission's views. She believed that
inviting educators to the hearing was insufficient and thought that
the FCC should have made a tentative reservation of channels based
on the interest shown at the joint meeting of the IER and NAEB.
"I think," she said, "that our duty to 'encourage the larger and more
effective use of radio in the public interest' requires us to make an
affirmative effort to make provision to insure that educators will be
able to make full use of television and to enter this field before the
spectrum becomes too crowded."[27]

The commission's invitation provided the legal basis, and
Hennock's dissent the moral basis, for decisions by educational
organizations to appear at the hearing. Attorneys for the NAEB
filed a notice of their intention to appear at the hearings. The NAEB
notice was supported by cofilings of the Association of Land Grant
Colleges and Universities, the Association of State University Presi-

dents, and the National University Extension Association. The U.S.
Office of Education and the National Education Association filed
requests for VHF channels for immediate use and UHF channels for
future use.[28]

The FCC decided to tackle the problem of color television first.
Hearings began in September 1949 did not end until the commission
accepted the CBS standards for a mechanical and incompatible color
system in October 1950.

The commission was then ready to begin hearings on other aspects
of the television question, including channels for education. The one-
year delay afforded persons interested in educational television an
opportunity to stimulate and organize support. Franklin Dunham,
director of the audiovisual education division of the OE, spoke to a
group of educators in Baltimore about educational television. He
said educators had three advantages in television: know how, show
how, and a reservoir of subject matter. He cited 18 colleges and
two school systems that were putting educational programs on commercial stations. Dunham thought this would be valuable experience
for educators who hoped to establish their own stations.[29]

The most forceful booster of educational television was a member
of the FCC, Commissioner Hennock. In 1949, other members of the
FCC had gone out of their way to support educators, by specifically
inviting them to build a case for the reservation of channels at FCC
hearings. Paul A. Walker, vice chairman of the FCC, had stated
to a group of educators, "I am for education. And I am for television.
I am personally anxious to see some provision for noncommercial
educational stations." Still, it was Hennock who stimulated, inspired,
and browbeat educators into requesting television channels and encouraged the American public to back the educators' request.
Born in Poland in 1904, Hennock had immigrated with her parents
to the United States at the age of six. She had a high regard for
formal education. She had what a close associate called a "Jewish
immigrant's love for education." Educational television was a natural
issue for her, therefore, and a good issue for the FCC's only female
commissioner as well. Hennock was a highly emotional woman,
whose pleading and shouting in closed sessions were not ineffective
in persuading reluctant commissioners to accept her point of view.
The intensity and persistence of her interest goaded educators and
government officials to prepare testimony, attend hearings, and
get what she thought they needed. She did not write well, but she
felt strongly. Her public addresses and her opinions on matters
before the FCC were written by assistants, but the conviction was
hers, as was the point of view. She spoke any time she had the
opportunity. In a speech to the IER, Hennock said: "I already am
on record as proposing to set aside certain channels for you educators

who are unable to come in at present because of financial reasons.
It seems to me necessary to reserve channels to protect the interests of educators. However," she continued,

> the FCC, as you know, realizes that a channel is very
> valuable property and it belongs to the public. With
> the scarcity of and the demand for channels, we cannot
> sit tight in Washington and reserve them for you unless
> you show some interest. I have asked you educators
> to evince your interest, to indicate your willingness
> to use them in the future. I want the channels set aside,
> and I want you people to come in and back up the United
> States Office of Education, the NEA, and the other edu-
> cational institutions who filed notice of appearance. I
> want you to write and phone the FCC to reserve these
> channels, and I ask that as many of you as possible
> appear before the Commission.[30]

Later at the meeting, Hennock said: "We at the FCC cannot and will
not impose from above our own individual ideas of what American
broadcasting shall be like." She begged educators to make their
influence felt. "You must do it, for nothing is so important to you
as educators and to our nation."[31]

When the FCC announced that it would resume its television
hearings on October 2, 1950, and scheduled testimony concerning
the reservation of television channels for educational television,[32]
Hennock stepped up her crusade. To the National Association of
Women Lawyers, she said:

> We are now about to allocate what is in all probability
> the last significant piece of spectrum which will be
> assigned for broadcasting purposes. This is the UHF
> band in which the Commission will authorize commer-
> cial television operation. I have urged that a portion
> of the frequencies available for television be reserved
> for the use of noncommercial educational institutions.

She urged her fellow lawyers to back her request. She felt that
educational stations would stimulate competition to provide better
programs on commercial stations. "Technical progress in television," Hennock declared, "is worthless unless it is put to good use."
In another typical speech, this time to the New York Women's Advertising Club, Hennock praised technical advances in television but
said programs were more important than technological progress.
She cited the hundreds of letters received by the FCC complaining

about programs and said: "Education can bring a great deal to television. Educators pioneered in radio; their contributions to television can be greatly superior." She advocated that 25 percent of the eventual 2,000 television channels be reserved for education and urged her listeners to back her suggestions.33

By 1950, a number of organizations had heard the call and felt the pressure from Commissioner Hennock and were preparing petitions and testimony, but their goals and procedure were contradictory. Some stressed nonprofit operation, and others stressed noncommercial. Dunham, of the OE, with the blessing of the NAEB and at the instigation of Commissioner Hennock, called a meeting in his office for October 16, 1950, to reconcile the differences. In attendance were representatives of those organizations that had indicated to the FCC their intention of appearing before the commission to request television channels for education. Recalling the fiasco at the FCC conference in 1934, when conferees reported conflicting versions of their problems and made contradictory requests for congressional action to reserve radio channels for education, these educators vowed their determination not to make the same mistakes again but to present a logical, unified case for both nonprofit and noncommercial stations.

THE JOINT COMMITTEE ON
EDUCATIONAL TELEVISION

With the advice of the OE, the cooperation of the NAEB, and with the insistence of Miss Hennock, the representation formed an ad hoc committee, the Joint Committee on Educational Television (JCET), to plan and coordinate the testimony to be given to the FCC. At the suggestion of Commissioner Hennock, former FCC General Counsel and U.S. prosecutor at the Nuremberg Trials, Telford Taylor, was employed to represent JCET before the commission. The decision to ask for nonprofit and noncommercial operations was overruled by Taylor, who shared the belief with Commissioner Hennock that asking for nonprofit operations would lessen the chances for FCC approval of the reservation of channels for education and complicate future relations with foundations, labor, the broadcast industry, and business.34

Senator John Bricker, trustee of Ohio State University, which was particularly interested in the prospects of educational television, introduced a resolution in the Senate in November 1950 directing the FCC to study the general problem of allocating television frequencies, and particularly his suggestion that the commission allocate one television channel in each state for noncommercial educational broad-

casting.[35] Bricker knew that the FCC was hearing testimony on the
question of allocating channels for educational television, and he used
the whip of congressional interest to keep it to its task.

The commission was probably predisposed to do something for
education before the hearing began, but it was never disposed to do
as much as Hennock hoped for or expected. It was necessary first
for educators to present a clear case showing the possibilities television held for education, demonstrating some interest in educational
television, and promising that channels would be used if reserved
for them. Then, it was essential for Commissioner Hennock to
wheedle, cajole, and threaten as much as possible out of her fellow
commissioners.

Coy's invitations triggered the NAEB resolution. The resolution
gave the FCC the excuse to invite educators to request television
channels. Its invitation and Hennock's exhortations gave educators
the inspiration to make such a request. The OE meeting turned
inspiration into organization.

The educational television phase of the FCC hearing lasted from
November 1950 to January 1951. Testimony from 76 witnesses—71
supporters of educational television and 5 opponents—filled 2,600
pages of the record.[36] The supporting witnesses appeared for the
JCET, which represented seven national education groups: American
Council on Education, Association for Education by Radio and Televi-
sion, Association of Land Grant Colleges and Universities, National
Association of Educational Broadcasters, National Association of
State Universities, National Education Association, and National
Council of Chief State School Officers. The opposing witnesses
appeared for National Broadcasting Company, Columbia Broadcasting
System, National Association of Broadcasters, and Television Broad-
casters Association.

Attorneys for JCET requested the FCC to reserve television
channels for educational stations to provide programs to schools
and cultural, educational, and entertainment programs for a general
audience. They suggested that the commission establish rules for
educational television substantially the same as those for noncommercial educational FM radio stations. In allocating channels, the JCET
asked for the use of one VHF channel in 168 metropolitan areas with
a population of 30,000 or more and in 46 primarily educational centers.
In such areas as New York City and Los Angeles, where all VHF
channels had already been assigned, the JCET asked that the commercial stations be required to give a percentage of their time to
educational programs. The committee asked that 20 percent of all
UHF assignments be made for educational stations. Each organization represented by the JCET then presented a written statement
outlining its general position regarding educational television.

Educators then attempted to show the scope and nature of the service that television could render. Educational broadcasters from Baltimore, Philadelphia, and other cities talked about their experiments with programs for classroom reception and their plans for the future. Some college broadcasters declared that some schools were prepared to begin an educational program service immediately; others said they were interested but did not yet have the money to begin broadcasting. They requested that their interests be protected so that they would not be excluded from broadcasting. Representatives of medicine and agriculture told of television's potential usefulness for educational programs in those fields. The FCC witnessed a demonstration of educational broadcasting to classrooms in Hagerstown, Maryland.

Finally, the JCET presented witnesses who stated what would be done if channels were reserved for educators. Witnesses reviewed the past history of educational AM broadcasting to show what happened when radio channels were not reserved for educators. Other witnesses used FM broadcasting as an example of what educators had done when channels were reserved. Other speakers testified concerning the nature of cooperation between commercial and educational broadcasters. They related that plans for educational television programs had been shelved to make room for commercially sponsored programs and that noncommercial educational programs had been canceled in favor of entertainment programs produced for advertisers. It was alleged that commercial television stations broadcast as few educational programs as possible and only to serve as a lightning rod to draw off public and official criticism. Researchers for NAEB testified that a week-long monitoring study of all New York commercial television stations identified a single half-hour program sponsored by an actual institution of learning and classified only 1 percent of the programming as designed primarily for children.

Probably in no other cause have American educators and their supporters demonstrated such unity of purpose and solidarity of action. Following this phalanx, commercial interests were restrained in their presentation.

They favored noncommercial educational broadcasting and approved educational television. Commercial broadcasters felt, however, that each application for a VHF channel should be considered on its merits and that a reservation of VHF channels for education would be a waste of the nation's resources. Broadcasters thought that the failure of educators to realize the full potential of AM radio substantiated their contention. There was no objection to educators being assigned UHF channels. It seemed clear that commercial broadcasters equated VHF television with AM radio and UHF television with FM radio. VHF and AM were firmly established as the

media for mass communication, while UHF and FM were thought of
as media for specialized audiences. Commercial interests, therefore, wanted all VHF channels for commercially sponsored programming.

The New York Times editorially inquired whether television
channels should be assigned to educators and replied that "the answer
is so obviously and urgently in the affirmative that the viewer might
wonder why any testimony is necessary."[37] The FCC was predisposed
to reserve channels for education. Educators showed a strong interest in television. Commercial broadcasters were not opposed to
educational assignments. The big question was, Where and how
many?

Resolutions in the House of Representatives and Senate directing
the FCC to study the allocation of channels for educational purposes
added impetus to the drive.[38] Commissioner Hennock maintained
the momentum of her crusade. At a meeting of the Women's National
Democratic Club in Washington, D.C., she argued for VHF and UHF
channels for education. Noting opposition to the proposal that the
FCC require television stations in New York City to share time with
educators, she stated that if the seven stations in New York provided
only three hours of programs each evening, they would require 294
half-hour entertainment programs. "Barnum, Cohan, and Ziegfield
working in shifts with the pick of all the entertainment on this bilious
green earth couldn't produce that many good shows." Hennock asked
her listeners to support the entire JCET proposal and to make their
support known to the FCC. To the Adult Education Council of Philadelphia, the New York Teachers and Parents Association, and the
U.S. Conference of Mayors, Hennock carried her message.[39]

NONCOMMERCIAL EDUCATIONAL
TELEVISION STATIONS

On March 21, 1951, the FCC announced its tentative decision to
supplement the 12 VHF channels with 70 UHF channels and to assign
209 stations in the VHF and UHF bands to noncommercial educational
television stations. The announcement stated:

In the Commission's view, the need for noncommercial
educational television stations has been amply demonstrated
on this record. The Commission further believes that
educational institutions need a longer period of time to
get prepared for television than do the commercial
interests. The only way this can be done is by reserving
certain channels for the exclusive use of noncommercial
educational stations.

It was obvious to the FCC that

> the period of time during which such reservations should
> exist is very important. The period must be long enough
> to give educational institutions a reasonable opportunity
> to do the preparatory work that is necessary to get
> authorizations for stations. The period must not be so
> long that frequencies remain unused for excessively
> long periods of time. The commission will survey
> the situation from time to time in order to insure that
> these objectives are not lost sight of.

In making the 209 assignments, the commission reserved one channel for a noncommercial educational station in all communities having three or more assignments. Where a community had less than three assignments, no reservation was made unless it was a primarily educational center. Commissioner Hennock thought the tentative assignments were insufficient to establish a nationwide educational service.[40]

The FCC established May 7 as the deadline for receiving written comments on the proposal, June 11 as the deadline for receiving written countercomments, and July 23 as the beginning of oral arguments. The commission later canceled the oral arguments.

On March 22, the day after the FCC announcement, the JCET was formally established. The committee received an initial grant of $90,000 from the Fund for Adult Education of the Ford Foundation to give legal assistance to educational broadcasters in preparing written comments and countercomments to the FCC proposed assignment plan. With additional grants, the JCET organized meetings, scheduled speakers, and issued publicity regarding educational television.[41]

The Federal Communications Bar Association, Trent Broadcasting Corporation, and station WKMH filed petitions with the FCC questioning, generally, the legality of the commission's proposal and, specifically, its authority to reserve channels for noncommercial educational television stations. Senator William Benton told his colleagues: "The commercial broadcasters have now challenged the 209 reservations. And I think all of you will agree that the commercial broadcasters have shown that they can exert very heavy pressure here in Washington." The FCC answered the petition on July 13 by tracing the development of its authority and affirming its determination to designate and reserve channel assignments for educational television.[42]

During the summer and fall of 1951, the FCC received thousands of written comments and countercomments on its table of tentative

assignments. The JCET assisted in preparing 834 sworn statements
on behalf of colleges, universities, state boards of education, school
systems, and public service agencies defending the general idea of
reserving television channels for education and specific channel
assignments.[43]

Opponents of educational assignments argued that educators had
not shown that they needed more time, that educator nonusage and a
limited audience would waste valuable spectrum space, and that
educators had no stable financial plans for utilizing television channels.[44]

In its final report and order of April 13, 1952, adopting the tentative proposal, the FCC replied that educational institutions must move
slowly, that reservation implied some nonusage and size of audience
was unimportant if the service was in the public interest, and that it
was not necessary for educators to prove their financial responsibility.
The FCC upheld all of its tentative individual assignments, despite
numerous protests against them. Not only did the commission uphold
its tentative assignments but in its final report increased the number
of educational station assignments from 209 to 242 (80 VHF and 162
UHF). The commission's rules and regulations regarding noncommercial educational television stations were substantially the same
as those for noncommercial educational FM stations and did not
require educational stations to operate on a regular schedule or
specify a minimum number of hours of operation. "To permit the
utilization of the Commission's limited personnel for the consideration and processing of the hundreds of applications for television
stations which will be on file,"[45] the FCC declined to consider any
petition to change the table of assignments for one year following the
effective date of the order unless the petitioner requested the assignment of an educational station to a town to which a channel had not
already been assigned.

In a dissenting opinion, Commissioner Hennock concurred with
the decision insofar as it adopted the principle of reserving channels
for educational purposes but dissented insofar as it failed to make
a more adequate and proper promise for education. It was her contention that the assignment plan failed to reserve enough channels to
make a nationwide educational network possible, failed to allot educational channels to one-fourth of the metropolitan communities in the
United States, and erred in allocating only one educational channel
for the 11 million people of New York City. She complained that the
assignments were primarily in the UHF range, for which broadcasting equipment and receivers were unavailable, and that 14 states
did not have a single VHF channel assigned for educational purposes.
Hennock said, "I am in complete agreement with the Commission's

action in finally adopting the principle of indefinitely reserving television channels for noncommercial educational purposes."46

Deservedly honored, lauded, and acclaimed, Hennock reigned at the 1952 meeting of the Institute for Education by Radio and Television (IERT). Hennock did not slow the pace of her campaign, however, for she told the audience, "You educators have been handed the ball. You have been granted the channels. You should now take advantage of the opportunity offered to you. Start where you are. The only way to learn how to do it is to do it. Let's get to work, on all levels," she continued. "Don't forget your applications. Don't be ashamed to come in with only a small amount of concrete programming planned. We will be happy to get you started televising educationally." Walker added this comment: "I hope with all my heart that you who have fought so brilliantly for the 242 educational television channels now reserved will rally your forces this afternoon to fight on to preserve the victory you have so nobly won."47 In an NEA Newsletter, Walker stated that competition for television channels was intense and urged educators to use the educational assignments because they could not be held indefinitely.48

The FCC was so eager to get educational television started that when Kansas State College of Agriculture and Applied Science applied for the first construction permit to build an educational station, although funds had not yet been appropriated for construction, a majority of the commissioners voted to waive its usual requirement for indications of financial qualifications and to issue a construction permit to Kansas State anyway. At the same time, the FCC issued three construction permits to the University of the State of New York for stations in Albany, Rochester, and Buffalo.49

The JCET received additional grants to assist educational institutions in planning educational television stations. The National Citizens Committee for Educational Television was organized with foundation help to promote educational community stations. The Fund for Adult Education gave $5 million to develop television as an educational medium.50

Out of the 1949 Allerton House Seminar meeting of 40 educational broadcasters in Monticello, Illinois, to establish an educational radio network came the idea to found a nationwide educational television network. During 1952, support for the network idea came from the OE, the American Council of Education, and Walker of the FCC. In November, with the financial support of the Fund for Adult Education, the National Educational Television and Radio Center was incorporated to exchange, evaluate, publicize, research, and create or acquire programs for distribution to noncommercial television and radio stations. Regular network service began on May 16, 1954.51

EDUCATIONAL ASSIGNMENTS: CONFUSION
ABOUT TIME LIMIT

The block of channels the FCC assigned to educational FM was
assumed to be an indefinite assignment. Commissioner Hennock, in
her dissenting views on the commission's final television report and
order, stated that she was "in complete agreement with the Commission's action adopting the principle of indefinitely reserving television
channels for noncommercial educational purposes."[52] Yet, a peculiar
misunderstanding arose over the time limit on the reservation of the
educational assignment.

Edgar Fuller, executive secretary of the JCET, in an article in
School Executive, stated that those accustomed to think about educational changes over a period of 10 to 20 years "will be discomforted
by the one year deadline" set by the FCC. He urged "prompt and
decisive action" before the FCC give the educational reservations
to commercial stations. Two and a half months later, Commissioner
Walker was quoted recommending that educators be prepared to argue
to the FCC that it was in the public interest to continue the reservations. William Jansen, superintendent of the New York City public
schools, called the FCC one-year time limit a "threat" that should
be opposed to the utmost. He cited the high cost of acquiring television broadcasting equipment and the fact that UHF transmissions
were not yet receivable as reasons why only 20 applications for educational broadcasting stations had been filed. The New York Educational
Television Institute resolved that the 242 television channels be "vested
permanently in the public domain." Walker told delegates to the
Southern Regional Conference on Educational Television that their
"overriding action" should be to file applications for permits to construct stations. Those not able to file immediately should be prepared
to prove to the FCC that it was in the public interest to continue to
reserve channels for education.[53]

The American College Public Relations Association, meeting in
Albany, urged a time extension for the educational assignments.
Walker asked delegates to the National School Boards Association,
meeting in Atlantic City, to mobilize behind the movement to build
noncommercial educational television stations and save the 242
assignments "from being lost by default." Speaking at Boston University Founders' Day Institute, Walker said he realized that educators
needed more time, but after June 2, 1953, commercial interests
could petition to have noncommercial assignments shifted to commercial assignments. On April 2, governors of 14 southern states
petitioned the FCC to extend its one-year deadline by at least two
years.[54] Having resigned as chairman of the FCC but remaining a
member for another year, Walker said to the IERT, "I urge you, as

forcefully as I can, to move ahead as rapidly as possible. For only
a channel in use—as against one still 'reserved'—can bring the American people the valuable type of educational programming of which
you are capable."55

At a hearing on educational television conducted by the Senate
Committee on Interstate and Foreign Commerce in April 1953,
Walker spoke not only of the advantages but of the necessity of educational television. Commissioner Hennock reported evidence of a
"commercial conspiracy" to make educators believe that the educational reservations were for only a year. She wanted it known that
the reservations were for "thirty years." Rosel H. Hyde, the new
FCC chairman, assured the committee "there is no time limit."56

Nevertheless the impression that educational assignments expired
on June 2, 1953, mushroomed, creating confusion among educators
and the general public. Senator Charles W. Tobey, chairman of the
Senate Committee on Interstate and Foreign Commerce, wrote the
FCC on April 28 and requested a statement of policy to dispel the
confusion regarding educational television channels. "I shall keep
a watchful eye on each and every one of these 242 channels for education," he warned, "and upon the slightest evidence that the FCC is
about to weaken and to delete one of them or substitute a substantially
less valuable channel for one of them, I shall call for a full investigation." On May 11, the FCC issued a public notice stating that
educational assignments were indefinite. The commission emphasized the need for noncommercial educational television stations
and the necessity for educational reservations because educational
broadcasters took more time to begin broadcasting. The FCC am-
biguously said "indefinitely" did not mean an "excessively long period"
and stated its intention "to survey the reservations from time to
time." As additional salve, the FCC announced it had made 16 additional channel assignments to noncommercial stations.57

Confusion over the time limit was the fault of the commission
itself. Its decision not to receive proposals for changes in the table
of assignments was designed to give the FCC a chance to catch up
with paper work after four years of hearings. It should have stated
this more explicitly. It should also have explained that the reservation of television channels was no different from any other FCC
decision—that is, it was always subject to revision after the proper
formalities—and that in considering petitions for changes of educational
television assignment, the FCC would be guided by those basic principles that led it to establish the educational reservations in the first
place. Walker's eagerness to get educational stations on the air
probably created more confusion than the ambiguity of the commission's statements. Walker was genuinely interested in educational
television, but in begging educators to start broadcasting and threaten-

ing them with losing their assignments to commercial interests, he
did more than create confusion. As a result of the misunderstanding,
educators took action before they were properly prepared and made
errors that dampened their enthusiasm. They did not have enough
time to organize their plans, to prepare adequately for financing,
to consider future programming, or to evaluate their philosophy of
television broadcasting.[58]

There is no evidence to support Commissioner Hennock's contention that the confusion over educational reservations was caused
by a commercial conspiracy. After June 2, no commercial interests
filed for educational assignments. Commercial stations actively
aided educational broadcasters by helping them to solve technical
problems and giving them $1,250,000 worth of buildings, towers,
and equipment.[59]

The FCC reported on June 30, 1953, that station KUHT, belonging
to the University of Houston and the Houston public school system,
was the first noncommercial station on the air, that 17 construction
permits had been granted, and that 29 applications for educational
stations were pending.[60]

Educators had reason to be thankful for their lady at court, but
they also had reason to fear changes that the influence and attitude
of new members of the FCC might bring. On June 18, 1954, eight
months after his appointment to the FCC, Robert E. Lee told the
District of Columbia Broadcasters Association that 80 percent of
the assignments to educational television had no applicants. Noting
network complaints that they could not get satisfactory outlets, he
wondered if the removal of educational assignments where their need
could not be demonstrated would not lead to the establishment of a
nationwide competitive television system. He favored educational
grants only if the applicant showed strong financial, technical, and
program ability to render satisfactory service. On October 28,
1954, less than a month after his appointment as chairman of the
FCC, George C. McConnaughey told a meeting of the NAEB that he
was disappointed by the response to educational television. Seven
stations were broadcasting; 33 stations were under construction;
and 16 applications were pending. He promised educators that he
would not set a deadline on reservations. Commissioner Hennock
was "amazed" at McConnaughey's statement chiding educators for
not using the channels available to them and asked why the chairman
had not cited the 1,400 unused commercial channels. Hennock said
educators were doing all in their power to acquire and use the
channels and told the NAEB not to fear that the FCC would give
noncommercial channels to commercial interests.[61]

FCC SHIFTS EDUCATIONAL CHANNELS TO
COMMERCIAL STATUS

On June 1, 1955, the FCC received the first petition seeking to shift a VHF educational channel to commercial status. In this case, the petition was denied because Des Moines, Iowa, already had three VHF stations and a civic organization was making tentative plans to use the educational assignment. In 1956, the commission shifted the educational assignment from VHF to UHF in College Station, Texas, because there was no interest in educational television in the foreseeable future and granted the VHF channel to a commercial interest. The FCC then deleted the educational assignment in Weston, West Virginia, and made the assignment to a commercial station. On September 27, 1957, the FCC unreserved the educational assignment in Eugene, Oregon, and assigned it to commercial status.[62]

When a reporter during a news conference on February 6, 1957, asked President Dwight D. Eisenhower what comments he had on the controversy over taking away channels assigned to educational television, the president said: "Well I have not had a recent study presented to me on this question; but speaking only from what I believe to be the eventual good of the United States, and not knowing as of now anything of many more channels being available through improvements of technique and equipment, I would say we must preserve channels for educational purposes."[63] Although the president apparently did nothing else to preserve the channels, Congress did.

Commercial interests thought they saw a trend toward the gradual elimination of the educational assignments, and so did Congress. Senator Richard Neuberger read a report of Commissioner T. A. M. Craven's plan to open for commercial applicants those television channels set aside for educators. Neuberger rebuked Craven in the Congressional Record. Craven replied that his plan was just an idea and that it actually "favored educational television," except where there was no indication of intended usage of channels for education, in which case the channels should be assigned to commercial usage.[64] The Senate Committee on Interstate and Foreign Commerce had said it would watch over the educational assignments. On March 15, 1957, the Senate committee invited the commissioners to an informal meeting of the committee. Each commissioner was asked his personal views on educational television. All agreed with the principle of educational television, but some said channels should not be reserved indefinitely. Craven said it was "foolish" to reserve channels where no interest was shown. The committee then told the commissioners what it thought about educational television. Senator A. S. Mike Monroney said to let commercial stations have any educational assign-

ments would be "robbery of coming generations." Senator William
A. Blakley said the channels should be reserved "indefinitely."[65]

The threat of congressional action against the FCC through
appropriations and appointments was unspoken, but the commission
got the point. In 1957 and 1958, the FCC denied petitions to change
educational assignments in Jacksonville, Florida; Durham, North
Carolina; Hartford, Connecticut; and San Antonio and Denton, Texas.
In 1958, the FCC reserved a channel in Carbondale, Illinois, for
education and assigned a second educational channel to Pittsburgh,
Pennsylvania. At that time, there were 257 channel assignments
reserved for educators.[66] Despite slowness on the part of educators
and disappointment in their progress on the part of the FCC, the
commission thereafter remained faithful to its pledge to reserve
channels for educators indefinitely and, by its faithfulness, continued
to contribute to the creation of educational television.

THE UHF PROBLEM

Although educators moved relatively quickly to use VHF channels
assigned to them, they moved slowly in using UHF channels. This
response was not peculiar to educators, however, for commercial
broadcasters did not take up UHF channels with alacrity either. The
reasons are complex, but the public was not impressed by the superior
quality of UHF television and did not purchase UHF receivers.

At a congressional inquiry into television problems, Ralph Steele,
executive secretary of the JCET, spoke of the UHF problem as it
related to educational broadcasting. He said educators had taken
many VHF assignments and wanted to expand into UHF broadcasting.
He explained that educators were reluctant to start UHF broadcasting
when the public was so indifferent that it refused to buy receivers.[67]

The FCC was acutely aware of the problem and investigated
several ways to expand the use of UHF and to equalize the use of the
more valuable VHF channels. Since a large number of channels
reserved for education were in the upper spectrum, anything done
by the commission to make the channels technically available to
audiences directly benefited educational broadcasting.

One of the many possible solutions investigated was to assign
all television broadcasting to UHF channels. In 1945, the FCC
thought all television broadcasting would eventually move to UHF.
While research in television broadcasting in the upper spectrum
was being conducted, millions of dollars were invested in VHF transmitting and receiving equipment. It would take a very brave commission to make this equipment obsolete.

In June 1956, the FCC called a meeting of television broadcasters and manufacturers for August 20 to establish the Television Allocations Study Organization (TASO). The FCC recognized the importance of UHF to educational broadcasters by naming a representative of the JCET as one of the five directors of the organization. TASO was asked to conduct a thorough research and development program to determine the capabilities and potentialities of UHF, so that the FCC could use the information as the basis of a study of the proposal that it switch all television broadcasting to UHF. The organization reported the results of its research in the spring of 1959.[68] The FCC decided that it could not in good conscience switch all television to UHF and sought further possible solutions.

The commission found that it was not possible to obtain additional VHF space used by the military and began a number of procedures in 1961 to solve the VHF-UHF problem. It established a high-power UHF transmitter on top of the Empire State Building in New York City to study the technical problems of reception in a canyon city. The study, which was begun in 1961 and completed in 1962, indicated that UHF could be received well in built up areas. The FCC hoped this would spur broadcasters to use UHF, take the pressure off the lower spectrum, and tempt viewers to buy UHF converters. In the summer of 1961, the commission gave notice of proposed rule making to expand the use of UHF by relaxing technical requirements to reduce the cost of broadcasting, require VHF stations to operate parallel UHF transmitters, make additional UHF reservations for education, and substitute pools of UHF channels in various cities in place of an intermixture of VHF and UHF channels. Late in 1961, the commission began procedures to delete the VHF channel in eight cities with one VHF assignment and to require all UHF broadcasting. The stations involved took their cases to court, and the commission dropped the pooling or deintermixture proposals in 1962.

Also in 1961, the FCC voted to initiate an inquiry to determine how, "in view of the incalculable benefits" of noncommercial educational broadcasting, it could make a VHF channel available to education in New York City and Los Angeles. John F. White, president of the National Educational Television and Radio Center in New York, asserted that the FCC action reflected a new realization on the part of the commission that educational television was entitled to "competitive" consideration along with commercial television. The proposed inquiry was terminated in 1956, after Educational Television for the Metropolitan area, with substantial help from the Ford Foundation, bought WNDT, a commercial station, and began a noncommercial educational service in the New York area and when the commission decided the educational need in Los Angeles could be met by UHF.[69]

When all-UHF, equalization, pooling, and deintermixture proved
illusory solutions to the UHF problem, the FCC turned to Congress
for help. The commission asked Congress to amend the Communications Act of 1934 to give it the authority to set standards for television-
receiving apparatus, with the understanding that all television sets
sold or transported in interstate commerce would contain a device
making the set capable of receiving all VHF and UHF channels. In
a period of years, the technical availability of an audience would be
established. The initial cost of the device would be about $30 for
each set, but the commission wanted the government to put the potential long-range social benefit of educational television ahead of temporary social hardship.[70]

THE ALL-CHANNEL LAW

The FCC offered a draft of suggested legislation during a television inquiry held by the Senate Committee on Interstate and Foreign
Commerce in February 1960, and Senator John O. Pastore introduced
a bill to that effect; however, the legislation got nowhere during the
Eighty-Sixth Congress.[71] In the summer of 1961, Senator Warren
G. Magnuson and Representative Oren Harris introduced identical
bills in their respective branches of the Congress, at the request of
the FCC, to give the commission the power to require that television
sets receive all 82 channels.[72] It was not until the second session
of the Eighty-Seventh Congress that action began to be taken.

The Senate held hearings in February, and the House held hearings in March. FCC Chairman Newton N. Minow said the legislation
was needed to make television broadcasting competitive on a national
scale, to establish three competitive facilities in all middle-sized
communities, to afford all communities of appreciable size an outlet
for local expression, and to institute a noncommercial educational
service throughout the country. Chairman Minow said that the
commission felt a "deep concern" for the full development of educational television and that the "growth and expansion of educational
broadcasting must be in UHF, making the growth of educational
television go hand in hand with the growth of the utilization of the
UHF."[73]

Educational broadcasting associations fully supported the bill
at the congressional hearings. David C. Stewart, director of the
Washington Office of the National Educational Television and Radio
Center and secretary of the Joint Council on Educational Broadcasting,
called the bill a "necessity" for educational broadcasting. William
G. Harley, representing the National Association of Educational
Broadcasters, and Robert C. Anderson, of the Joint Council, sup-

ported the measure, as did the commercial networks and associations of commercial broadcasters.[74]

In a special message to Congress regarding the protection of consumer interests, President John F. Kennedy urged passage of the bill and mentioned its importance to educational television.[75] Congress passed the law in June, and President Kennedy signed it on July 10, 1962.[76]

The FCC drew up standards for all-channel television receivers and set April 30, 1964, as the effective date of its ruling.[77] As the FCC standards went into effect, President Lyndon B. Johnson commended the all-channel act and said the law would "bring to millions of American homes a wider range of noncommercial educational television."[78] At the request of the Electronics Industries Association, the FCC, in February 1963, established a group (later called the Committee for the Full Development of All-Channel Broadcasting) to provide a forum for persons interested in UHF broadcasting. The committee, composed of representatives of the FCC and various groups, including the NAEB and the National Educational Television (NET) network, was asked to furnish insights into the problems of all-channel broadcasting so that the FCC could take appropriate action. By including on the executive committee Richard B. Hull, chairman of the board of directors of the NAEB, the commission and the committee recognized the important stake educational television had in all-channel broadcasting.[79]

REALLOCATION OF UHF CHANNEL ASSIGNMENTS

With the all-channel law passed and with the expectation that there would be a gradual accretion of UHF stations, the FCC in 1963 pursued the course laid out in 1961 to reallocate all UHF channel assignments. The commission had endorsed a request by the NAEB for research funds from the Department of Health, Education and Welfare (HEW) to conduct a study of electronic computer techniques in the development of a television channel assignment plan. The study showed that while there were limits in the capacity of the computers to make complex judgments, the rapidity with which it could examine assignment plans outweighed the limitations. Consequently, the FCC contracted with the UNIVAC Division of Sperry-Rand Corporation to develop a computer program, to be delivered in October 1964, which would result in an efficient assignment plan for UHF television. On June 3, 1965, the commission issued for comment a revised table of UHF allocations. The FCC had used the computer to assess the impact of each assignment on the potential

channel assignments for each city that would leave the largest number
of channels available for assignment to other cities. The table made
1,000 assignments, and half of them were for education. The country
was not saturated, however, except for certain metropolitan areas,
and education had not reached its limit, for there was room for many
more assignments when needed on channels 14 to 69 in the UHF
band.[80]

The NAEB commented that the plan was inadequate because it
did not reserve every possible assignment. It felt that educators
needed the security of knowing that they would always have a certain
number of assignments reserved for them. The FCC in adopting the
plan with slight modifications on February 9, 1966, denied the contention of the NAEB. The commission said it had reserved channels
in every case where educator interest had been shown or contemplated
and had included channels to provide 50 statewide networks, even
when no interest had been demonstrated. The FCC once again declared
its interest in noncommercial educational broadcasting and stated
that it had not reserved every possible assignment in order to give
it the flexibility of being able to assign a channel exactly where
educators wanted a new channel when they needed it. The FCC further
pointed out that the table of allocations purposely did not include the
top 14 channels in the UHF band. In 1965, the commission indicated
that it wished to save that spectrum space for a new class of low-
power community stations serving the local interest in a commercial
or noncommercial capacity.[81] The low-power UHF television station
envisioned by the FCC would provide education with hundreds of additional outlets.

CONTINUED COMMITMENT OF THE FCC TO
EDUCATIONAL BROADCASTING

The Broadcast Bureau of the FCC experienced a modest reorgani-
zation on October 18, 1961, which demonstrated the commission's
commitment to educational broadcasting. The former Economics
Division of the bureau was renamed the Research and Education
Division, and the Educational Broadcasting Branch was established,
at the suggestion of NAEB, as a new part of that division. Hyman H.
Goldin, chief of the Research and Education Division, founded the
Educational Broadcasting Branch and explained its responsibilities.
This organization was charged with the responsibility of studying
the immediate and long-range needs of educational AM, FM and TV
broadcasting and making recommendations to the commission, analyzing the factors encouraging or hindering applications for stations,
studying FCC rules and making recommendations for revisions and

additions, studying FCC applications and report forms to see if they best met the requirements of the commission and educators, coordinating with those in the rule-making and other branches of the FCC to facilitate the development of educational services, providing liaison with broadcast organizations to provide them with information regarding FCC procedures and to learn of their plans, coordinating with other government agencies concerned with educational television, and serving as a clearinghouse for information with respect to congressional and other inquiries regarding trends and developments in educational broadcasting. [82]

The Educational Broadcasting Branch acted as liaison with the public, educators, and governmental organizations and improved the relations between the commission and educators and, especially, educational broadcasting organizations. Specifically, the Educational Broadcasting Branch developed a close relationship with the NAEB and the National Education Association and, by speechmaking, established ties with other national organizations.

The branch was responsible for the revision of FCC forms that was made effective December 3, 1962. The commission adopted separate forms for noncommercial educational broadcasts that relaxed and simplified the reporting requirements in applying for authority to construct or make changes (FCC form 340), applying for station licenses (form 341), applying for renewal of licenses (form 342), and reporting ownership (form 323E). The new forms removed the commercial aspects of the old forms and made them more flexible and palatable for educators. [83]

In order to disseminate information about FCC policy and government programs affecting educational broadcasting, the branch published information bulletins. Information Bulletin 16-B, regarding educational television, was issued in December 1963 and revised in June 1966; Information Bulletin 21-B, concerning educational radio, was issued in September 1966.

It was a recognition of the need of government agencies to cooperate in the distribution of information and services to the public that led Robert L. Hilliard, chief of the Educational Broadcasting Branch, to form, in 1965, the Inter-Agency Broadcast Media Group. Representatives of 20 federal departments and agencies jointly promoted the activities of their organizations in providing program material, grants, and contracts for educational radio and television.

The commission made several less publicized rulings that assisted educators in the establishment of statewide, regional, and nationwide networks. The FCC, in 1963, ruled favorably on a petition from the National Educational Television and Radio Center to allow educational broadcasters to use existing microwave facilities of closed circuit educational television systems to transmit program material to noncommercial educational television stations and to allow operators of closed circuit systems to use the auxiliary facilities of broadcasting stations to transmit program material to their closed circuit systems. On January 11, 1964, the FCC authorized the first statewide educational translator system by granting the request of the University of Utah to construct 18 UHF translator stations to rebroadcast VHF signals from KUED, a noncommercial educational television station broadcasting on channel 7 in Salt Lake City. After conducting initial experiments in a school in Plainedge, Long Island, New York, the commission, on July 25, 1962, announced that based on the suggestion of McIvor Parker, supervisory electronic engineer of the Rules and Standards Division, Broadcast Bureau, FCC, it proposed to establish a new class of service to promote educational television. The FCC suggested that the 1,990-2,110 or the 2,500-2,690 megacycle band be used to transmit visual and aural instructional material from a central transmitter to schools or other selected receiving locations where students, teachers, or others were assembled for formal education, training, or instruction. At the receiving location, the signal would be converted to a regular broadcasting channel for reception on a standard, mass-produced television set. The number of channels available to a community would be sufficient to permit sending different subjects simultaneously to different classrooms, and the cost would be less than wire or microwave closed circuit television for the same purpose.[84] The commission believed the new service would be useful for subject material; training in special skills; safety programs; rehabilitation of the aged, infirm, or mentally ill; clinical studies; new arts and crafts; keeping professionals and semiprofessionals abreast of new developments; in-service training of teachers; instructional materials for shut-ins; entertainment or cultural affairs; and administrative traffic.[85]

Since the maximum number of UHF broadcasting channels available to a community was ten, and with four to six of these reserved for education, the commission felt that there would not be enough broadcasting channels available to educators for broad community service and adult education and for instructional television for simultaneous transmissions of a variety of subjects to different classrooms. By proposing a system for transmitting to a small number of preselected or fixed receivers rather than to the community at large, the FCC was suggesting, in effect, a private communications system among schools, which would relieve the anticipated demand for more broadcast channels than were available. In the lower band, 10 transmissions were possible in each community; in the upper band, 15 or 16 transmissions were possible. The FCC's brainchild was to be called Instructional Television Fixed Service (ITFS).[86]

About 100 parties responded to the commission's request for comments. The respondents were overwhelmingly in favor of the proposal; only 4 parties were opposed. Fifty educational organizations endorsed the proposal, and, although no equipment was then available, they generally preferred the upper-spectrum space, because more channels would be available. Based on this support, the FCC adopted its proposal and established the ITFS in the upper band effective September 9, 1963.[87]

In February 1965, the Educational Broadcasting Branch of the FCC held a meeting in Washington, D.C., for those concerned with the ITFS. The commission learned uncoordinated planning in urban areas was creating an incipient shortage of channels. At the recommendation of the participants in the meeting, the FCC established, on October 11, 1965, a National Committee for the Full Development of Instructional Television Fixed Service, which held its first meeting on November 4. Commissioner Lee was permanent chairman, and the membership was made up of about 20 representatives of state and local governments, educational, charitable, religious, civic, and welfare agencies, and other nonprofit organizations. The committee had four regional chairmen, who were responsible for setting up state and local committees. Although some broadcasters saw the ITFS as a financial threat to their over-the-air programming and opposed it, some 1,000 people were active in the work of the national committee and took a lively interest in the 33 authorizations and the four systems operating at that time.[88]

The FCC did not limit itself to group action in having an impact on noncommercial educational broadcasting. Commissioners as individuals showed concern for the development of educational broadcasting. To the New York State Broadcasters Association, Commissioner Lee stated, "I have virtually stumped the country in an effort to encourage the implementation of the channel assignments by educational authorities." Chairman E. William Henry urged educators at the 1963 meeting of the NAEB to take a "position on issues of public importance, and provide programs for that large audience whose tastes are not often met by commercial outlets."[89]

Money has always been a chronic problem for educational broadcasters, and while the FCC had no money of its own to offer, the commission affirmed this point as a group and as individuals. As will be seen, the FCC testified to congressional committees on the needs of educators for funds. The commission said that noncommercial broadcasters should have an opportunity to experiment with different kinds of financing and approved the use of courtesy credit lines for corporations that underwrote the costs of programming educational broadcasts. To the International Radio-Television Society, an organization of men in advertising, commercial broadcasting, publishing, and industry, Chairman Henry said "that educational

television should permanently struggle for subsistence is intolerable."
Educational broadcasting is "entitled to look to you for a portion of
its financial support," and "if you have already done much, you should
do more." As a result of this speech, the society formed a committee
to see what the private business community could do to help educational television in a practical way.90 The committee held a half
dozen sessions and prepared promotional material for educational
stations but did not do anything in a direct way to meet the chronic
need for money.

When asked in 1934 what change the establishment of the FCC
would have on communications, knowledgeable spokesmen declared
that the philosophies and personalities of the individual commissioners
would have more to do with changes than the establishment of the
commission. Their statements were borne out in the creation of
educational television. Personally convinced that educational television was in the public interest, members of the FCC performed
services far beyond their normal duties to create educational television. Prall, Hennock, and Walker invited and exhorted educators to
appear at FCC hearings and build a case for the reservation of television channels for education. Educators built a strong case, and
the commissioners rewarded their efforts by giving them what they
asked for. Hennock and Walker continued their campaign, by urging
educators to use the channels assigned to them. Thus, the philosophies and personalities of individual members of the commission
were influential in making FCC policy to create, protect, and defend
the reservation of television channels for educators. After these
commissioners left the FCC, the specter of congressional interest
kept new members of the FCC committed to the policy, even though
they were perhaps less philosophically dedicated to the idea. After
1961, the commission again became quite sensitive to the needs of
educational broadcasters, and on its own initiative and in response
to petitions from educators reaffirmed by word and deed that noncommercial educational broadcasting was a special concern of the
FCC.

NOTES

1. Sydney W. Head, Broadcasting in America (Boston: Houghton
Mifflin, 1956), p. 154 (hereafter cited as Head, Broadcasting).
2. Public Law 69-632.
3. Federal Radio Commission, Annual Report, vol. 3 (Washington, D.C.: U.S. Government Printing Office, 1929), pp. 55, 56.
4. E. B. Kurtz, Pioneering in Educational Television 1932-1937
(Iowa City: State University of Iowa, 1959), pp. vii-ix; New York
Times, May 20, 1938.

5. New York Times, July 13, 1930, September 20, 1936, December 13, 1936; Federal Communications Commission, Official Report of Proceedings, In the Matter of: The Allocation of Frequencies above 30,000 KC and the Review of Present Frequency Allocations, Docket 3929 (Washington, D.C.: Ward and Paul, 1936).

6. New York Times, April 28, 1940.

7. Federal Register, IV, 2244; New York Times, April 9, 1939.

8. Federal Register, IV, 4975; V, 934.

9. Ibid., V, 1189; New York Times, March 24, 1940.

10. Congressional Record, LXXXVI, A1886, A1887.

11. New York Times, November 10, 1940.

12. Federal Communications Commission, Television Report, Order, Rules and Regulations, May 3, 1941, mimeographed (1941); Federal Register, VI, 2282.

13. New York Times, July 2, 1941; Federal Register, VII, 3248.

14. New York Times, February 24, 1944.

15. Federal Communications Commission, Official Report of Proceedings, In the Matter of: Allocation of Frequencies to the Various Classes of Nongovernmental Services in the Radio Spectrum from 10 KC to 30,000,000 KC, Docket 6651 (Washington, D.C.: Ward and Paul, 1944).

16. Federal Communications Commission, Report of Allocations, January 15, 1945, mimeographed (1945).

17. Federal Communications Commission, Report of Allocations from 25,000 KC to 30,000,000 KC, May 25, 1945, mimeographed (1945).

18. New York Times, October 13, 1945, January 18, 1946.

19. Federal Register, XII, 2282.

20. Ibid., 5673; XIII, 2589.

21. Ibid., XIII, 2629.

22. Ibid., 5782.

23. Billboard (August 21, 1948).

24. Federal Register, XIII, 5861, 6124.

25. Richard B. Hull, "The History Behind ETV," NAEB Journal 17 (February 1958): 29 (hereafter cited as Hull, "History"); Richard B. Hull, "A Note on the History Behind ETV," Educational Television: The Next Ten Years (Washington, D.C.: U.S. Government Printing Office, 1965), pp. 339-40 (hereafter cited as Hull, "Note"); see also Robert B. Hudson, "Allerton House: Twenty Years After," Educational Broadcasting Review 4, no. 1 (February 1970), pp. 35-39.

26. Federal Register, XIV, 4483, 4484.

27. Ibid., 4485, 4486.

28. Hull, "History," p. 29; see John Walker Powell, Channels of Learning: The Story of Educational Television (Washington, D.C.: Public Affairs Press, 1962).

29. New York Times, March 12, 1950.

30. Josephine H. MacLatchy, ed., Education on the Air:
Twentieth Yearbook of the Institute for Education by Radio (Columbus:
Ohio State University, 1950), pp. 24, 25, 103, 104, 113, 114.

31. Ibid.

32. Federal Register, XV, 6049.

33. New York Times, September 16, 1950, November 16, 1950.

34. Hull, "History," p. 29; Hull, "Note," 340; W. Wayne Alford,
NAEB History, vol. 2, 1954 to 1965 (Washington, D.C.: National
Association of Educational Broadcasters, 1966), pp. 6–11.

35. Senate, Joint Resolution 81–208; Congressional Record,
SCVI, 15943.

36. Federal Communications Commission, Official Report of
Proceedings, In the Matter of: Amendment of Section 3.606 of the
Commission's Rules and Regulations, Docket 8736 et al. (Washington,
D.C.: Ward and Paul, 1950–51), pp. 15743–18337 (hereafter cited
as FCC, Amendment of Section 3.606).

37. New York Times, November 26, 1950.

38. House of Representatives, Joint Resolution 82–148; Senate,
Resolution 82–127; Joint Resolution 82–28.

39. New York Times, February 2, 1951, February 16, 1951,
March 20, 1951, March 24, 1951.

40. Federal Register, XVI, 3072–82; see Robert A. Carlson,
"1951: A Pivotal Year for Educational Television," Educational
Broadcasting Review 1, no. 2 (December 1967), pp. 47–55.

41. New York Times, May 1, 1951; Robert B. Glynn, "Public
Policy and Broadcasting," Television's Impact on American Culture,
ed. William Y. Elliott (East Lansing: Michigan State University
Press, 1956), p. 199 (hereafter cited as Glynn, "Public Policy and
Broadcasting"); see Robert A. Carlson, "Establishing Educational
Television as a Viable Institution: The Early Leadership of E. Scott
Fletcher," Educational Broadcasting Review 2, no. 3 (June 1968),
pp. 45–52; see also Ford Foundation Activities in Noncommercial
Broadcasting 1951–1976 (New York: Ford Foundation, 1976).

42. Federal Register, XVI, 5852; New York Times, May 16,
1951; Federal Register, XVI, 7518.

43. Glynn, "Public Policy and Broadcasting," p. 200.

44. FCC, Amendment of Section 3.606, Comments and Countercomments.

45. Federal Register, XVII, 3905–4093.

46. Ibid.

47. Josephine H. MacLatchy, ed., Education on the Air:
Twenty-Second Yearbook of the Institute for Education by Radio and
Television (Columbus: Ohio State University, 1952), pp. 111, 112,
120.

48. New York Times, June 16, 1952.

49. Ibid., July 26, 1952.

50. Ibid., July 14, 1952, November 25, 1952, September 8, 1952.

51. Robert B. Hudson, "Allerton House 1949, 1950," Hollywood Quarterly 5 (Spring 1951): 238; New York Times, May 4, 1952, July 8, 1952, November 14, 1952; Harry K. Newburn, Emphasizing Educational Television (Ann Arbor, Mich.: 1956), p. 15.

52. New York Times, August 31, 1952, November 13, 1952, November 14, 1952, December 12, 1952.

53. Ibid.

54. Ibid., January 24, 1953, February 13, 1953, March 11, 1953, April 3, 1953.

55. Josephine H. MacLatchy, ed., Education on the Air: Twenty-Third Yearbook of the Institute for Education by Radio and Television (Columbus: Ohio State University, 1953), p. 17.

56. Senate, Committee on Interstate and Foreign Commerce, Hearing on Educational Television, 83 Cong., 1 Sess.

57. Congressional Record, XCIX, A2514, A2515.

58. Glynn, "Public Policy and Broadcasting," p. 197.

59. New York Times, June 7, 1953, August 3, 1953.

60. Federal Communications Commission, Annual Report, vol. 19 (Washington, D.C.: U.S. Government Printing Office, 1953), p. 94.

61. New York Times, June 19, 1954, October 29, 1954, October 30, 1954.

62. Federal Communications Commission, Annual Report, vol. 21 (Washington, D.C.: U.S. Government Printing Office, 1955), p. 100; Federal Communications Commission, Annual Report, vol. 22 (Washington, D.C.: U.S. Government Printing Office, 1956), p. 102; Federal Communications Commission, Annual Report, vol. 23 (Washington, D.C.: U.S. Government Printing Office, 1957), p. 113.

63. Public Papers of the Presidents of the United States. Dwight D. Eisenhower, 1957 (Washington, D.C.: U.S. Government Printing Office, 1958), document 28.

64. Congressional Record, CIII, A1119, A1342.

65. New York Times, March 16, 1957.

66. Federal Communications Commission, Annual Report, vol. 24 (Washington, D.C.: U.S. Government Printing Office), pp. 108, 109.

67. Senate, Committee on Interstate and Foreign Commerce, Television Inquiry, 84 Cong.

68. Television Allocations Study Organization, Engineering Aspects of Television Allocations: Report of the Television Allocations Study Organization to the Federal Communications Commission, March 16, 1959, mimeographed (1959).

69. Federal Register, XXVI, 2812; New York Times, March 30, 1961; Federal Register, XXX, 8759.

70. House of Representatives, Committee on Interstate and Foreign Commerce, Hearing on HR8031, HR9267, HR9277, HR9291, HR9293, HR9322, HR9349, HRes450, HRes457, HRes469, 87 Cong., 2 Sess. (hereafter cited as House, Hearing on HR8031).

71. Senate, Committee on Interstate and Foreign Commerce, Television Inquiry, 86 Cong.; Senate, Bill 86-3115.

72. Senate, Bill 87-2109; House of Representatives, Bill 87-8031.

73. House of Representatives, Hearing on HR8031, 87 Cong., 2 Sess.

74. Senate, Committee on Commerce, Hearing on S2109, 87 Cong., 2 Sess.

75. House of Representatives, Document 87-364.

76. Congressional Record, CVIII, 10565, 12325, 13110.

77. Federal Register, XXVII, 9222-9225, 11698-11700.

78. Public Papers of the Presidents of the United States, Lyndon B. Johnson, 1963-1964 (Washington, D.C.: U.S. Government Printing Office, 1965), document 173.

79. Senate, Committee on Commerce, Hearing for Program Report from Federal Communications Committee, 88 Cong., 1 Sess.; Federal Register, XXVIII, 1379-1380, 3793.

80. Federal Communications Commission, Annual Report, vol. 30 (Washington, D.C.: U.S. Government Printing Office, 1964), pp. 68-69; Federal Communications Commission, Annual Report, vol. 31 (Washington, D.C.: U.S. Government Printing Office, 1965), p. 111 (hereafter cited as FCC, Annual Report, vols. 30 and 31).

81. Federal Register, XXX, 2932-2952.

82. Ibid., XXVI, 10193; Federal Communications Commission, Annual Report, vol. 28 (Washington, D.C.: U.S. Government Printing Office, 1962), pp. 63-64 (hereafter cited as FCC, Annual Report, vol. 28); Hyman H. Goldin and Keith M. Engar, "The FCC's New Educational Broadcasting Branch," NAEB Journal 21 (May-June 1962): 1-3.

83. Federal Communications Commission, Annual Report, vol. 25 (Washington, D.C.: U.S. Government Printing Office, 1959), p. 72; Federal Register, XXVII, 6172-6173, 7993, 11948-11950.

84. Federal Communications Commission, Annual Report, vol. 29 (Washington, D.C.: U.S. Government Printing Office, 1963), p. 73; FCC, Annual Report, vol. 30, p. 73; FCC, Annual Report, vol. 28, p. 64.

85. Federal Register, XXVIII, 64.

86. McIvor L. Parker, "Technical Aspects of the Proposed ETV Fixed Service," NAEB Journal 12 (May-June 1963): 18-24; Federal Register, XXIX, 7022-7024.

87. Federal Register, XXVIII, 8103-8114; Senate, Committee on Commerce, Hearing for a Status and Progress Report from the Federal Communications Commission, 89 Cong., 1 Sess.; FCC, Annual Report, vol. 30, p. 73.

88. Federal Register, XXX, 13174; FCC, Annual Report, vol. 31, pp. 112-13.

89. New York Times, March 8, 1961, November 21, 1963.

90. New York Times, April 3, 1965, October 3, 1964, April 1, 1965.

CHAPTER

5

THE CONGRESS AND THE
DEPARTMENT OF HEALTH,
EDUCATION AND WELFARE—FUNDS

LEGISLATION EXPEDITING UTILIZATION OF
TELEVISION FACILITIES FOR EDUCATION

Not only did Congress keep a watchful eye on education's television channels, it passed legislation to expedite the utilization of television facilities for education and to provide funds directly and indirectly for educational broadcasting. Congress enacted laws to construct and equip educational stations, to pay for research in educational broadcasting, to make surplus property available to stations, and to increase the potential audience of educational broadcasts. Congress also passed a host of other laws providing extensive amounts of financial assistance to elementary, secondary, and higher education, and at least seven of these authorized grants, administered through the Office of Education, which could be used for educational broadcasting.

Leonard H. Marks, legal counsel to the National Association of Educational Broadcasters, convinced his colleagues in the association that they should seek federal funds to build stations in order to use the channels reserved for them. Apparently, this course of action had not occurred to them before because of the general antipathy to federal involvement in education. Marks talked with Senate Majority Leader Lyndon B. Johnson on a social occasion in 1956 and convinced him that educational broadcasters needed aid. Johnson had a personal business interest in commercial television and a deep commitment to public education. He arranged for Marks to meet with Senator Warren G. Magnuson of the state of Washington, who was chairman of the Commerce Committee, which had jurisdiction over legislation dealing with communications. Magnuson agreed to introduce a bill and hold hearings to determine the needs and the kind of support that

could be generated. Marks prepared a draft of the legislation, and
in March 1967, Senator Magnuson introduced a bill in the Senate
authorizing the appropriation of $1 million to each state and territory
to provide educational television facilities. The proposal was for a
grant by which the federal government would provide funds for the
acquisition and installation of television equipment if the states or
their agencies provided land and buildings for educational stations
and agreed to operate and maintain the equipment. The bill authorized
the commissioner of education of HEW to make grants to organizations
or states that secured authority to broadcast from the FCC and satisfied the commissioner of education that the organization or state
would operate and maintain the station; that the operation of the
station would be under the control of a state agency or officer primarily
responsible for the supervision of public instruction, a nonprofit
agency organized to engage in educational television, a state educational television commission, or a state or university; and that the
station would be used only for educational purposes.[1]

On April 24 and 25, the Senate Committee on Interstate and
Foreign Commerce held hearings on the bill.[2] Educators insisted
that their problem was one of financing and not one of interest or
zeal. They recalled the dramatic effect the grants from the Fund
for Adult Education had on the establishment of the first educational
television stations and declared that federal grants would produce
even more spectacular results, by establishing a pilot station in each
state for the understanding of television's potential in education.
Educational television, it was believed, would help correct shortages
in classrooms and teachers. The Senate committee asked the FCC
for its opinion on the bill, and the FCC said that the question of
appropriations was primarily one of fundamental substantive policy
for the judgment of Congress but added that it was the commission's
opinion that the problems of educational television were basically
financial. When asked for its counsel concerning the bill, HEW stated
that it opposed the bill because it did not believe federal appropriations were necessary in view of continued progress in building educational television stations.[3] The department was less convinced of
the progress in educational television than it was influenced by the
conservative fiscal policy of the administration of President Dwight
D. Eisenhower. The Senate passed the bill on May 29, 1958.[4]

The House of Representatives Committee on Interstate and Foreign Commerce held hearings on the Senate bill and two similar
House bills[5] on July 15 and 16. Testimony from educators, the FCC,
and HEW was essentially the same as at the Senate hearing.[6] The
House measure, identical to the Senate bill, was reported out of
committee on August 15[7] but was swamped in the jam of legislation
at the end of the second session of the Eighty-Fifth Congress.

At the first meeting of the first session of the Eighty-Sixth Congress, Senator Magnuson reintroduced his bill to grant $1 million to each state and territory to expedite the utilization of educational television. It was identical with the bill that the Senate passed during the previous session of Congress, except that the states or their agencies were required to request the funds within five years after the passage of the law.[8] The Committee on Interstate and Foreign Commerce held hearings on the bill on January 27 and 28, 1959.[9] Educators urged Congress to pass the bill; the FCC repeated its contention that the problems of educational television were primarily financial, saying, "There is no information that a Federal program is necessary to assume continuing development of educational television or that there is an inability to finance the acquisition and installation of transmitting equipment," and recommended that the bill not be enacted.

On April 13, the Senate passed the bill, despite the statement of Republican Senator Everett McKinley Dirksen that the bill would destroy the surplus in the federal budget and open the door to federal control of educational television.[10]

The Committee on Interstate and Foreign Commerce of the House of Representatives held hearings on the Senate bill and seven similar House bills to expedite educational television.[11] The hearings in May were a rehash of previous congressional hearings on the subject.[12] On June 4, the committee shelved the bill, pending further hearings after Congress adjourned. In November and December, the House committee held supplemental field hearings in various parts of the United States.[13] The committee visited educational television stations, saw television demonstrations, and heard the opinions of educational broadcasters, college and school administrators, and state officials. Spokesmen unanimously testified that the FCC should reserve channels for education over an extended period and that Congress should assist in the development of educational television grants, loans, or matching grants on a one-time or long-range basis.

The House committee wrote a new bill, patterned after the Hospital Survey and Construction Act, to assist states in surveying their needs and developing programs for the construction of educational television facilities and to assist through matching grants in their construction. The bill authorized the appropriation of $10,000 to each state, if matched by the state, to survey the state's need for educational television and to draft a comprehensive program of development. Each state taking advantage of the act would be required to submit its program to HEW within three years after the passage of the act. HEW was authorized to pay 50 percent of the cost of new installations and 75 percent of the cost of enlarging or expanding existing facilities, with a maximum payment of $750,000 to each state. The FCC was authorized to provide such assistance in carrying out the provisions of the act as HEW might request. Stations owned and operated by an agency or officer responsible for state public instruction, a state educational television authority, a state college or university, or a nonprofit community educational television organization were eligible to participate in the state development program.[14]

The Committee on Interstate and Foreign Commerce approved the bill on March 24, 1960, and reported it to the House of Representatives, but a tie vote in the Rules Committee on May 12, 1960, kept the bill from reaching the floor of the House and killed the bill for the eighty-sixth session of Congress.[15]

The Eighty-Seventh Congress convened in January 1961, and among the first bills introduced in both chambers were measures to provide financial assistance for the construction of educational television facilities.

On January 6, Senator Magnuson reintroduced his bill to provide $1 million to each state to acquire and install equipment for educational stations. The bill was referred to the Senator's Committee on Interstate and Foreign Commerce, where hearings were held March 1 and 2.[16] Senator Magnuson commented that President John F. Kennedy had voted for identical bills on two separate occasions while a member of the Senate and implied that he had more hope of success under the new Democratic administration. Representatives of the National Association of Educational Broadcasters, National Education Association, American Council on Education, Joint Council on Educational Broadcasting (the new name of the reorganized Joint Council on Educational Television), National Educational Television and Radio Center, and Radio Corporation of America dusted off their old notes and testified for the third time in favor of the same bill. FCC Commissioner Frederick W. Ford asserted more positively than had been done previously that the commission endorsed the objectives of the bill. Chairman Newton N. Minow, in a letter to Senator Magnuson, joined in urging the use of federal funds for the purpose. Secretary of Health, Education and Welfare Abraham Ribicoff, however, in a letter to the senator, recommended against passage of the bill until his department had had a chance to study the most effective methods of providing federal assistance to education. Despite Ribicoff's request for more time, the Senate passed the bill for the third time on March 21.[17]

Members of the House of Representatives offered seven bills to establish a program of federal assistance for building television facilities for educational purposes. Three were the same as the Senate bill for direct grants, and four provided for matching grants. The Committee on Interstate and Foreign Commerce held hearings

in March and May.[18] Representative Kenneth A. Roberts of Alabama
supported the idea, because of his personal interest and because of
the interest of Alabamians, as demonstrated by their having set up
the first statewide educational network. Robert W. Hemphill, a
representative from South Carolina, also supported a program of
grants, based on the success of educational television in his native
state and because of limited sources of revenue for school purposes
in South Carolina. FCC Chairman Minow declared: "The Commission
is most anxious to cooperate in any program which will assist the
development of educational television." He felt that there was a
"real need for financial assistance to educational television" and
stated that he "wholeheartedly endorsed the use of Federal funds to
aid in improving or establishing educational television for broadcasting facilities." A letter from Commissioner Rosel H. Hyde declared,
"I would recommend that Congress provide financial aid for educational
television as a means of expanding our educational facilities and as
a manner of improving our national communications service." Having
had two months since the Senate hearings to review the various suggestions for providing financial assistance to education and having
been told by the White House to either testify in support of the legislation or not testify at all, Secretary Ribicoff told the House hearings
that the Kennedy Administration "strongly favors a nationwide system
of educational television." Quoting President Kennedy's education
message of February 21, Ribicoff said "our twin goals must be a
new standard of excellence in education and the availability of such
excellence to all who are willing and able to pursue it." The secretary concluded his remarks with: "The achievement of these two
goals could be hastened by the legislation now before us." Ribicoff
supported matching rather than direct grants.[19]

The House Committee passed a bill similar to the Senate bill
calling for direct grants in August, but the bill did not come to the
attention of the House Rules Committee until January 1962.

In his education message of February 6, 1962, President Kennedy
declared: "I urge the Congress to take prompt and final action to
provide matching financial grants to the states to aid in the construction of state or other nonprofit educational television stations."[20]
Thereafter, events moved more swiftly.

By a 337-68 vote, the House of Representatives passed an amended
version of the committee bill on March 7. The House measure called
for matching grants, as the president had requested; therefore, it
was necessary for a Senate and House conference committee to consider the bills passed by the respective house of Congress and come
up with a compromise measure.[21]

The conference committee noted that 273 channels had been
reserved by the FCC for education and only 62 were in use. The

committee reported: "There is great danger that unless the process
of getting educational television stations on the air is speeded up,
the demand to use these channels for commercial purpose may become irresistible, and thus they will be irretrievably lost to education." To speed up the process, the committee compromised on a
bill to authorize matching grants up to $1 million for each state to
aid in purchasing equipment and constructing educational television
facilities. Congress was authorized to appropriate up to $32 million
over a five-year period beginning with fiscal year 1963. The bill
required the FCC to give all needed assistance to HEW that was
required to administer the measure. HEW was instructed to make
grants of 50 percent of the cost of construction of new facilities and
25 percent of the cost of existing facilities to state or local educational
supervisory agencies, state educational television agencies, and tax-
supported colleges, universities, or nonprofit organizations set up
to advance educational television.[22]

The conference report was agreed to in the Senate on April 16
and in the House two days later.[23] When President Kennedy signed
the Educational Television Facilities Act on May 1, 1962, he said,
"I am delighted to approve an act which will do so much to assist
in the growth of this important educational medium."[24] Vice President Johnson observed the signing ceremony. He had been keeping
in touch with the bill ever since he introduced Marks to Senator
Magnuson in 1956 at the beginning of the six-year legislative struggle
to obtain federal funds for educational broadcasting facilities. Secretary Ribicoff lauded the act and Chairman Minow said, "I couldn't
be more pleased."[25]

Congress adjourned in 1962 without appropriating any of the
money authorized in the law, and it was not until May 1, 1963, that
Congress got around to appropriating one and one-half of the $32
million authorized. HEW told Senator John O. Pastore on April 26
that rules and regulations were completed, application forms had
been printed, a large number of potential applicants were ready to
proceed, and the opening date of acceptance of applications was
established as two weeks from the day funds were appropriated.[26]
On May 15, HEW began processing applications for funds.

During the five fiscal years, Congress appropriated all the
authorized funds and HEW disbursed them. Senator Magnuson
announced in 1966 that his committee would hold hearings in the
spring of 1967 to consider whether the Educational Television Act
should be extended and more money appropriated for educational
television facilities.[27]

Eleven years after the FCC reserved channels for education,
Congress acted to help solve a critical problem for noncommercial
educational broadcasters—money. Through the lean years of fiscal

appropriations, educators had their champions in Congress, but they
got no financial help. When a new administration began looking for
ways to assist education with federal funds, these champions consolidated the interests of the White House, HEW, FCC, and educational
broadcasting associations behind their protracted effort and acquired
federal funds for educational television facilities.

It should be recalled that two months after Congress passed the
Educational Television Facilities Act of 1962, Congress passed an
amendment to the Communications Act of 1934 that increased the
potential audience of educational UHF stations. The All-Channel
Receiver Act provided that television sets in interstate commerce
must be capable of receiving UHF as well as VHF transmissions.
Both laws were part of President Kennedy's legislative program and
indicated an interest in noncommercial educational broadcasting on
the part of the executive as well as the legislative branches of the
federal government.

Further indicating the interest of Congress in noncommercial
educational broadcasting was a law signed by President Kennedy in
1962 to make independent educational radio and television stations
eligible to receive surplus government property.[28] Congress
approved the Federal Property and Administrative Service Act in
1949 to transfer surplus property to tax-supported school systems,
schools, colleges, and universities and other nonprofit educational
institutions held to be exempt from taxation. Under this law, a number of schools and colleges received surplus broadcasting equipment.
Florida College in Tampa, for example, got a broadcasting station
and sound control booth for a new auditorium through donations of
surplus property from several Florida air bases.[29]

Some organizations for technical reasons had been left out.
At the request of HEW, Congress revised the law in 1962 to make
independent nonprofit educational stations eligible.[30] This action
had a minuscule effect on the large problem of financing educational
television facilities, but it was indicative of the interest engendered
in Congress for noncommercial educational broadcasting.

Noncommercial educational television needed money, a lot of
money. Among the sources available for these funds was the federal
government, and Congress controlled the federal purse. Over a
period of years, Congress developed an interest in noncommercial
educational broadcasting. In an amendment to the Communications
Act of 1934, it increased the potential audience for educational broadcasts. In the Educational Television Facilities Act, it made money
available for educational television facilities. In the Federal Property
and Administrative Services Act of 1949 and amendments to the act,
it made surplus property available to educational stations.

THE OE's IMPACT ON EDUCATIONAL
TELEVISION

Except for a few years in the late 1930s, when it made important contributions, the OE did not have a significant impact on educational broadcasting until Congress passed a number of laws dealing with education, beginning with the National Defense Education Act in 1958.

In 1952, after the FCC reserved channels for educators, the OE gave an anguished cry in its annual report.

> The United States Office of Education has a rare opportunity for creating a climate in which a new educational medium can flourish. The present resources of the Office of Education are not adequate to do the job expected of it and for which it can rightly be held accountable. It needs to add personnel of high caliber and to undertake cooperative research programs for the development of television for educational purposes.[31]

During the next year, a government reorganization forced the Radio and Television Services Section to discontinue its radio script and transcription service and to break up its files of reference materials on radio.[32] For the next five years, the OE had an even less significant impact on educational broadcasting than before.

Staff specialists advised on educational projects in many parts of the United States and cooperated with educational institutions in planning and producing programs. The Radio and Television Services Section organized the Joint Committee of the OE and the Radio-Electronics-Television Manufacturers Association on Teaching with Radio, Audio, Recording, and Television Equipment to study ways of using communications equipment in education. Three earlier studies dealt with a single class of equipment and described what educators were doing with the equipment. The fourth study, begun in 1953, took the reverse approach. It started with the instructional jobs schools had to perform and determined how the jobs might be facilitated by the use of various types of communications equipment.

In 1958, the OE combined the Audiovisual Section and the Radio and Television Services Section into a new organization, which it called Audiovisual Aid to Education. The audiovisual section conceived of its role in educational broadcasting to be to cooperate with organizations concerned with educational television, to issue directories of university courses in broadcasting, to publish bibliographies and lists, to assist applicants for broadcasting licenses, to give advice on organizing and financing stations, to review the results of

uses of educational television, to maintain contact with researchers
and experimenters, and to participate in workshops for training
teachers in the use of educational television. One of the first activities of the reorganized section was to sponsor a three-day National
Conference on Educational Television in May 1958, attended by representatives of 51 national organizations. The conference explored
new developments and trends and attempted to set principles to serve
as guidelines for future developments.[33]

The audiovisual section had hardly been organized a year when
Congress passed a law that made it possible for the OE to come out
of its 20-year slump and become a vital force in educational broadcasting. The National Defense Education Act (NDEA) of 1958, in
Titles III and VI, emphasized new educational media for the improvement of instruction in selected subject areas and, in Title VII (Educational Media Research), provided for federal support through the
OE for research and dissemination of information regarding all
educational media. Title VII authorized the expenditure of federal
funds

> through grants or contracts to conduct, assist, or foster
> research and experimentation in the development and
> evaluation of projects involving television, radio, and
> motion pictures which may prove of value to elementary,
> secondary, and higher education and in the development
> of new and more effective techniques and methods for
> utilizing television, radio, and motion pictures, for
> training teachers, and for presenting academic subject
> matter.[34]

Congress appropriated $500,000 for such research and experimenta-
tion in the first year of the act. When a subcommittee of the House
of Representatives Committee on Education and Labor held hearings
to determine public response to the National Defense Education Act
the next year,[35] administrators from HEW reported that they had
received approximately 200 proposals, requesting $20 million for
research and experimentation in television, radio, and motion pictures. Because the demand from educators was so great and the
proposals so worthy of consideration, they urged Congress to appropriate more money for educational media research. At last, the
OE had the funds and the authority to enter the field of educational
broadcasting in the manner and with the means it had wanted and
deemed essential.

Scrapping Audiovisual Aids to Education in the Division of State
and Local School Systems, the OE organized, in the Division of
Statistics and Research Studies, an Educational Media Branch, with

two sections. The Research Section was set up to administer Part A
of Title VII, which charged HEW with responsibility to conduct
research and experimentation in the uses of new educational media
through grants or contracts.[36]

In accordance with Section 761(a) of the National Defense Education Act, the Educational Media Branch appointed an Advisory Committee on New Educational Media, which met twice a year to review
and approve Part A proposals and to make recommendations regarding
the implementation of Part B. In fiscal years 1959 and 1960, the
committee approved 116 project proposals, costing $7 million.
About half the grants concerned television for large group instruction
and teaching machines for individualized learning. For a number of
years, 60 to 70 grants were made annually, totaling between $4 and
$5 million. Not all of these projects dealt with educational television,
of course, but in the first seven years, more than $8 million was
spent for studying, planning, and reporting about educational broadcasting.[37] In addition, almost 40 contracts were awarded during
the same period for the dissemination of information. Grants under
Part A were divided into three categories: Unlimited Grant Program,
Small Grant Program, and Institutional Research Grant Program.
Grants in the first category were limited in size and scope only by
appropriations and the availability of funds. Second-category grants
were usually made to individuals for projects not lasting more than
18 months or costing more than $7,500; third-category grants were
usually made to institutions for the same length of time and not in
excess of $10,000. Part B grants were not categorized.[38]

A number of research and dissemination projects are listed
below in order to give a representative sampling of those dealing
with educational broadcasting. They and all the others were named
and described in an annual publication of the Dissemination Branch
entitled "Title 7, New Educational Media, News and Reports."

speech improvements in elementary schools in Hawaii through the
    use of television
effects of television on retention
supplementation of television high school physics with correspondence
    courses and student teachers
effectiveness of guidance instruction by television
determinants of audience formation and reactions to television college-
    credit courses
distribution of visual aids on a university campus by low-power UHF
    television
role of state and regional networks in educational broadcasting
survey of television equipment and facilities used for purpose of
    instruction

demonstration of in-service teacher training in audiovisual education
    by television
use of television for education in medicine and dentistry
demonstration of use of FM radio network to facilitate conference
    technique of communication among institutions of higher education
dissemination conference on principles and practices in use of televi-
    sion in education
evaluation of procedures for individualizing group instruction by
    television
physiological factors of television viewing
survey of uses of television for application to teacher education
depth seminars on projected uses of television in education for the
    next decade
planning, construction, and evaluation of media for teaching high
    school and junior college science via television
evaluation of communication media used in adult liberal studies
    programs
characteristics of students enrolled for credit in telecast college
    courses
learner-participation techniques in a programmed course on elemen-
    tary government and civics via television[39]

    In addition to "Title 7," the OE has produced other publications.
In 1959, Franklin Dunham, then chief of Radio-Television, wrote
"Educational Teleguide: References for Education by Television."
It listed books on television, publications by the government, foundations making grants, closed circuit educational television systems,
educational television stations, colleges and universities offering
courses in television, colleges granting credit for network television
courses, and school districts and schools making regular use of
television. In the same year, the OE published a promotional piece
on "New Educational Media Programs," which it revised in 1962
and again in 1963, with a selected bibliography of government documents on educational media, as well as a description of its Title VII
activities. For a number of years after 1961, Gertrude G. Broderick
prepared a list entitled "Educational AM and FM Radio, and Educational Television Stations by State and City." It also reprinted in
1962 the proceedings of a symposium it had jointly sponsored with
the Institute for Communications Research of Stanford University
in November 1959. Stanford University first published in 1960 the
proceedings of the symposium on the state of research in instructional
television and tutorial machines.[40]
    In 1960, the OE sponsored a conference on the educational uses
of television at Ohio State University that was attended by representatives of 20 states. A year later, educators and broadcasters from

41 countries attended a seminar at Purdue University sponsored by
the OE, the UN Educational, Scientific, and Cultural Organization,
and others. Participants reviewed trends and examined the issues
involved in the use of television as an educational medium and as an
instrument of national policy.[41]

What seems to be the most important and provocative results of
the OE's activities in the area of noncommercial educational broadcasting began with the commissioning of four studies and the appointment of an Educational Media Study Panel.

C. Walter Stone, director of the Educational Media Branch,
decided in late 1960 to commission four studies regarding educational
broadcasting. The branch asked the National Educational Television
and Radio Center to make an audience study of eight stations in six
different situations. It requested the NAEB to survey the plans of
educators to determine the needs for the exchange of teaching materials
used on television. It contracted with the Institute for Communications Research at Stanford University and its subcontractors to study
copyrights, personnel needs, program quality, financing, school
and equipment design, and instructional use of television. An Educational Media Study panel was formed to hear testimony, review the
reports of the studies, and make recommendations within a year.[42]

In December 1961, the panel issued a report and urged a national
policy for the development of educational television. The report
stated that financial support was needed from public and private funds,
that federal action was needed to assure that all television sets received both VHF and UHF signals, that a nationwide talent search
and training program was needed to keep a full supply of personnel,
that nationwide research and evaluation was needed to increase the
worth and efficiency of educational television, and that there was a
need for national and regional exchanges for teaching materials for
television.[43]

A fuller statement of the thinking of specialists on the future of
educational television, with complete reports of task forces operating
under the general direction of Wilbur Schramm of the Stanford Institute
for Communications Research, was contained in Educational Television: The Next Ten Years. Published originally in 1962, the book
was reprinted by the U.S. Government Printing Office with revisions
in 1965.

The long-range results of the various studies, reports, and
publications were uncertain, but two studies—the NAEB survey and
the University of Nebraska study (described below)—achieved notable
results and promised an even greater impact on educational broadcasting in the future.

Vernon Bronson of the NAEB made a state-by-state survey for
the OE of the future needs of education for television channel alloca-

tions. The survey included colleges and universities, school systems, state departments of education, civic and government leaders, and operating educational television stations. Bronson found that educators planned to use television not only for formal education but for continuing education at every stage of life as well. School systems anticipated a greater use of the medium than colleges and universities; 95 percent of the schools reporting stated that they had curriculum deficiencies or teaching needs that could be met or helped by educational television. The survey found that educators preferred to use VHF channels for community communications and UHF channels to supplement their curricula. Bronson came to the conclusion that educators would need 1,197 channels to meet anticipated demand. To the 88 UHF channels and 187 VHF channels reserved when the report was published in 1962, the author determined that 97 VHF channels and 825 UHF channels would need to be added, for a total of 1,197 channels. Not only did the survey estimate the number of channels needed, but it provided a method for acquiring the additional channels. Bronson programmed a computer with the FCC's table of allocations, the characteristics of television broadcasting, and the anticipated needs of educators and produced a table of "additional availability," containing 48 VHF channels and 608 UHF channels.[44]

Anthony J. Celebreeze, secretary of Health, Education and Welfare, sent the report to the FCC to be used as suggested criteria for considering future applications for channels.[45] The commission was so impressed by Bronson's use of a computer to examine assignment plans that it established a computer program of its own. As previously described, the FCC used a computer to reallocate all UHF assignments in 1965. Using the technique Bronson developed with a computer and the information he elicited from educators on anticipated future need, the FCC made half of its 1,000 UHF assignments to educators and indicated that the computer could find many more channel assignments when educators were ready to make full use of television broadcasting.

The NAEB survey was an important document in substantiating the need for channels and in justifying further FCC assignments. The application of computer technology to channel assignments should be of considerable importance to commercial and noncommercial stations. Their requests for channels should be more rapidly and efficiently processed and their individual needs more nearly met.

The second study to produce demonstrable results began with the question, "How can effective television material be made more readily available to schools?" Jack McBride and W. C. Meierhenry of the University of Nebraska had a contract in 1960 with the OE to determine how to locate and gather useful instructional television material, how to insure the continued production and availability of

such material, and how to exchange the material generated. Their
report, published in 1961, suggested that the OE establish national
and regional centers for the exchange of instructional television
material.

The OE had had a successful experience 20 years before in
exchanging radio scripts and transcriptions. Commissioner of
Education Sterling M. McMurrin announced that National Defense
Education Act funds would be used to establish an exchange. In 1962,
the OE negotiated a contract with the National Educational Television
and Radio Center to set up a national exchange called the National
Instructional Television Library and two regional exchanges. The
University of Nebraska organized the Great Plains Instructional
Television Library, and the Eastern Educational Network in Boston
organized the Northeastern Regional Instructional Television Library.
The national library in Washington, D.C., planned to work closely
with the regional libraries and to cover the areas not included in the
Great Plains and northeastern regions.

When the National Instructional Television Library surveyed its
intended area of operations, it discovered that few programs were
available and that the existing sources for appropriate programs
could not supply the need. Consequently, in 1964, the National
Education Television and Radio Center withdrew from its contract
with the OE, which subsequently contracted with the Indiana University Foundation to set up a national organization to acquire and
distribute videotapes of courses from grade school to college and
to give assistance in developing new courses.[46]

The Indiana University Foundation received $1,104,652 in
August 1965 to establish the National Center for School and College
Television. It was the largest grant to that date made by the OE
under Title VII, B, of the National Defense Education Act. The
grant was for two years. It was felt that after five years, the center
would be self-supporting.[47] The new national center retained the
regional centers at Lincoln, Nebraska, and Boston and established
another regional center in San Francisco, operated by the Western
Radio and Television Association.

The OE in 1962 contracted with the Educational Media Council,
which subcontracted with a textbook publisher, to produce Educational
Media Index. This comprehensive directory of educational materials,
including videotapes, was revised periodically and was quite useful
as a key to the holdings of the national and regional centers of videotaped instructional material.[48]

With centers devoted to the acquisition and distribution of videotaped courses, with even more reserved UHF channels, and with the
Instructional Television Fixed Service, the federal interest in the
instructional aspects of noncommercial educational broadcasting was

comprehensive. It was up to educators to prove that the interest of
the federal government was well placed by using the facilities that
some of their leaders had fought for and gained.

Stanford University's Institute of Communications Research
directed a number of studies for the OE on the future of educational
television. Televised instruction created problems of copyright,
royalties, and compensation to teachers, which the American Council
on Education studied. The NAEB studied personnel needs of educational stations. It identified those persons available and discovered
shortages in management and engineering. The Educational Media
Study Panel, in reviewing the study, recommended that station
personnel receive broader training than production skills and arranged
with the University of Pittsburgh and the Alameda County, California,
schools to help develop guidelines for training. Sources of money
for educational broadcasting were studied by Brandeis University in
1963 and by an NAEB conference in Washington, D.C., in 1964.
WGBH, in Boston, utilized the FM radio network to demonstrate the
use of FM radio for the conference technique of communicating among
institutions of higher learning.[49]

In addition to the Title VII provisions of the National Defense
Education Act for research and dissemination of information regarding educational media, subsequent changes in the law directly affected
educational broadcasting. In 1960, Congress extended the law and
amended Title II for the improvement of teaching of science, mathe-
matics, and modern languages by matching funds for equipment and
supervisory services to authorize schools to purchase television
receivers. The scope of NDEA Institutes for Advanced Study was
broadened to include educational media specialists. In the summer
of 1966, institutes were held in 37 locations for advanced study for
education media specialists, including advanced study in the use of
educational television.[50]

A number of other laws administered in whole or in part by the
OE had provisions for grants or loans that could be used for various
aspects of educational broadcasting. The Cooperative Research
Act of 1954 (Public Law 83-531) provided federal assistance to improve elementary and secondary school curricula. One project used
funds appropriated under the act to design a fully automated reading
and arithmetic curriculum, utilizing television in part. Most of the
measures were passed as part of President Johnson's legislative
program for the Great Society.

The Manpower Development and Training Act of 1962 (Public
Law 88-204), as amended in 1963 and 1965, authorized the OE to
pay the costs of purchasing, maintaining, and repairing instructional
equipment. This presumably included anything from television sets
to closed circuit or ITFS systems.

The Higher Education Facilities Act of 1963 (Public Law 88-204) provided under Title I, grants for 40 percent of the cost of constructing or improving undergraduate classrooms, libraries, and laboratories; under Title II, grants for one-third of the cost of graduate academic facilities; and, in addition, under Title III, loans to cover up to 75 percent of the total cost of such facilities. Receivers, special wiring, studios and other accoutrements of educational broadcasting could be included in academic buildings.

In the Library Services and Construction Act of 1964 (Public Law 88-269), Congress made provisions for federal funds to be used to construct, expand, remodel, or alter library buildings and to acquire equipment. Libraries could engage in broadcasting, producing, and receiving educational television programs, and this act would provide funds to do so.

The Elementary and Secondary Education Act of 1965 (Public Law 89-10) provided financial aid to educational broadcasting directly and indirectly. Title I provided financial assistance to local school agencies for the education of children of low-income families and specifically authorized funds to be spent for educational radio and television should anyone apply. Title III established supplementary educational centers and services and suggested that the services could include educational television and radio, as well as psychological testing, remedial education, and audiovisual aids. Two other titles of the act provided for indirect aid. The second title, to purchase instructional materials, enumerated documents, tapes, records, physical facilities, and equipment as eligible items. The fourth, to foster educational research and training, suggested the building and equipping of national and regional research facilities, which could include experimentation and research in educational broadcasting.

The Higher Education Act of 1965 (Public Law 89-329) also could be interpreted to provide assistance for the use of educational broadcasting. If one were to use educational television for library training, one could obtain funds through Title II for audiovisual aids, tapes, recordings, and other needed library material. If one were to use educational broadcasting to improve undergraduate instruction, one could obtain assistance under Title IV to acquire modern teaching equipment, including television, and to train teachers in the use of the new technology.

The OE urged educational broadcasters to meet their obligation to use their medium for assistance to the whole community and to address all types of special audiences, as well as schoolchildren. It challenged educators to use their imagination and broaden the services performed by educational television by employing federal funds designed to increase economic opportunity and improve the conditions of life of groups of people with special problems. It

specifically encouraged broadcasters to use television to meet the
objectives of the Manpower Development and Training Act of 1962,
the Public Welfare Act amendments of 1962, the Vocational Rehabilitation Act amendments of 1963, and the Economic Opportunity Act of
1964. Commissioner of Education Francis Keppel reemphasized this
point in a speech to educational broadcasters in December 1964.
The OE urged educators to follow through with recommendations of
the Commission on Heart Disease, Cancer, and Stroke that television
programming support federal efforts in the health field. HEW publicized that aspect of the Appalachian Regional Development Act of
1965 which provided funds to meet part of the nonfederal share in
federal matching grants, such as the educational television facilities
program. The OE also kept in touch with a Peace Corps educational
television project in Colombia and an NAEB project in American
Samoa.[51]

The OE also alerted scholars and broadcasters to the provisions
of the National Foundation of the Arts and the Humanities Act of 1965
that authorized studies of ways to make better use of educational
television, radio, and films. The National Council on the Arts,
established by the act, made its first awards in August 1966. It
gave $875,000 on a matching basis for educational television, the
largest single federal grant for educational broadcasting. The award
was shared by Educational Broadcasting Corporation, National Educational Television, and educational television stations for the development of national programming in the arts.[52]

When Congress passed the Educational Television Facilities Act
in 1962, it made HEW responsible for administering the law. The
director of the Educational Television Facilities Program, Bureau
of Educational Assistance Programs, Office of Education, was dele-
gated the authority to carry out the program. He had a staff to
provide informational material, prepare rules and regulations,
process applications, and make grants on a matching basis for 50
percent of the cost of new construction and 25 percent of the cost of
eligible apparatus owned on the date the application for funds was
accepted for filing. By the end of fiscal year 1966, and the fourth
year of the five-year assistance program, the department had made
grants in the amount of $23 million. Congress appropriated for
grants and administration $1,500,000 in fiscal year 1963, $6,500,000
in 1964, $13,000,000 in 1965, and $8,826,000 in 1966. Of the 114
noncommercial educational television stations broadcasting on
June 30, 1965, 29 new stations had come on the air with federal
assistance, and almost 50 old stations had improved or expanded
their services with federal funds. Twenty-five stations receiving
federal help were in various stages of construction.[53]

Indicating the importance of educational television to the total program of HEW, John W. Bystrom was appointed in 1965 to the newly created position of assistant for educational television to the assistant secretary of Health, Education and Welfare for Education. NAEB President William G. Harley had suggested the need for such a position. Bystrom's responsibilities were to coordinate department programs and activities in educational broadcasting. It was a significant change in emphasis from only a few years before when two staff persons cared for the needs of educators interested in radio and television, and it was an accurate reflection of the federal interest in noncommercial educational broadcasting in the executive branch of the government.

The OE had the money, personnel, and programs for which it gave an anguished cry in 1952, and after the enactment of the National Defense Education Act and Educational Television Facilities Act, it achieved notable results. The ebullient spirit in the OE needed to be fed by an overwhelming demand from educators for the goods and services that the OE was able to provide.

NOTES

1. John E. Burke, "The Public Broadcasting Act of 1967: Part I: Historical Origins and the Carnegie Commission," Educational Broadcasting Review 6, no. 2 (April 1972): 107-08; Senate, Bill 85-2119.

2. Senate, Committee on Interstate and Foreign Commerce, Hearing on S2119, 85 Cong., 1 Sess.

3. Senate, Report 85-1638.

4. Congressional Record, CIV, 9802.

5. House of Representatives, Bill 85-12177, Bill 85-13297.

6. House of Representatives, Committee on Interstate and Foreign Commerce, Hearing on S2119, 85 Cong., 2 Sess.

7. House of Representatives, Report 85-2636; Congressional Record, CIV, 17931.

8. Senate, Bill 86-12.

9. Senate, Committee on Interstate and Foreign Commerce Hearing on S12, 86 Cong., 1 Sess.; Senate, Report 86-56.

10. Congressional Record, CV, 5757, 5775.

11. House of Representatives, Bill 86-32, Bill 86-1981, Bill 86-2926, Bill 86-3043, Bill 86-3723, Bill 86-4248, Bill 86-4572.

12. House of Representatives, Committee on Interstate and Foreign Commerce, Hearing on S12 and Other Bills, 86 Cong., 1 Sess.

13. House of Representatives, Committee on Interstate and Foreign Commerce, Summary of Supplemental Field Hearings on S12 and Other Bills, 86 Cong., 2 Sess., passim.

14. House of Representatives, Report 86-1466.

15. New York Times, March 25, 1960, May 13, 1960.

16. Senate, Committee on Interstate and Foreign Commerce, Hearing on S205, 87 Cong., 1 Sess.

17. Congressional Record, CVII, 4368.

18. House of Representatives, Committee on Interstate and Foreign Commerce, Hearings on HR132, HR5099, HR5536, HR5602, HR654, HR965 and HR2910, 87 Cong., 1 Sess.

19. Ibid.

20. Public Papers of the Presidents of the United States. John F. Kennedy, 1962 (Washington, D.C.: U.S. Government Printing Office, 1963), document 37 (hereafter cited as Public Papers, Kennedy, 1962).

21. Congressional Record, CVIII, 3555.

22. House of Representatives, Report 87-1609.

23. Congressional Record, CVIII, 6636, 6937; Public Law 87-447.

24. Public Papers, Kennedy, 1962, document 166.

25. New York Times, May 2, 1962.

26. Congressional Record, CIX, 7568.

27. Congressional Record, CXI, A6163.

28. Public Law 87-786; Congressional Record, CVIII, 23543.

29. House of Representatives, Government Operations Committee, Evaluation of Donable Property Program, 89 Cong.; Public Law 81-152.

30. House of Representatives, Government Operations Committee, Donation of Surplus Personal Property to Educational Institutions, 87 Cong.

31. Federal Security Agency, Office of Education, Annual Report, 1952 (Washington, D.C.: U.S. Government Printing Office, 1953), p. 25.

32. Department of Health, Education and Welfare, Office of Education, Annual Report, 1953 (Washington, D.C.: U.S. Government Printing Office, 1954), p. 178.

33. Department of Health, Education and Welfare, Office of Education, Annual Report, 1958 (Washington, D.C.: U.S. Government Printing Office, 1959), p. 174.

34. Public Law 85-864.

35. House of Representatives, Committee on Education and Labor, Hearing on Administration of National Defense Education Act of 1958, 86 Cong., 1 Sess.

36. Department of Health, Education and Welfare, Office of Education, Annual Report, 1959 (Washington, D.C.: U.S. Government Printing Office, 1960), p. 159.

37. Department of Health, Education and Welfare, Office of Education, Annual Report, 1960 (Washington, D.C.: U.S. Government Printing Office, 1961), p. 215.

38. Department of Health, Education and Welfare, Office of Education, Annual Report, 1965 (Washington, D.C.: U.S. Government Printing Office, 1966), pp. 298-300 (hereafter cited as HEW, Annual Report 1965).

39. Department of Health, Education and Welfare, Office of Education, "Title 7 [National Defense Education Act] New Educational Media, News and Reports," 1-8 special editions (1961-65).

40. Department of Health, Education and Welfare, Office of Education, "New Teaching Aids for the American Classroom . . ." (Washington, D.C.: U.S. Government Printing Office, 1962).

41. New York Times, August 13, 1960, October 5, 1961.

42. Department of Health, Education and Welfare, Office of Education, Educational Television: The Next Ten Years (Washington, D.C.: Government Printing Office, 1965), pp. viii-ix (hereafter cited as HEW, Educational Television).

43. Department of Health, Education and Welfare, Office of Education, National Policy for Educational Television, Report and Recommendations Submitted to the Commissioner of Education by the Educational Media Study Panel (Washington, D.C.: U.S. Government Printing Office, 1961).

44. Department of Health, Education and Welfare, Needs of Education for Television Channel Allocations, Survey by NAEB (Washington, D.C.: U.S. Government Printing Office, 1962).

45. New York Times, August 24, 1962.

46. Edwin Cohen, "A Center for ITV," American Education 2 (June 1966): 22-24; New York Times, January 12, 1962.

47. New York Times, August 24, 1965.

48. Department of Health, Education and Welfare, Office of Education, Annual Report, 1962 (Washington, D.C.: U.S. Government Printing Office, 1963), p. 284 (hereafter cited as HEW, Annual Report, 1962); Department of Health, Education and Welfare, Office of Education, Annual Report, 1964 (Washington, D.C.: U.S. Government Printing Office), p. 261.

49. HEW, Annual Report, 1962, pp. 283-86.

50. Department of Health, Education and Welfare, Office of Education, "NDEA Institutes for Advanced Study . . . Manual for Preparation of Proposals under Title IX" (Washington, D.C.: U.S. Government Printing Office, 1965).

51. HEW, Educational Television, p. ix; New York Times, December 8, 1964.

52. New York Times, August 30, 1966.

53. HEW, Annual Report, 1965, pp. 300-01; Department of Health, Education and Welfare, Office of Education, Annual Report, 1966 (Washington, D.C.: U.S. Government Printing Office, 1967), p. 169.

6

THE CONGRESS AND
THE PRESIDENT—
PUBLIC BROADCASTING

In addition to the channels that the Federal Communications Commission had reserved, the new classes of service that the commission established and contemplated establishing, the programs for research and dissemination in new educational media and for the construction of educational television facilities that Congress provided and the Office of Education in the Department of Health, Education and Welfare administered, there were still at least three great needs in noncommercial educational broadcasting. Educational television needed large sums of money for local and national programming, complete interconnection of stations, and a wider commitment on the part of educators and the public.

THE FORD FOUNDATION AND
EDUCATIONAL TELEVISION

Aimed specifically at the need for a national interconnection of stations and a large sum of money for programming, and based primarily on its large financial commitment to educational television and an offer by the American Broadcasting Company, was a proposal of the Ford Foundation to the FCC in 1966. Between 1952 and 1966, the Ford Foundation granted about $100 million to educational television. By far, the largest percentage of its television grants in that period were for the establishment of a national educational network. The Ford Foundation on its own and through the Fund for the Advancement of Education gave nearly $30 million to the National Educational Television and Radio Center. Begun in Ann Arbor, Michigan, in 1954, the foundation poured $6 million into the operation in the first five years. When the center moved to New York City in 1959, the

119

foundation gave $5 million in the next five years. After 1963, the
Ford Foundation gave the National Educational Television and Radio
Center $6 million a year to provide about five hours of quality pro-
grams each week by videotape to the more than 100 educational
television stations around the country. The foundation's support
was not limited to National Educational Television, however. It
supplied funds to activate channels, to develop statewide networks,
to support instructional programming, and to assist community-
sponsored stations. Its commitment to educational broadcasting was
great, and its financial support exceeded that of the federal government.[1]

In 1965, ABC filed with the FCC a proposal to use a communications satellite in synchronous orbit around the earth to relay programs
to its affiliated stations rather than to use the coaxial cable and microwave facilities of the common carriers. The company, on May 14,
1965, stated that it would make a satellite relay channel available
to educational television stations without charge if it were allowed
to launch a multichannel satellite.[2]

John F. White, president of the National Educational Television
and Radio Center, immediately hailed the suggestion as helping to
solve the "nagging financial problems" of broadcasting. Richard D.
Heffner, professor of communication at Rutgers University, in a
speech to the Institute for Education by Radio-Television at Ohio
State University in June 1965, said the use of communications satellites could "make educational television throughout the country
economically viable for the first time."[3]

The Communications Satellite Corporation (COMSAT) chartered
by Congress in 1962 to participate in an international consortium to
provide worldwide communication by satellite, filed objections with
the FCC to the ABC proposal. COMSAT interpreted the Communications Satellite Corporation Act of 1962 to mean that the FCC had the
power to license domestic satellite communications system to
COMSAT but that Congress would have to give the FCC the power
to license any other corporation to provide the service. The FCC,
in March 1966, noted the ABC application and the COMSAT opposition
and invited interested parties to file comments. The commission
asked respondents to address their remarks to three questions:
Does the FCC by law have the power to license domestic noncommon
carrier communications-satellite facilities? What would be the
effects of such an authorization on COMSAT? Is it in the public
interest to grant such an authorization?[4]

In response to the invitation of the FCC for the comments of
interested parties, the Ford Foundation made an electrifying proposal.[5] Noting that a first-rate national noncommercial network
service was much needed and that the existing means of supporting

educational television were inadequate, McGeorge Bundy, president of the foundation, called for a new level of action. Bundy suggested that a nonprofit corporation be formed to place four communications satellites in orbit over the United States, one in each time zone, to relay commercial and noncommercial television signals across the country. Television programs would be beamed 22,300 miles to an electronic sphere in synchronous orbit with the rotation of the earth, and the satellite would beam programs back to earth, where they could be received over a wide area for rebroadcasting over conventional television transmitters to ordinary television receivers. Bundy suggested that the nonprofit corporation could provide cost-free a system of regional and national noncommercial network service. He further suggested that because satellite communications would be considerably cheaper than traditional ground communications, the nonprofit corporation could pass on the major share of the savings for commercial broadcasters to noncommercial broadcasters for television programming. The Ford Foundation president estimated that commercial broadcasters spent $65 million a year for conventional facilities to relay radio and television and that the cost of satellite communications would be $20 million a year. He felt that $30 million could be given to noncommercial educational programming and that in ten years, $60 million would be available.

Fred W. Friendly, television adviser to the president of the Ford Foundation and former president of the News Division of the Columbia Broadcasting System, created the idea of providing a free channel to educational television and using a large share of the savings for noncommercial programming. The idea was supported in the comments filed with the FCC by 80 pages of social, technical, and economic analysis in exhaustive detail.

The Ford Foundation model suggested that the communications satellites carry 11 television channels: 1 channel for noncommercial informational and cultural programs, 4 instructional television channels, and 6 commercial channels. The analysis argued that COMSAT had an exclusive right to international satellite services but that the act which created COMSAT anticipated additional systems to meet unique national needs, which the FCC had the authority to license. The foundation analysis determined that the loss of revenue from cable and microwave relay facilities would amount to less than one percent of the income of common carriers, whose income increased by four percent a year.

Bundy stressed that the Ford Foundation had no intention of operating the proposed Broadcasters' Non-Profit Satellite. He made clear that the foundation's interest was only that the FCC not hand over satellite communications to the commercial common carriers without first studying all possible alternatives, of which the foundation's proposal was one.

Reaction to the Ford proposal was immediate. COMSAT, in a brief filed with the FCC, declared that it was the sole chosen instrument of Congress to operate communications satellites. The American Telephone and Telegraph Company (AT&T), chief of the common carriers, in a brief filed with the commission, stated that a nonprofit system was against "expressed national policy" and would be a burden to its customers. The American Broadcasting Company, the National Broadcasting Company, and the Columbia Broadcasting System voiced approval of the foundation model in principle. The Department of Health, Education and Welfare said it supported vigorously a satellite system that would offer major advantages to educational broadcasting. President of National Educational Television White declared it a "giant stride forward." Senator John O. Pastore, chairman of the Communications Subcommittee of the Senate Commerce Committee, held informational hearings on the Ford proposal on August 17 and 18.[6]

After the Senate hearings, James McCormack, chairman of COMSAT, and Joseph V. Charyk, president of COMSAT, drafted a new proposal, which incorporated and extended the Ford suggestion. Whereas the foundation advocated two satellite systems, COMSAT proposed a single satellite system for all domestic communications, including telephone, telegraph, commercial television, facsimile, and computer data. The corporation suggested that it garner part of the savings generated by using communications satellites rather than ground circuits and pass the savings on to a private organization to be used for educational programming. It also incorporated free service for educational broadcasting in its satellite scheme. When Senator Pastore asked for constructive alternatives instead of criticism of the Ford plan, he got one from COMSAT.[7]

REPORT OF THE CARNEGIE COMMISSION ON
EDUCATIONAL TELEVISION

While the Ford Foundation was generating its ideas, a second group was also at work on another set of proposals. A Carnegie Corporation-funded group with the backing of President Lyndon B. Johnson was preparing a report that would ultimately transform educational broadcasting. It was not only the quality of the proposals but the sure political skills of the president and key members of Congress turning important proposals into public law that made the Carnegie Commission report the most significant development in educational broadcasting since Freida B. Hennock used her political skills to reserve television channels for education.

Educational Television Stations (ETS), a division of the National Association of Educational Broadcasting, held a conference in December 1964. HEW sponsored the meeting, which was called the "National Conference on Long Range Funding of Educational Television Stations." Conference participants realized that educational television had reached a plateau and that only the infusion of money from a new source would rescue it from its stalled position and push it on to new heights. As a result of these deliberations, the conferees decided that only a national commission with the backing of the president of the United States would obtain the attention the subject deserved and result in long-range funding. A delegation was charged to meet with President Johnson and solicit his support.[8]

A group of educational broadcasters met at the White House and made its plea. C. Douglass Cater, Jr., played a key role for the president in getting interested parties together to advance the proposal. John W. Gardner, secretary of HEW and former president of the Carnegie Corporation, made important contacts with the corporation, as did C. Scott Fletcher, former head of the Fund for Adult Education and senior consultant for ETS.

In November 1965, the Carnegie Corporation awarded a foundation grant, eventually worth $500,000, to form the Carnegie Commission on Educational Television. Headed by James R. Killian, Jr., president of the Corporation of the Massachusetts Institute of Technology, the commission was given 18 months to appraise educational television, as well as the technical and financial limitations under which it operated, and to publish a report of its findings and recommendations.[9]

Alan Pifer, acting president of the Carnegie Corporation, in announcing the grant, said: "We are asking for an overall appraisal of educational television—including technical, organizational, financial, and programing considerations—a prescriptive definition of Educational Television's role in contemporary America and recommendations as to how that role can be filled."[10]

President Johnson endorsed the Carnegie study in a letter to Pifer, which was made public. He said:

> Educational Television has an important future in the
> United States and throughout the world. There is an
> urgent need to project the requirements for the future if
> we are to meet the educational, social, and cultural
> demands. This will call for a recommendation on not
> only the facilities and finances of educational television,
> but also the manpower and organization.[11]

While there had been other committees, reports, hearings, conferences, and recommendations, the report of the Carnegie Commission on Educational Television gave promise of special importance. Educational television—its problems and potentialities—

had never before had such attention from the chief executive of the
United States. President Johnson had a prior connection to broadcasting as a former television station owner, but the substantial
impetus was his concern for education. During his years as president,
his knowledge of the legislative process and his vital interest in
education for all Americans from the very young to the very old
resulted in the most comprehensive body of legislation for federal
aid to education ever passed in Congress. The laws included:

the Higher Education Facilities Act, which provided for grants and
    loans for classroom and library construction
the Economic Opportunity Act, which authorized work-study aid for
    needy students and created Project Upward Bound
the Higher Education Act of 1965, which authorized federal funds for
    guaranteed student loans, for colleges to buy instructional equip-
    ment, for educational opportunity grants to needy students, for
    library materials and librarian training, for the Teacher Corps,
    for aid to developing colleges, and for colleges to become in-
    volved in community service
the National Sea-Grant Program and College Act, which provided
    for aid to marine research at designated colleges
the International Education Act, which authorized federal funds
    for centers for international studies and for improving under-
    graduate studies of international affairs
the Education Professions Development Act, which authorized funds
    for the training of educational personnel from grade school
    teachers to college administrators
the Higher Education Amendments of 1968, which refined student-aid
    programs and created new programs of aid for college use of
    educational technology, for cooperative education, for law
    schools, and for graduate education, as well as extending earlier
    legislation.

President Johnson clearly foresaw in the promised Carnegie report
the prospects of recommendations for legislation that would contribute
to, and round out, his legislative program on education.
    Perhaps as important in the long-run success of turning recom-
mendations into realities was the leadership of Killian. Not only did
he lead in the formation of recommendations and the espousal of the
essential ideas, but as shall be seen, he was called upon to rescue
the implementation of the commission's recommended program from
the political interference of a later president. Among the other lead-
ing educators who served with Killian on the commission, and lent
their prestige and perception to it, were James B. Conant, former
president of Harvard University; Lee A. DuBridge, president of the

California Institute of Technology; David D. Henry, president of the
University of Illinois; and Franklin Patterson, president of Hampshire
College, Andover, Massachusetts.

Commissioners discussed their work with network officials,
foreign broadcasters, and foundation staffs. They talked with Congressional leaders, including Senator Warren G. Magnuson, chairman
of the powerful Committee on Commerce (with jurisdiction over broadcasting) and strong advocate for providing federal funds for educational
broadcasting facilities. In addition to the educators on the commission,
other educators, and specifically educational broadcasters and educational broadcasting groups, were consulted.[12]

When the commission finished its work in about a year, advance
copies of the report were sent to Gardner and Cater. At a White
House staff meeting, they recommended the report as consonant with
the president's goals for educational broadcasting. Cater then discussed the report with President Johnson, who liked what he heard
and instructed Cater to begin drafting a statement to be included in
the forthcoming State of the Union Address. In that address to Congress on January 10, 1967, Johnson stated: "We should develop
educational television into a vital public resource to enrich our homes,
educate our families, and to provide assistance in our classrooms.
We should insist that the public interest be fully served through the
Nation's airways."[13]

Two weeks later, the Carnegie Commission on Educational
Television issued its report to the nation. In a book entitled Public
Television: A Program for Action, the commission stated that a
well-financed and well-administrated educational television system
serving the entire United States had to be created if the needs of the
American people were to be served. It called for a system that was
nowhere in existence but which would be "a new and fundamental
institution in American culture."[14] The commission felt that commercial television, being national and mass-market oriented, was
not serving the full needs of the people and urged that noncommercial
educational broadcasting stress local and regional diversity. In
order to achieve such diversity, the control of noncommercial television had to be in the hands of local stations, a crucial point in later
discussions, and programs had to be produced throughout the country,
another crucial point. Symbolic of the shift in attitude was the name
proposed for the system—Public Television. The commission felt
that the instructional or educational aspects of television ought to be
extended but took a much enlarged view of the role of noncommercial
stations.

Specifically, the Carnegie Commission on Educational Television
made the following statement and recommendations:

The commission's strong view was the the fundamental unit of public television should be vigorous and independent local stations. Each station should be the product of local initiative and local support and should decide for itself what and when it wanted to broadcast. Federal funds, however, would be needed to build, expand, and upgrade facilities and to pay for programming.

To provide partial support to these independent local units, the commission recommended the formation of a federally chartered, nonprofit, nongovernment organization, called the Corporation for Public Television (CPT). The CPT would serve local stations but neither operate nor control them. The corporation's primary responsibility would be to finance programs and their distribution. The corporation would support the production of programs by National Educational Television, a second national program production center, independent producers, and the 20 larger public stations in metropolitan areas for programs of local as well as national interest. The corporation would also provide funds for local production. In regard to distribution of programs, the federally chartered corporation would provide facilities to interconnect public stations. Interconnection was not intended to be like a commercial network, whereby a central authority decided what was to be produced and when it was to be seen by simultaneous transmission on affiliated stations. Interconnection of public stations was to be a service to facilitate communication among the stations and to exchange program material for live broadcast or for delayed broadcast if and when the local stations chose to use the program material provided. It was thought that conventional long lines and microwave facilities of commercial carriers would be used immediately and that a communication satellite would be used when technology made it feasible. Also, part of the recommendation was that Congress act to allow communication carriers and communication-satellite companies to offer preferential rates or free service to public broadcasters.

The corporation would be further charged to conduct research and to develop different types of programs, new techniques of production, and innovations in television technology. The Carnegie Commission also envisioned that CPT would recruit and train technicians, artists, and other specialized personnel.

To finance the corporation, Killian's group advocated a federal excise tax on new television receivers to bring in $50 million a year immediately and $100 million annually in ten years. A tax on the manufacturer's list price would advance from two percent to five percent in ten years. The corporation would also be authorized to receive private and foundation funds for current operating expenses and for endowment. It was proposed that a trust account be established in the Treasury Department to receive revenues from the tax and forward the funds directly to the corporation without congressional approval. The commission was searching for a way to provide federal funds and, at the same time, isolate CPT from political influence and maneuvering. To further isolate the corporation from political influence, it was recommended that six board members be appointed by the president and six be appointed by the board itself.

The commission asked Congress to provide funds from general tax revenues and charge HEW with disbursing the funds, to increase the number of public stations on the air, to enlarge the facilities in existence, to upgrade the equipment in use, to contribute to basic operating costs of each station, and to support more extensively instructional television. It specifically urged that the Educational Broadcasting Facilities Act be extended. It observed that with minor exceptions, the total disappearance of instructional television, as it then existed, would leave the American educational system fundamentally unchanged. It recognized the problems that a lack of trained personnel and a lack of equipment presented, but it felt that instructional television had never been made a part of the educational process. Since instructional television was only incidentally or occasionally used in the classroom, partly because of scheduling, it suggested that cassettes be provided, so that teachers could preview material, use it when needed, and stop and start as appropriate. Nevertheless, the commission recommended that a study be made of how television could best serve education.

By 1980, the commission foresaw an annual budget of $270 million for public television, exclusive of instructional costs—the budget would be met by $104 million from the CPT, $91 million from HEW, and $75 million from state, local, institutional, and foundation sources.

Public Television: A Program for Action transcended all previous analyses of noncommercial and educational broadcasting (NCEB), and it established at least five principles that would dominate the discussion and development of educational broadcasting. First, the principle of adequate funding was asserted. Whatever the source of funds, public television was going to need substantial amounts of money with no strings attached. It established the principle of decentralization, that is, public television would not be a fourth network built on the model of commercial networks. The third principle followed from the second. Local stations would be self-sustaining, yet capable of contributing to other stations. They would be the governors of the system; they would decide what was best for themselves and for public television. The fourth principle included a change in concept. Television would be in the broadest interest of all segments of the public—not just educational. Finally, while calling for an expanded role in public television for the federal government, the commission

established the principle of isolation from government interference.
The commission recommended the formation of a federally chartered
agency to receive tax money, disburse it, and serve local stations,
as well as to expand HEW operations to provide facilities and operating
funds. The commission realized the inherent dangers of executive
and legislative meddling in so sensitive an opinion maker as television
and built safeguards into its recommendations to isolate the stations
and the corporation from government interference in general decision
making and program producing; its recommendations to isolate the
provision of funds from the annual appropriation process of Congress
and the appointment of half the members of the board of CPT from
presidential appointment and Congressional approval were specific
examples.

Because of the Ford Foundation proposal in early August 1966,
the Carnegie Commission proposal in late January 1967, and presidential endorsement, momentum for public television was at an all-time
high. Public broadcasting attracted national attention, as the supporters of a national commission in educational television had expected,
and the feeling among supporters was that something positive would
result.

Opposition to details developed, but not to the general scheme.
The Electronic Industries Association, manufacturers of television
receivers, opposed the tax on receivers, because it felt that a benefit
to the general public should not be borne by a tax on one industry.
The American Telephone and Telegraph Company, chief provider of
long lines and microwave relay in the United States, opposed providing
free channels or lower rates for interconnecting stations, because it
did not think public television should be subsidized by the users of
commercial facilities, such as commercial television and long-
distance telephone. It suggested the use of its facilities at nonpeak
hours at already established cheaper rates to transmit program
material for later use. Congressman Charles S. Johnson, in a letter
to the president, suggested that the money "should come from mean-
ingful fees to be paid annually by radio and television stations for
licenses granted them by the Federal Communications Commission."[15]

SUPPORT FOR THE CARNEGIE
COMMISSION PROPOSALS

Support for the Carnegie Commission proposals was widespread.
Bundy endorsed the commission recommendations and lent to them
the prestige of the Ford Foundation, which had poured millions of
dollars into public television in supporting local stations, had established NET as a production center, and had just announced a $10

million grant to interconnect stations to demonstrate the feasibility
of live broadcasting. The presidents of the commercial television
networks endorsed the Carnegie Commission proposals in principle.
Secretary of HEW Gardner voiced his approval. Hundreds of public
broadcasters communicated their interest in the Carnegie recommendations, and congressional leaders in the support of a federal role
in public broadcasting let their interest in the proposals be known
also.[16]

President Johnson, having tested the reaction to the work of the
commission his office had helped to arrange, announced in his 1967
budget message that he would soon propose legislation to "extend and
expand federal support for educational television."[17] Cater, presidential adviser on education and health, took a key role in fashioning a
strategy that would adopt the attractive principles of the proposals
and avoid difficult specifics.

Consequently, in his February 28 special message to Congress
on health and education, President Johnson said, "I am convinced
that a vital and self-sufficient national television system will not only
instruct, but inspire and uplift our people." He went on to say:
"Non-commercial television today is reaching only a fraction of its
potential audience—and achieving only a fraction of its potential worth.
Clearly," he said, "the time has come to build on the experience of
the past 14 years, the important studies that have been made, and
the beginning we have made."[18]

He asked Congress to do three things: create and fund a federally
chartered corporation; provide money for the construction of facilities;
and authorize a study of instructional television. The president urged
Congress to establish the CPT to receive public and private funds,
so that it might support local stations, underwrite the production of
individual programs or series, and bear the costs of interconnecting
stations. He wanted the corporation to function like a private foundation, free from government control, and proposed that the operation
of the corporation be directed by 15 public board members appointed
by the president and of sufficient stature to protect the corporation
from government interference. He asked Congress to appropriate
$9 million for the first year's operation, thus postponing the question
of later funding for further study and future recommendation. The
president asked Congress to approve $3.3 million in the current
fiscal year and $10.5 million in the next fiscal year to construct
noncommercial radio and television broadcasting facilities. He further
requested $500,000 for HEW to sponsor a major study of the value
and potential of instructional television.[19]

Thus, the president adopted the attractive principles of the
Carnegie Commission report and avoided the difficult specifics.
He simplified the arguments for an expanded role of the federal

government in public broadcasting before going to Congress and left
the corporation with the task of coming to grips with specifics and
of serving as a focal point for building a consensus and for continued
championing of public television. Significantly, he added radio to
the concerns of the corporation and to HEW. He left the Ford Foundation proposals for a communications satellite system and the establishment of an educational television and radio network to further
study of Congress and the executive branch (not just the FCC) and
endorsed the Carnegie Commission emphasis on localism. Just as
Hennock had become the federal patroness of educational television
in her drum beating for the reservation of television channels for
education, President Johnson became the federal patron for a much
expanded role for the national government in public broadcasting.
His knowledge of Congress and his use of political skills to maneuver
the Congress produced the most significant legislation for public
broadcasting to date. Yet, by concentrating on the obtainable and
leaving difficult questions to the further building of consensus and
the gaining of additional experience, he left unanswered questions
that would plague educational broadcasting for almost a decade.[20]

THE PUBLIC BROADCASTING ACT OF 1967

Senator Magnuson, himself a federal patron of educational television because of his leadership in the congressional passage of the
Educational Broadcasting Facilities Act in 1962, introduced in the
Senate on March 5 a bill written by Dean W. Coston, deputy undersecretary of HEW, which provided the details of what President
Johnson had outlined in his message on education and health.[21]
Before giving attention to the congressional hearing on the bill, it
would be well to sketch the state of television in America at the time
and to discover what measures were taken to build support for its
congressional hearing.

Eighty million Americans regularly watched television in 1967,
and 94 percent of the households in the United States possessed at
least one television set. There were 600 commercial television
stations, and 500 of them were affiliated with one of the three commercial networks. Revenues in 1965 exceeded $2 billion, and profits
before taxes equaled $500 million. In addition to the commercial
stations, there were 125 noncommercial stations—80 of which were
affiliated with schools and colleges and 40 of which were community
affiliated.[22] These 125 stations were chronically underfinanced,
personnel shortages existed, those stations with UHF assignments
were developing slowly, and the quality and range of coverage varied
widely from station to station. Yet, with the stimulus of $32 million

from the federal government over a ten-year period, the system had
grown astonishingly. When Congress passed the Educational Broadcasting Facilities Act in 1962, only 21 noncommercial educational
broadcasting stations were on the air. In 1967, however, nearly
two-thirds of the population of the United States could receive noncommercial broadcasting, NET was providing a national program
series, there were patches of intercommunication, and a corps of
dedicated men and women were at work on both a paid and a volunteer
basis.23 It was on the foundation of federal assistance and station
achievement that influential members of Congress expected to build
when the Senate began hearings on the bill.

It was also essential to build a consensus before holding public
hearings. Nothing moves a bill through Congress or a decision through
a regulatory agency more easily than fundamental agreement among
those affected by the bill or decision. This had been amply demonstrated. The fiasco of discordant voices at the FCC hearings in the
1930s on assigning AM frequencies to education, the symphony Hennock orchestrated at FCC hearings on the assignment of television
channels to education, and the ready agreement of educational television broadcasters at congressional hearings on the promise of federal
funds for building television facilities were in the minds of those
preparing for the hearings. In this instance, Cater, of President
Johnson's staff, continued to play a key role in building such a consensus. He operated a command post in the White House basement
to coordinate the efforts of those favoring the adoption of the proposed
legislation.

Three important meetings were held in March and April 1967
that consolidated support for the bill. The NAEB sponsored a meeting
in early March addressing the question of long-range financing of
educational television. The conference members clearly preferred
the Carnegie plan, stressing local station autonomy and financing
stability, to the Ford plan, stressing a strong network. The conferees
feared at that stage in the development of public television network
news and Sunday night spectacles would not ease the severe financial
problems of the rest of the week. They also felt that the Ford Foundation plan for a domestic satellite system was visionary and so far in
the distance as to have little significance for their immediate prob-
lem.24 The Johnson staff had examined all that had been said in the
past year, talked to the people involved, and in consultation with
them formed a plan that could move ahead without delay and leave
for the future troublesome problems, such as long-range funding,
on which there was no agreement. Much to the credit of the Ford
Foundation, Bundy pledged his support for this course of action and
stressed that the foundation and the commission had similar objectives.
He told the NAEB meeting, "We shall be in this business this year,

next year, and until there is no further need for our support."25
In a speech to the International Radio and Television Society, Robert
W. Sarnoff, president of the Radio Corporation of America, the
largest manufacturer of television receivers and the parent company
of the National Broadcasting Corporation, endorsed the Johnson
administration plan. He emphasized the importance of adequate and
stable financial support on a permanent basis "from public sources."26
The National Association of Broadcasters met in early April. Vincent
T. Wasilewski, president of the organization, endorsed the Carnegie
proposals, while warning that the proposed system had the "potential
of being a government propaganda agency." Speaking to the convention, Rosel H. Hyde, chairman of the FCC, endorsed the administration proposal and opined that the keys to success of the national
communications system were "corporate independence, local autonomy,
[and] financial adequacy." He too felt that the thorny problem of
permanent financing could be put off for future study.27 With what
supporters hoped was solid support for fundamentals and willingness
to postpone the nagging problem of long-range funding and a mechanism
to keep government from intruding in programming, the hearings
began.

The bill that would be the subject of the hearings was in three
parts or titles. Title I in effect extended the Educational Broadcasting Facilities Act and authorized an appropriation of $10 million for
the fiscal year ending in 1968 and such sums as necessary for the
next four years. It stipulated that not more than 12.5 percent of
each amount appropriated could be awarded within a state and that
the federal share of any project could not exceed 75 percent. Previous
legislation provided that not more than $1 million could be awarded
to one state and that the federal share of a project be limited to 50
percent. The title applied to radio facilities, as well as television,
which had been the sole concern of previous legislation.

Title II asserted that it was in the public interest to encourage
the growth of educational television at the local and national level
and that it was necessary to complement and assist a national policy
that would most effectively make noncommercial educational radio
and television service available to all the citizens of the United States.
To facilitate these aims, a private corporation would be created.
The organization would be called the Corporation for Public Television,
with a board of 15 selected from the fields of education, cultural and
civil affairs, and the arts, including radio and television. The commission would elect annually a chairman from its membership and
appoint a president. The corporation would be charged with ten
responsibilities:

1. to facilitate the full development of educational broadcasting and make programs, obtained from diverse sources, available to noncommercial educational broadcasting stations
2. to assist in establishing and developing one or more systems of intercommunication, so that all stations could broadcast the programs if and when they so desired
3. to assure a maximum freedom from interference regarding program content
4. to obtain grants
5. to contract for program production
6. to contract for interconnections
7. to provide funds to local stations to aid in programming and operating costs
8. to develop a library and archives
9. to encourage the creation of new stations
10. to conduct research

The title authorized the appropriation of $9 million for fiscal year 1969.

Title III authorized HEW to conduct a study of educational and instructional television broadcasting. It specifically mentioned these topics for study: the quality and content of existing programs and how they could be improved; financial factors involved in the use of instructional television in educational institutions; relative advantages and disadvantages of using instructional television, as compared with other media; advantages and disadvantages of closed circuit television; the relationship between instructional and educational television; and new technology not then available for general use. The bill also stated that the Communications Act of 1934 should not be construed to prohibit U.S. common carriers from rendering free service or reduce prices for interconnection. It also emphasized that educational broadcasting should be free from federal direction, supervision, or control.[28]

With Senator John O. Pastore of Rhode Island, a longtime friend of educational broadcasting, presiding as chairman, the Subcommittee on Communications of the Committee on Commerce held hearings for eight days between April 11 and 28.[29] Those giving testimony were constituted in six categories: government officials, representatives of the Carnegie Commission and the Ford Foundation, educational broadcasters, common carriers, commercial broadcasters, and representatives of educational organizations.

Government witnesses included senators and representatives and officials from HEW, the FCC, and the National Foundation on the Arts and Humanities, Senator Pastore opened the hearings with

his observation that the Educational Broadcasting Facilities Act had
proven its worth but that noncommercial educational broadcasting
remained chronically understaffed, underfinanced, and underprogrammed. He felt that the time was then ripe to move dramatically
not only for more facilities but also for higher-quality programs and
services. He noted that there had been proposed a number of different plans for financing but cautioned that the witnesses ought to be
careful about recommending taxes, because taxes were the province
of the Finance Committee of the Senate and the Ways and Means
Committee of the House. He urged the witnesses to help get the new
program started through his committee and let other committees
handle taxes at the proper time or the bill would be lost. He urged
support for the interim bill under discussion, lest the issue become
confused and the bill lost. This was his strategy throughout the hearing, and the 696 pages of testimony record his determination to keep
the witnesses to the subject of the bill at hand rather than concentra-
tion on future methods of financing. Representative Claude Pepper,
a former teacher still vitally interested in education, stressed the
need for educational broadcasting to be free from government interference and for public money to stimulate private initiative. He
was the first of several witnesses who testified to the importance of
including provisions for radio in the legislation. Senator Vance
Hartke, a member of the committee from Indiana, which had a strong
educational television system, emphasized the importance of the
local stations and the essential need for local option to select programs available from national sources and for local production. He
was skeptical that so long as Congress decided how programs were
to be funded, Congress would exercise power over programming.
He was also leery of the potential threat to local stations and local
programming from the proposed corporation, which he saw as yet
another level of bureaucracy not subject to congressional oversight,
not audited by the General Accounting Office, and not responsible to
the Bureau of the Budget. Senator Norris Cotton was concerned
about the proposal to establish another trust fund in the Treasury
Department like the trust fund for highway construction. He felt
that if another such precedent were established, it would lead the
way to proposals for trust funds for airport maintenance and water
pollution and that Congress would lose control of appropriations and
spending. Several members of the committee were also on the
Appropriations Committee, and he felt that this particular proposal
would have trouble being enacted if brought up in the future. Committee member Senator Hugh Scott disdained passing money through
HEW, which had so many axes to grind and was so constantly lobbying
in Congress for funds that it might not actually push for this program.
Secretary Gardner, however, avowed his support for the bill. He

pointed out that the facilities which had been built through earlier
legislation were "an incomplete monument to a great hope" without
programs to be broadcast. He felt that public broadcasting was a
potential source of greatly diversified television and criticized commercial television broadcasters for giving inadequate attention to
cultural matters. FCC chairman Hyde wholeheartedly endorsed the
legislation, saying that it gave promise of a real breakthrough for
educational television. He expected three principles to be established
in the legislative history of the bill: adequate financial support, complete independence for corporation policy judgments, and local autonomy in choice of programming. He referred to FCC docket 16495
on the legal, technical, and policy questions regarding domestic uses
of satellite communication, including educational broadcasting, and
hoped that the committee would leave these matters to the commission
and concentrate on the legislation under discussion. He specifically
urged that the FCC be confirmed in its authority to establish preferential or reduced rates for the interconnection of educational broadcasting stations. Roger L. Stevens, chairman of the National Foundation
on the Arts and Humanities, lent strong support to the proposed
legislation and saw its enactment as the "opening of a new and extra-
ordinarily creative era in American radio and television." He pointed
out that the foundation had made sizable grants to noncommercial
television programming and cited, as an example, a recent grant of
$870,000 for the American Film Institute; he said his organization
was studying the possibility of creating a radio repertory company.

James D. O'Connell, special adviser to the president and director
of the Office of Telecommunication Management, expressed his complete satisfaction with the soundness of the bill and repeated the
White House contention that it was wise at that point to avoid the
hazards of committing large expenditures to a national system of
domestic satellite interconnection or making long-range financing
proposals until the requirements had been better developed and other
essential experience gained.

In their testimony, representatives of important government
agencies gave strong support to increasing the federal role in noncommercial educational broadcasting.

Next, Killian and other members of the Carnegie Commission
testified as to the recommendations of the commission and as to their
high regard for the bill, which would turn the best of their recommendations into legislation. Killian pointed out that the Carnegie Commission had studied the objectives of educational broadcasting and
had established a set of recommendations based on uniquely American
mores and traditions rather than on noncommercial services provided
in other countries, such as Great Britain and Japan. He said the
foundation of the American system must be strong and energetic local

stations. He also said that public television must provide abundant
programming to allow local stations a wide diversity of choice to
meet the needs of the local community. Only a national institution
could provide an abundance of high-quality programs and leadership
for all. Killian stressed the similarity of purpose and essential
agreement between the Ford Foundation proposal and the Carnegie
Commission recommendations. He said the only real difference
was that the Ford Foundation raised questions of national policy
regarding commercial satellite but that CPT could live with any
domestic satellite system.

Killian then explained the commission's point of view on the
essential elements of the legislation. To establish a service of the
magnitude envisioned, substantial annual sums would be needed from
federal, as well as state, local, and private, sources. He emphasized that federal funds must be provided in such a way as to isolate
public broadcasting from government influence or interference. He
felt that annual appropriations could only be a temporary expedient.
As to the composition of the corporation board, he believed the principle of insulation was more important than the mechanics of appointment. He would support any method of appointment that guaranteed
insulation from legislative or executive control. Further, he explained
the corporation's concept of interconnection as a mechanical means
of distributing program choices to local stations and not as a fixed
service in the manner of commercial networks. Killian pointed out
the need for local operating funds and repeated the corporation's
suggestion that such funds be channeled through HEW from regular
tax sources, since not enough money would be available to the corporation for both programming and operations. His final point was that
the committee was not talking about instructional television. It was
describing a new concept of public broadcasting that went far beyond
the classroom to every home for a great diversity of programming.
While recognizing the importance of classroom television and supporting the study of such uses of educational television, he and the
commission felt this was the responsibility of HEW and should be
funded through HEW from tax revenues and the usual appropriation
processes. DuBridge and other members of the commission also
gave their support to the legislation under consideration and pointed
out the similarity between the Carnegie and Ford proposals. Hyman
H. Goldin, of the Carnegie Commission staff, testified regarding
projected costs and predicted an annual need of $270 million. Of
that sum, the corporation would need $100 million—$70 million for
programming and $30 million for interconnection, training, and
publicity; HEW would need $100 million annually for support of opera-
tions; and state and local governments and private donors would
provide an additional $70 million for local operation.

Bundy, speaking for the Ford Foundation, voiced his complete support for the pending bill. He said it took into account what could be enacted and what could reasonably wait for future enactment. Bundy also emphasized his strong support of the Carnegie Commission report and recommendations and reaffirmed his conviction that in a domestic satellite system lay a special promise and opportunity for a new level of diversity and a solution for partial funding of corporation activities. He was pleased that the bill left the way open for the use of domestic satellites and provided no bar to free or reduced rate for interconnection. Friendly, television consultant to the foundation and former producer of news and public affairs programming on commercial television, opposed any plan that would provide news programs funded from federal sources and preferred private sources for such programs, believing that producers would thus be protected from federal influence. He was fearful, moreover, that annual appropriations would be continued indefinitely as the course meeting the least resistance. He felt that manufacturers of television equipment had mounted an antitax campaign, that commercial stations had started an antitax on station franchise efforts, and that common carriers had an antidomestic satellite tax campaign that would eventuate in a "consensus of the negatives" to provide annual appropriation to the corporation from general tax revenues, with the concomitant result that news and public affairs programming would be unduly influenced.

When educational broadcasters began to testify, they tended to talk more about specifics of operations rather than in generalities and high principles. And it was when specifics were mentioned that divergence of opinion emerged. These differences were significant, because they reemerged over the course of the next few years and because the executive branch exploited these differences for its own purposes. The question that was unanswered in April 1967, and remained unanswered, was whose hand would be on the switch sending programs over the noncommercial airwaves. Potentially, there were four hands: the producers of programs, such as NET in New York (funded by the Ford Foundation); the interconnecter, whose role and function were as yet undefined; the funder of programs and operations at the national level, which was proposed as CPT; the local station; or possibly a combination among the four.

White, president of NET, said the corporation should assume a high-policy role and make grants to entities such as NET to decide what programs to produce, produce them, and then interconnect the stations to distribute them. Killian reentered the discussion to urge revision of the legislation if necessary to "free educational broadcasting from centralization and rigidity of a network system" and to allow the corporation to determine when to interconnect. But John Kier-

maier of station WNDT, and president of the Eastern Educational
Network, had earlier said the individual stations intended to preserve
their autonomy and would not countenance a national hand on the interconnections. E. William Henry, a former member of the FCC vitally
interested in educational broadcasting and a member of the board of
directors of NAEB, warned that the corporation must have the power
to make "midnight decisions" or it would lose its influence. He
observed that the normal independence of single stations was ample
to guarantee against dictation. Fletcher, representing ETS, a branch
of NAEB, and chairman of a second national conference on long-range
financing of educational television stations, said it had been the unanimous view of delegates to that meeting that the corporation not be
involved in operations but limit its activities to reviewing programs
and making grants. Senator Pastore wanted to postpone this kind of
discussion among educational broadcasters and develop a consensus
of support for essential ideas, for he said: "Let's come out of here
with legislation and not a debate."[30]

The testimony of Edwin G. Burrows, chairman of NAEB, and
Jerrold Sandler, executive director of its educational radio division,
had the sanguine effect of broadening the legislature under discussion
when they urged the inclusion of educational radio in the bill. Burrows
endorsed the Carnegie Commission recommendation and talked about
the Wingspread Conference on Educational Radio as a National Resource, which had issued a research report entitled "The Hidden
Medium: A Status Report on Educational Radio." Sandler pointed
out that the hearing was the first time that a champion of educational
radio had had an opportunity to be heard at a major hearing on educational broadcasting and urged that radio be included in the grants for
educational broadcasting facilities, in the concerns of the corporation
to be formed, and in the study of instructional uses of broadcasting.
He cited several examples of what educational radio was doing with
very limited amounts of money to support it. He mentioned activities
in connection with the improvements of education after the desegrega-
tion of schools in the South; he described a two-way radio exchange
between physicians learning new developments in medicine; and he
explained multiplexing, whereby one or more services could be broadcast to special audiences while broadcasting to a general audience
from the same transmitter with one frequency assignment. Senator
Pastore, by far the best-informed person regarding broadcasting on
the panel, expressed astonishment and delight at these developments.
He called the hearings "a labor of love." Originally, representatives
of HEW and others were opposed to the inclusion of radio in the legislation for fear that to do so would siphon off funds needed for television;
however, the testimony and enthusiasm of these witnesses were deciding factors in changing the scope of the legislation and in changing

the name of the corporation from Corporation for Public Television
to the Corporation for Public Broadcasting (CPB).

When hearings reopened on April 25, the lead-off witnesses
represented the common carriers. AT&T engineering vice president
Kenneth G. McKay repeated an offer made the previous week to cut
by as much as 50 percent the cost of microwave relay of program
material in off-peak hours for rebroadcast. This was in line with
the Carnegie Commission recommendation that local stations have
an abundance of programming available to them for broadcast at such
time as they felt appropriate and that interconnection be provided
free or at reduced rates. In a newspaper account, Everett N. Case,
chairman of NET, pointed out that it would still be cheaper to ship
videotape to local stations by express as was the current practice,
and Bundy said the proposal did not answer the need for instant and
simultaneous interconnection and transmission in evening hours.
The FCC later adopted the basic AT&T proposal but modified it for
greater reliability and convenience. Representatives of Communications Satellite Corporation and Western Union Telegraph Company
expressed the intent of the corporations they represented to provide
domestic satellite interconnection as soon as regulatory agencies
cleared the way. It was Senator Pastore's view that a decision on
the type of distribution ultimately to be used should not stand in the
way of passage of the bill.

The presidents of the three commercial broadcasting networks
supported the proposed legislation. Frank Stanton of CBS said the
proposal was conceived and structured so as to isolate the corporation from financial reprisal should some of the broadcasts irritate
the corporation and the public. He also supported the idea of a tax
on new television sets. Leonard H. Goldman of ABC opposed the
tax but approved the system. NBC President Julian Goodman thought
the "bill established principles on which a system of noncommercial
broadcasting can flourish."31

Representing the educational complex of the United States,
spokesmen for the Joint Council on Educational Telecommunication
testified in favor of the bill. Organized in the late 1940s as the Joint
Council on Educational Television to pioneer the assignment of
spectrum space for educational television, the organization had
changed its name to the Joint Council on Educational Telecommunica-
tions. Constituent members included, among others, the American
Association of School Administrators, American Council on Education,
Association for Higher Education, Council of Chief State School
Officers, the National Association of Educational Broadcasting,
National Association of State Universities and Land Grant Colleges,
National Educational Association of the United States, and National
Educational Television. As such, it represented a broad base of

support for the pending legislation. A dozen or more other organizations and individuals testified in support of the legislation as the hearings wound down to an end on April 28.

The hearings were as important in the future for what they achieved as for what they did not achieve. They established public broadcasting and superimposed it as a new industry on an old one—educational broadcasting. They gave noncommercial broadcasting a scope far beyond instructional television. They did not, however, provide for long-range financial support. They did not establish a mechanism to keep government from interfering in programming. These two problems would plague public broadcasting for eight years, while the White House worked behind the scenes both for and against its interests and Congress annually breathed life but not health into the corporation.

The Subcommittee on Communications and the Committee on Commerce quickly considered and unanimously passed the bill, [32] and Senator Pastore took it to the floor of the Senate on May 16. Called the Public Broadcasting Act of 1967, to reflect the inclusion of radio as well as television in all its provisions, the bill provided for a five-year extension of the Educational Broadcasting Facilities Act, with a first-year appropriation of $10.5 million; a Corporation of Public Broadcasting, with nine appointed members of the board of directors and six elected by the appointed members; and an initial appropriation of $9 million. It provided for one or more systems of noncommercial educational television and radio broadcasting, one or more systems of interconnection, and a complete study of instructional television and radio, including broadcasting, closed circuit, cable, instructional television fixed service, and two-way communication of data links and computers.[33]

In opening the floor debate, Senator Pastore called the bill one of the most important to be considered in Congress that year. He declared that enough progress had been made to reveal the potential of educational broadcasting, but observed once again that the service was underfinanced, understaffed, and underprogrammed. It was his hope that the bill would make it possible to provide full noncommercial broadcasting to all families in the United States. He recalled that more than 80 witnesses appeared at the televised hearings and that while many variants of details had been discovered, all supported the legislation and all agreed that the matter was urgent and the time for passage had come. Senators emphasized the need for adequate safeguards to prevent government control of program content and local station choice of programming. Senator Charles Percy, former chairman of the Fund for Adult Education, which as a Ford Foundation activity had poured millions of dollars into educational television, spoke of the need for a national commitment for the further development and growth of this very exciting medium. The bill passed without dissent. Senators Mike Mansfield and Ralph Yarborough commented on the outstanding job Senator Pastore had done to steer the bill through the upper house.34

The identical bill, when brought to the attention of the House of Representatives,35 did not have so easy a time. Whereas the Senate concerned itself with general principles, the House concerned itself with specifics and allowed the matter to become a partisan issue. The Committee on Interstate and Foreign Commerce, chaired by Representative Harley O. Staggers, held hearings from July 11 to 21.36 The witnesses and their testimony were essentially the same as at the Senate hearing, and the testimony filled more than 800 pages. The real debate occurred when the committee took up the bill in early August. The committee had no real quarrel with extending the Educational Broadcasting Facilities Act, which Secretary Gardner described as legislation that "pleased about everyone" or with authorizing a study of instructional broadcasting, although by strict party vote of 18 to 13, the committee rejected a Republican bid to kill the whole bill. The committee members of both parties were particularly concerned about possible government control and about the ultimate cost and long-range funding. International and national events had also intervened between the hoopla of January and the House Committee considerations of the bill in August. Anxiety over the Vietnam War, the possibility of a 10 percent income tax surcharge, and summer riots in urban areas had intervened. Educational broadcasters themselves had done little, except to appear when invited at the hearings. They left most of the work to skillful White House manuevering and congenial leadership. The New York Times suggested that the broadcasters should have articulated their goals and said what they were going to do rather than say, "Give us the money and we will show you what we can do." The paper also suggested that a greater emphasis on teaching and learning would have eased the way with certain members, such as Clarence J. Brown of Ohio, where instructional television was strongly utilized. More organized constituent support, more pledges of money, and more people of prominence speaking out in favor of the legislation would have been helpful. The momentum had definitely been allowed to sag.37

Reflecting these concerns about government control and long-range costs and funding, the committee adopted a number of amendments sponsored by Representative William L. Springer, the ranking Republican member of the Committee on Interstate and Foreign Commerce, as the price of Republican support. To counter possible government control, the bill was amended to allow no more than 8 members of the 15-person presidentially appointed board to belong to one political party. It also forbid editorializing or support of, or

opposition to, political candidates, although under the FCC's Fairness
Doctrine, commercial stations could do so. The amendment also
required "objectivity and balance" in each program or series. To
show their concern for the lack of long-range funding provisions and
the unanswered questions about its future level of federal financing,
the bill authorized funds for only one year, thus putting pressure on
the administration to devise its long-range funding plans quickly.
Other changes included a three-year authorization for 75 percent
matching grants for radio and television facilities grants ($10.5 mil-
lion in fiscal year 1968, $12.5 million in fiscal year 1969, and $15
million in fiscal year 1970) and a limit of 8.5 percent of the authorization to any one station in order to broaden the opportunity to receive
grants. It strengthened the language to forbid the corporation from
engaging in program production and network operation. It allowed
one or more systems of interconnection to protect statewide interconnection and forbid the corporation from dealing directly with
commercial carriers for interconnection. Finally, the revised bill
defined educational broadcasting as "primarily designed for educational
and cultural purposes and not primarily for amusement and entertainment purposes."[38]

The document reporting the bill to the House of Representatives
reflected continuing dissatisfaction, inasmuch as it contained additional minority views. The minority report criticized the "we must
have it now no matter what the shortcomings" attitude of the majority.
The report stated there was not enough emphasis on instructional
use of radio and television in the school and home and too little concern for long-range financing. The minority said all of the following
methods of long-range financing should be taken into consideration
in devising extended financial support of the system:

1. license fees for television sets
2. acceptance of advertising on educational television
3. conversion of educational television to pay television
4. operating a pay television subsidiary service to cover the cost
    of noncommercial television
5. revenue or franchise tax on commercial television
6. earmarking ordinary income tax payments of commercial televi-
    sion for educational television
7. excise tax on new television sets.

Representative Pepper presented the amended bill when it reached
the floor of the House on September 21. He said, "I have had a long
time association with educational television and radio and I am an
ardent supporter of the enormous educational potential of educational
television and radio." Representative Torbert H. Macdonald, who

was a very effective behind-the-scenes negotiator for public broadcasting, as well as a public spokesman, described the bill as "one
of the most significant achievements of the 90th Congress" and
declared that the time had come "to take steps to produce higher
quality and more diverse programs." Representative Staggers de-
lineated the provisions of the bill. He described titles I and III as
noncontroversial and expressed the opinion that Title II had been
greatly improved after committee discussion and amendment. As
to long-range financing, he felt that no one could tell what future
needs would be and that a "clearer view" of such needs would be
discernible after the proposed corporation "had gained operational
experience." In the meantime, he said, the annual appropriation of
funds was the only alternative.[39]

All of the introductions did not belay harsh criticism, however,
even from supporters of educational broadcasting. Representative
Brown repeated, as he would continue to do so, his strong concern
that instructional television not be overshadowed by the new concept
of public broadcasting. Representative Howard W. Robison of New
York, himself a strong supporter of educational television, favored
adopting only titles I (extending the grant program for broadcasting
facilities) and III (authorizing a study of instructional broadcasting).
He felt that educational television was a familiar concept, which had
already won for itself wide public and congressional acceptance and
support, but that public broadcasting, while intriguing, was a controversial matter, including new issues of public policy not yet resolved.
Representative Albert W. Watson of South Carolina, professing himself an ardent supporter of the system of educational television in
his home state, moved to drop both titles II and III. He called the
proposed CPB a "Frankenstein monster," which could turn into a
government propaganda machine. Watson felt that the corporation
would compete directly with local educational television programs
and indirectly for local support funds. The House rejected his amendment by only 9 votes (111 for the amendment, 120 against). A motion
to recommit the legislation to committee was rejected by 27 votes.
In a final roll call vote, the House passed the bill 265 to 91.[40]

Since the Senate and House bills differed, a conference of representatives of both houses met to come to agreement on one bill. At
the conference meeting, the Senate conferees agreed to all the House
changes, the most significant being the ban on editorializing, which
limited the ability to make searching inquiry into public affairs and
the definition of educational broadcasting as primarily designed for
educational and cultural purposes. Excellence, however, was needed
in all areas, including amusement and entertainment, as well as the
need for objectivity and balance, which placed restraints on noncommercial broadcasting beyond those required of commercial stations
by the FCC's Fairness Doctrine.[41]

The conference bill of October, while more specific than the legislation introduced in March, still addressed itself to basic principles and left unanswered the question of government control and long-range financing. The bill passed both houses of Congress only eight months after its introduction, which was considered a record for legislation authorizing appropriations.[42] New ideas are not usually so quickly adopted. It was passed so quickly because of the backing of the high-level prestigious Carnegie Commission, because of the success of the Educational Broadcasting Facilities Program, and because the controversial aspects of the bill had been removed. Most importantly, the bill's passage was a mark of President Johnson's determination to make a record for himself as "education president" and to his legislative skills in working for the bill personally and through Cater and Senators Magnuson and Pastore and Representatives Staggers and Macdonald.

In the East Room of the White House, with the Marine Band playing and nearly 300 dignitaries in attendance, President Johnson signed the bill into law on November 7, 1967.[43] Extolling the law as providing a "wider and stronger voice" to educational radio and television and proudly announcing that Killian and Milton S. Eisenhower had agreed to serve on the board of the Corporation for Public Broadcasting, Johnson was not satisfied to bask in the adulation of the invited guests. He said the legislation was only "the beginning" and declared:

> I think we must consider new ways to build a great network for knowledge—not just a broad system, but one that employs every means of sending and of storing information that the individual can use. Think of the lives that this would change: . . . eventually this Electronic Knowledge Book could be as valuable as the Federal Reserve Bank. A wild and visionary idea? Not at all. Yesterday's strangest dreams are today's headlines and change is getting swifter every moment. I have already asked my advisers to begin to explore the possibility of a network for knowledge—and then to draw up a suggested blueprint for it.[44]

CPB FUNDING

After the signing, the Carnegie Corporation pledged $1 million to the CPB. Other pledges included $25,000 from the United Automobile Workers, $100,000 from the Communications Workers of

America, and $1 million from the Columbia Broadcasting System.45
President Johnson's personal pledge to support the corporation and
propose long-range funding were not kept, however. His thoughts
turned away from the network of knowledge to the entanglement of
the Vietnam War.

As costs of the Vietnam War mounted, rumors circulated in
Washington and the press in January 1968 that funding requests for
public broadcasting would be slashed far below the Congressional
authorization. As the difficulties of finding an equitable and acceptable solution to the question of long-range financing became more
apparent, the rumor also circulated that an answer to the question
would be deferred until after the presidential election in November
of that year.46 Educational broadcasters were asking why it was
taking so long to establish the CPB and appoint a president and new
members of the board of directors.

President Johnson in his budget message delivered to Congress
in late January asked for a supplemental appropriation of $4 million
(rather than the $9 million authorized) in seed money to fund the
activity of CPB during the remainder of the fiscal year. He also
asked that a new law be passed extending the life of the corporation
for one year and authorizing an appropriation of $20 million. He
announced that no funds were being requested for educational broadcasting facilities during the fiscal year (although $10.5 million had
been authorized) but that the full authorization of $12.5 was being
requested for fiscal year 1968/69.47 Early the next month, Johnson
said in his education message to Congress:

> We have acted also to launch an historic educational
> force in American life: public broadcasting—
> noncommercial radio and television services devoted
> first and foremost to excellence. Last year the Con-
> gress authorized the Corporation for Public Broadcast-
> ing. This year we must give it life. I recommend that
> the Congress approve the funds needed in fiscal 1968
> and fiscal 1969 to support the initial actions of the
> Corporation for Public Broadcasting.
>   Last year I stressed the importance of a long
> range financing plan which would ensure that public
> broadcasting would be vigorous, independent and free
> from policy interference or control. The problem in-
> volved is complex. It concerns the use of the most
> powerful communications medium in the world today.
> It should not be resolved without the most thorough
> study and consultation.
>   I am asking the Secretary of Health, Education
> and Welfare, the Secretary of the Treasury, and the

Director of the Bureau of the Budget—who have been
studying this problem since the law was enacted—to
work with the Board of Directors of the Corporation
for Public Broadcasting and the appropriate committees
of the Congress to formulate a long range financing plan
that will promote and protect this vital new force in
American life.[48]

And so the rumors were correct: funds for the fiscal year would be
cut and the proposals for long-range funding postponed. Organization
also began slowly, for Cater had difficulty finding a person to recommend to President Johnson as chairman who was suitable to the
supporters of public broadcasting.

The president announced in mid-February that Frank Pace, Jr.,
would be nominated as chairman of the board of directors of CPB.
Pace had been secretary of the army and director of the Bureau of
the Budget and at the time of his nomination was president of International Executive Service Corporation, a Peace Corps for business.
He brought to his prospective job a thorough knowledge of government,
and certainly of the budget process. Pace cautioned against expectations of overnight miracles and described the corporation as a
"gradually growing social asset that could add to the nation's awareness of the democracy's strengths and resources in information and
the arts."[49]

Late in February, the president announced the name of the other
14 nominees for the board of directors. It was a very impressive
list of Americans from government, the arts, education, and business, who would win easy approval from an already receptive Senate
and enhance the chances of getting the corporation moving to accomplish its responsibilities.[50]

At the confirmation hearing on March 8 before his Committee on
Commerce, Senator Magnuson said: "I consider this one of the finest
groups of Americans ever put together on one board." He was enor-
mously pleased at the progress that had been made since he first
introduced in 1967 a bill to provide grants for the construction of
educational broadcasting facilities. Killian acknowledged as "enor-
mously helpful" the consultations he had had with Senators Magnuson
and Pastore. Pace, whose illness and hospitalization had further
delayed organization of the group, sent a statement that cautioned
against expectations of quick development. He said the corporation
must lay the groundwork, experiment, and move forward slowly
based on experience. He cautioned that "the corporation can be
effective only if it is truly independent."[51] The hearing went extra-
ordinarily well, ignoring the news that President Johnson had with-
drawn his request for a supplemental appropriation to fund the

corporation during the remaining three months of the fiscal year. Only four days later, on March 12, the Senate unanimously approved the slate as the first 15 directors of the CPB.*

On March 22, Senator Magnuson arose in the Senate to offer a technical amendment to the Public Broadcasting Act of 1967. He explained that Congress had authorized $9 million for CPB in fiscal year 1968 but that the board had been appointed at such a late date and that the corporation was just getting organized (indeed, it was not even incorporated yet) that it was not practical to appropriate any funds for 1968 (not even the supplement appropriation of $4 million President Johnson requested in his budget message). Therefore, why not just change the date for the authorization of funds from 1968 to 1969. He reminded the Senate that the president had said HEW, the Bureau of the Budget, the secretary of the Treasury, and CPB were at work on the long-range funding problems and assured the members that the Bureau of the Budget and HEW supported the technical amendment. Without committee hearing or Senate debate, Senator Magnuson in a few minutes' time led the Senate to extend the life of the Corporation for Public Broadcasting by one year with an authorized appropriation of $9 million.52

It was not quite so easy in the House of Representatives. Congressman Macdonald's Subcommittee on Communications and Power of the Committee on Interstate and Foreign Commerce held hearings on a bill to extend the corporation and appropriated funds for one year, and again the committee issued majority and minority views on the bill.

Appearing at the March 27 hearing were officials of the government, CPB, and educational broadcasters.53 Citing delays in nominating directors and subsequent delays in organization, including the hospitalization of Pace, representatives of HEW, the FCC, and the Bureau of the Budget recommended a one-year extension.

Why were no funds being requested in that year for facilities construction? Coston, deputy undersecretary of HEW, offered the explanation that changes in the law regarding matching grants for educational broadcasting facilities construction had necessitated such extensive changes in procedures that no funds could be disbursed but that $10.5 million was requested for fiscal year 1969.

---

*The original members were Frank Pace, Jr., Robert S. Benjamin, Jack J. Valenti, Milton S. Eisenhower, James R. Killian, Jr. (six-year terms); Joseph A. Bierne, Michael A. Gammino, Oveta Culp Hobby, Joseph D. Hughes, Carl E. Sanders (four-year terms); and Roscoe C. Carroll, Saul Haas, Erich Leinsdorf, John D. Rockefeller, III, Frank E. Schooley (two-year terms).

What progress was being made in developing plans for long-range funding? William D. Carey, assistant director of the Bureau of the Budget, a member of the team looking into the matter, said a number of meetings had been held. The team established the principles of trying to minimize the budgeting and appropriation cycle, to require a public accounting at reasonable intervals, and to provide sufficient resources to get the job done. Specifically, they had been studying a tax on television receivers at point of manufacture, a tax on the gross revenues of commercial broadcasters, and properly insulated funds from general federal revenues. In regard to a tax on receivers, he said this was fair, because the purchasers were the direct beneficiaries, yet it was unfair, because purchasers did not benefit in proportion to the amount paid for the set and because such a tax would be regressive for the poor. The second consideration, a tax on gross revenues of commercial stations, seemed fair, because the spectrum was a public resource and a portion of the returns from its use could be used to support public television. Yet the cost of the tax could be passed on to consumers through increases in the cost of advertising on television, and this was regressive also, since the items advertised on television accounted for a larger share of those with low incomes. The third possibility was based on the assumption that public broadcasting would benefit the entire nation and, therefore, be funded from public revenue gotten through the income tax, which was not regressive. Strict budgetary control would be required, but several methods were feasible for providing federal tax revenue and still maintaining insulation from government interference. One method would be to establish a trust fund in the Treasury Department and appropriate money three years in advance. Another suggestion was to authorize automatic payments to the fund when Congress took action to prevent or control such payments. Finally, the team was considering a plan for automatic federal payments equal to donations received by all the stations in the system. It was felt that such a matching program had been successfully used in other programs and would provide an incentive to the private sector to contribute to public broadcasting. Carey felt that a lot of progress had been made, and the congressmen agreed. Indeed, except for the refinement of some details, ideas expressed in this hearing were to be enacted in 1975.

Joseph D. Hughes, a Pittsburgh banker and chairman of the Pennsylvania Commission on Public Television, who represented the CPB for the recuperating Pace, explained that Pace had held a meeting with commercial and noncommercial broadcasters, that the board had met informally after their nomination, and that on that very day, the corporation had been formally incorporated.

Representatives of NAEB were disappointed that no funds had been requested for construction during the fiscal year and said that many stations had matching money in hand to build or expand facilities with the expectation that authorized funds would be available. Quick passage of the pending legislation was urged in order to recruit staff and receive private funds for CPB. Spokesmen for the National Citizens Committee for Public Broadcasting also testified. This organization, backed by the Ford and Carnegie foundations and supported by 100 famous education, cultural, and civic leaders and many other less well-known persons, was a citizens' lobby for public broadcasting. Its membership included Newton N. Minow and Henry (former FCC commissioners), James M. Gavin (former military man), Arthur Miller and Paddy Chayefsky (playwrights), Leonard Bernstein (conductor), Kingman Brewster, Jr., and Lee DuBridge (college presidents), Myrna Loy (actress), Maria Tallchief (dancer), and many others. Thomas P. V. Hoving, director of the Metropolitan Museum of Art, lead the group, whose purpose was to generate grass roots excitement for public broadcasting and to lobby for legislation for federal support of television. It was a group that had the potential to meet a long-felt need for organized support in addition to that of educational broadcasters.

The committee report for the majority recommended a one-year extension of the law, and the minority report recommended against such action. The majority pointed out that the organization was just getting organized and needed a chance to show what it could do. It also referred to the meetings that had been held and the progress which had been made regarding long-range funding. The minority, on the other hand, made their point that neither the Carnegie report nor the Ford proposal favored direct congressional appropriation. They went on to declare that there could be no urgency, since President Johnson had been in no hurry to appoint the director, that a fiscal emergency existed because of the need to pay for the Vietnam War, and that no money should be provided until there was a financing plan.[54] The House of Representatives would decide.

In the meantime, the Ford Foundation announced a $20 million grant to noncommercial television and radio in 1968 to "sustain the enterprise during this critical time" when federal funding was not soon expected and to help it "move to a new level of excellence."[55] The money was made available for the production of specific series, general support, NET, support of Public Broadcasting Lab's political coverage, radio, and the soon-to-be-heard-of producer of "Sesame Street"—the Children's Television Workshop. Program ideas were to be submitted to a panel, which would make awards. There was some grumbling that the money would have been better spent by distributing it to stations to make their own decisions at the grass roots level rather than to these national organizations and through the centralized procedures.[56]

The House took up the bill to continue CPB for a year in late
April. Proponents and opponents took the positions detailed in the
committee report, and although there were differences of opinion,
there was little heat until Representative John R. Rarick called the
proposed operation a "runaway brainwashing monster." Still, the
House passed the bill 241 to 133—a smaller margin than the previous
year.[57] The president signed the bill ten days later.[58]

The House Appropriations Committee recommended $4.3 million
for construction but nothing for CPB, since the House had not yet
considered an authorization bill for CPB at the time the Appropriations Committee met. The Senate Appropriations Committee, on the
other hand, recommended an appropriation of $4.3 million for con-
struction and $6 million for CPB ($9 million was authorized). It was
hoped that in the inevitable conference between the two houses, a
compromise could be worked out to provide initial funding for the
corporation. The National Citizens Committee for Public Broadcasting issued a report in July, entitled "State of Public Broadcasting,"
which encouraged full funding, and it had a positive effect. After
what Senator Jacob Javits called "a very profound struggle," the
conference committee in October included in its final bill a $5 million
appropriation for CPB.[59] If this strategy had failed, the momentum
in public television would have been lost.

The FCC took the initiative to establish the interconnection of
educational broadcasting stations. Acting under the authority of the
Public Broadcasting Act of 1967, the commission issued a notice of
proposed rule making in September 1968 to begin a six-month experiment, from December 1, 1968 to May 31, 1969, to interconnect 57
points for two hours a night, Sunday through Thursday, from 8:00 p.m.
to 10:00 p.m. at about 40 percent of the standard rate.[60] The negotiations with AT&T that followed ended with a joint announcement in
November by the FCC and the CPB. The service was to be comparable in all respects to that provided commercial users, except for
the reduced rate. AT&T would use standby equipment maintained
for emergencies, and the commercial carriers could preempt the
equipment if needed to replace service on regular lines. AT&T could
recover the loss by including the true cost in its interstate rate base.
The commission had the authority to establish the service free to
educational broadcasters and to allow AT&T to recover the entire
cost through its interstate rate base; however, the commission bowed
to the wishes of the common carrier rather than to those of the financially starved stations in setting reduced rates. In December, Public
Broadcasting Laboratory would use the interconnection on Sunday
evenings for experimental programs begun the previous year with
Ford Foundation backing. In January, NET would provide two hours
of evening service to 150 stations Monday through Thursday. The

Ford Foundation would bear the $500,000 cost and CPB would pay the other half.[61]

When the NAEB met at Thanksgiving, the members had reason to rejoice and reason to be apprehensive.[62] They were grateful to Congress for appropriating funds for construction through HEW and for programming through the CPB and to the FCC for arranging interconnection. But they noted with apprehension that the corporation had been unable to find a president and felt that the absence of strong leadership was apt to be noticed in Congress. They noted with satisfaction that the concept of grass roots determination of what was to be shown locally was part of the law, yet they also observed that New York organizations were likely to dominate what programs were served on the interconnection. Public Broadcasting Laboratory provided Sunday night programs; NET with CPB and Ford Foundation money provided Monday through Thursday evening service; and Children's Television Workshop, using an $8 million grant from the Office of Education and other funds from the Carnegie and Ford Foundation, would serve preschoolers. Members of the association began to realize that the corporation would have little left from its initial appropriation to make grants to local stations after contributing to the cost of interconnection and programming for the evening hours. Educational broadcasting also realized that they had an equipment problem. Few stations had videotape equipment; therefore, their managers had to show programs as they came over the interconnection in the evening, possibly interrupting an existing schedule, or lose forever the opportunity to broadcast the program. Finally, the nation had just elected Richard M. Nixon president of the United States. Because President Johnson had made public broadcasting a matter of personal concern, it was fairly certain that President Nixon's position would be crucial to the future of public broadcasting as well. Nixon's position at that point was unknown.

Public broadcasting needed time to clarify objectives, resolve conflicting interests, and reduce what Lester Markel of the New York Times called a "plethora of double images,"[63] lest the system languish and possibly perish. The executive and legislative branches and the regulating agencies cooperated during 1969 to provide time to organize and resolve some of the concerns.

In February, the corporation took an important step in meeting those concerns with the appointment of John W. Macy, Jr., as president. Macy, widely respected in Washington, D.C., had been in government service since 1938, except for a three-year stint as executive vice president of Wesleyan College in Connecticut from 1958 to 1961. Most recently, he had been chairman of the Civil Service Commission. The purpose of the corporation, he said, was to strengthen, not dominate, local stations. He believed the corpora-

tion should not decide what went over the interconnection nor should
it be the judge of individual programming. The corporation would
be based in Washington, so as to deal effectively with Congress and
the executive branch for long-range funding and to avoid the appear-
ance of being tied to the production facilities and foundation headquarters in New York City.[64]

The corporation had to establish a position in a field in which at
least five centers of power had already been established and in which
local stations also wanted a responsible role. The five centers of
power that had to be accommodated were the Ford Foundation, interconnecters, Eastern Educational Network, Carnegie Corporation,
and the Big Eight (see below). The Ford Foundation provided millions
of dollars each year for program production and was principally
responsible for Public Broadcasting Laboratory (PBL), which dominated Sunday evening programming, and NET, which supplied week
night programming. The interconnection, involving delicate negotiations between AT&T, Ford Foundation, NET, and CPB, was just
getting started. The Eastern Educational Network of stations from
Boston to Philadelphia were interconnected for programming directly,
with Channel 13 in New York City as the flagship. The Carnegie
Corporation had established philosophical leadership through the
Carnegie Commission and was deeply interested in the Children's
Television Workshop but was having trouble getting morning viewing
times, since many stations provided in-school instruction at that
period of the day. The Big Eight television stations in Boston, San
Francisco, Los Angeles, New York, Pittsburgh, Chicago, and Philadelphia, with superior production facilities and a workable exchange
agreement, were a challenge to PBL and NET. Reconciling the
ambitions and interests of all concerned was a formidable task.[65]

A major breakthrough came in April, when the Ford Foundation
and the CPB held a joint news conference to report the results of
intense negotiation. The foundation announced that while it would
continue to make large grants to public broadcasting, it was reverting
to a role of "junior partner." The Sunday night programming would
include local and regional segments, with production headquarters
to be in Washington rather than New York City. The foundation would
help to establish, in conjunction with radio station WETA in Washington, D.C., a major production center concerned with public affairs
programming. A closer cooperation would be developed between
NET and Channel 13 in New York. The corporation would establish
within 90 days a separate entity to be called Public Broadcasting
Service (PBS). This new organization would manage the interconnection and consult with stations and producers to determine what would
go into the interconnection and at what time. The foundation announced
another grant of $20 million, including $5 million to be divided among

15 independent stations. Thus, the leadership in public television
passed from the Ford Foundation to the corporation.[66]

White resigned as president of NET, saying he was opposed to
establishing a second national production center in Washington until
the NET met minimum needs. A group of NET and Public Broadcasting Laboratory personnel, some of whose jobs were threatened by
the change, formed the Association of Public Television Producers
in opposition to federal involvement in noncommercial educational
television through annual grants to CPB.[67]

The announcement of the intent to form the Public Broadcasting
Service as a subsidiary of CPB immediately raised objections from
those station managers who feared the establishment of a fourth network patterned on the commercial system. They thought it fallacious
to assume that the whole country needed or wanted to see the same
programs at the same time. They were worried that programming
decisions would be based on trying to please as many people as possible rather than on valuing local differences. Others argued that to
achieve the quality of programming and the impact so urgently needed
required mass simultaneous circulation of programs. They further
pointed out that their lack of production facilities and trained personnel severely limited local production and that their lack of recording
equipment made rescheduling impossible. These difficulties made
scheduling for immediate transmission inevitable until such time as
funds from the corporation and private sources were available for
local production to make alternative programming a possibility.

EXTENDED AUTHORIZATION FOR THE
CONSTRUCTION PROGRAM AND THE CPB

For the first time since 1967, the Senate held hearings (in late
April and early May) on the extension of authorization for the facilities
construction program and the CPB and for oversight of development
in public broadcasting. The committee had under consideration a
bill drawn up by the Johnson Administration to extend the facilities
program for five years, with an authorization of $15 million the first
year, and to extend the CPB for five years, with an authorization of
$20 million for 1970. Senator Pastore explained that the three-month
old administration had not had time to consider long-range financing
and that another annual appropriation was necessary. Pastore encouraged the officials of the corporation and gave them advice on
how to handle the economy-minded House of Representatives. Senator
Hartke felt that the request was "a drop in the bucket" and that Congress
was still only giving "lip service to this important medium." Senator
Magnuson agreed, saying, "I suppose the defense department spills

this much money in a week. In educational television we're talking
about a value to the American people that you can't measure in dollars
and cents."68

Secretary of HEW Robert Finch sent a letter to the committee
supporting the legislation in behalf of the Nixon Administration but
recommending that the committee authorize $10 million, twice the
current appropriation, instead of $20 million. He stated there were
many other high-priority demands for funds and that the administration and CPB had begun to examine alternatives for a viable procedure
of long-range funding and was particularly interested in devising a way
"to encourage private enterprise to contribute."

There was no doubt that the committee or the Senate would vote
to extend the authorization and provide funds generously. The larger
purpose of the hearing was to establish a record of what had been
accomplished and what needed to be done.

Chairman Hyde of the FCC reported that the AT&T had been
preempting without notice equipment used for public broadcasting
interconnection and that the commission had requested that a 48-hour
notice be given in the future before such preemption. He also reported
that the experimental interconnection had been made permanent,
effective July 1, 1969.

Senator James B. Pearson noted that Dick Netzer, chairman of
the Department of Economics of New York University, had completed
a research report on long-range financing commissioned by the
National Citizens Committee.69 Netzer analyzed several proposals,
including an excise tax on new television sets, which he rejected as
the last choice because the rate of production and therefore tax
receipts fluctuated widely; a direct tax on television receivers in
use like the British system, which he rejected as too difficult and
expensive to enforce; surplus revenue from a nonprofit domestic
satellite system, which was acceptable, particularly because free
interconnection would be available but the total amount of revenue
produced would be inadequate; advertising charges, which would
destroy the noncommercial aspects of public broadcasting; and a
4 percent tax on the gross receipts of commercial broadcasters,
which he recommended because of the dependability of the source
as the potential for a substantial yield of money. He observed that
the television industry would strongly object to all the alternatives
he analyzed.

Pace reported progress in unifying the public television stations
and in establishing an interconnection of 138 stations five nights a
week. He announced that each station was receiving an unrestricted
grant of $10,000 to augment their ability to meet local needs and that
the amount would be raised to $30,000 the following year. He re-
marked that the new administration had not really had a chance to

take "a hard look" at the corporation and expressed his willingness
to go along with the administration recommendation that its budget
for the following year be $10 million.

Representatives of the NAEB called attention to the continuing
problem of UHF stations in a letter to Senator Pastore. The organization praised the federal requirement that all television viewers be
able to receive UHF transmissions but said that tuning was difficult
and should be as easy for UHF as it was for the twelve VHF channels.

Joan Granz Cooney talked about her forthcoming program,
"Sesame Street" for preschoolers. It was to be the most thoroughly
researched, tested, and studied program on television. Considering
the fact that Commissioner of Education Harold Howe spent $5 million
on the program the first year, it was also the most thoroughly federally subsidized. Fred Rogers, producer and principal performer of
"Mister Rogers' Neighborhood," described his program for children
with such feeling that it brought "goose bumps" to Senator Pastore
and an assurance that his testimony alone would guarantee a committee
vote for $20 million.

In quick action, less than two weeks after the conclusion of the
hearing, the Senate, on May 13, passed without objection a bill to
extend the construction program for five years (1971-76), with an
authorization of $15 million for fiscal year 1970 and such sums as
might be necessary for the other four years, and to extend the CPB
for one year, with a $20 million authorization for fiscal year 1970.[70]

The House of Representatives held hearings in June.[71] Macdonald
chaired the deliberations, which had both Democratic and Republican
support. Administration officials said that a $10 million authorization
would be consistent with the level of development, and the CPB representative agreed. Pace declared that the nine months needed to
select a president and additional months to select a proper staff had
been worth the wait. Macy felt a sense of excitement, ferment, and
expectation within the industry and was pleased with growing administration interest in the corporation's progress.

William G. Harley, president of NAEB, was concerned that so
little money had been made available for the educational broadcasting
facilities construction program. Congress in 1967 authorized $38
million for the project—$10.5 million in fiscal year 1968; $12.5 million
in 1969; and $15 million in 1970. In 1968, no money was appropriated.
In 1969, $4.3 million was appropriated. In 1970, Johnson requested
$5.6 million in his budget, but Nixon cut the request to $4 million.
These minuscule appropriations and requests were doing great damage
to educational broadcasting. They needed the full amounts to make
use of the programs being produced and distributed. They needed
funds to expand coverage by adding new stations; they needed funds
to expand the coverage and transmission quality of existing stations;

they needed funds to buy equipment to use the interconnection, to videotape material so that it could be rebroadcast or broadcast at times different from when the material came over the interconnection, and to produce programming.

Congress had very little opposition to this effort. It was so popular, in fact, that some congressmen thought it was coupled legislatively with the CPB to make the latter easier to swallow. The Nixon White House, and particularly HEW, did not give the program sufficient support. HEW was more concerned with program material—"software," to borrow a computer science term—than with buildings and equipment—"hardware." Congressmen would point this out at appropriation committee hearings and would approve more money for the program than HEW requested.

Reporting on a conference held April 9, representatives of ETS explained what local control meant to station personnel. They said, local control "means an effective station voice from beginning to end, in the conception, development, selection, and the distribution of national and regional programing. The option to reject what is offered is not enough."[72]

The corporation had formed an Advisory Committee of National Organizations (ACNO) to assist the corporation in determining the range of interests public broadcasting would serve. Eighteen national organizations had joined. The advisory group would also serve as a committee link back to the organizations the advisors represented. It would also serve as a lobby at congressional hearings and to elected representatives and government officials. More would be heard from this group as its membership expanded and activities became organized.

The subcommittee and the full committee unanimously agreed to send to the House of Representatives a bill to extend the educational broadcasting facilities program for three years, with authorized appropriations of $15 million each year, and to extend CPB for one year, with an authorized appropriation of $20 million. During friendly floor debate in September, Representative Macdonald emphasized the importance of the facilities program in stating that four out of five public television broadcasting stations had received a grant, that the number of states without any public television had been reduced during the life of the program from 15 to 3, and that for every federal dollar spent, 11 state, local, or private dollars had been spent in the program. Representative Staggers, speaking for the Committee on Interstate and Foreign Commerce, said it was "one of the most effective programs within our jurisdiction." Representative Springer expressed his displeasure with the backlog of needs and requests that had built up over the preceding three years and accused the executive branch of not pushing hard enough to turn authorization into appropriation.[73]

In regard to CPB, Representative Springer, the ranking Republican member of the Commerce Committee, pointed out that President Johnson had not recommended a long-range funding plan as promised and that President Nixon had not yet had the time; therefore, he was going along with year-to-year authorization until a permanent solution was forthcoming. He noted that the bill called for twice as much money as the executive branch had requested and doubted that the full amount could be obtained but would go along with the larger sum just in case CPB could convince the White House.

Representative Daniel E. Button of New York introduced an amendment to the bill to require CPB to allocate half of its appropriation to public television stations in the form of unrestricted direct grants for station operation. The past year, the corporation had allocated $10,000 to each station; in the coming year, it expected to allocate $30,000, but the amendment would have required $50,000. It was explained that basic costs for administration, production, and interconnection prohibited such a large percentage for direct grants but that grants larger than $50,000 per station were expected when long-range financing was settled and the corporation had more money to disburse. The proposition had been twice defeated in committee votes and was defeated in the full body as well.

The House approved the bill as presented to it by a comfortable bipartisan margin of 280 to 21.[74] The Senate concurred with the changes, and President Nixon signed the bill into law on October 27, 1969.[75]

While the legislative process was producing a bill to extend the authority of the CPB, the corporation established PBS and National Public Radio (NPR), and the FCC tackled the problem of preemption of interconnection equipment.

INTERCONNECTION

After months of deliberation, James Day, president of NET; Hartford N. Gunn, Jr., chairman of the board of ETS and general manager of WGBH in Boston; Kenneth A. Christiansen, chairman of NET affiliates from the University of Florida; and CPB officials reached agreement on interconnection. They agreed to establish PBS as a subsidiary of CPB, with a separate board of directors and chief executive officer. The board was to be composed of five representatives of public television stations elected at the NAEB convention, one from CPB, one from NET, and two from the public. Macy said the combination would "provide proper balance between station interest and public interest."[76] It would begin operation on January 1, 1970, and would have responsibility to handle the mechanics of inter-

connection, select programs for the interconnection (but not produce
any programs), and allocate time periods when programming would
be sent out over the interconnecters (which the station could accept,
reject, or postpone showing). It was a compromise that attempted
to reconcile the difference between NET, the chief producer of programming, which wanted to make the decisions, and the individual
stations, which wanted to avoid a fourth network on the commercial
model.[77]

The Public Broadcasting Act of 1967 awakened educational radio
broadcasters to an opportunity for expansion and service that they
had previously not even considered. With funds available for facilities
and programs, station operation and personnel training, a whole new
era opened for them. To take advantage of the opportunity and to
maximize their efforts, educational radio broadcasters organized
with more fervor and clearer purpose. The National Educational
Radio Division of the NAEB met in Madison, Wisconsin, in August
1969. The division represented 425 noncommercial stations and
had a small staff at NAEB headquarters in Washington, D.C. The
delegates recommended to CPB that it establish an independent entity
to be known as National Public Radio, which would produce programs
and handle station interconnections. A 12-person board would direct
the affairs of NPR. Nine members would be station managers (one
elected from each of the nine established regions), and three would
be public members (elected by the nine station managers).[78]

Working with Al Hulsen, director of radio projects for CPB,
the radio broadcasters established guidelines for NPR and criteria
for individual station support for operating expenses. To receive
operating support, public radio stations were expected to broadcast
with at least 250 watts power, to have adequately equipped control
rooms and stations, to employ a minimum of three full-time professional broadcasters, and to broadcast at least eight hours a day, six
days a week, 48 weeks a year. The criteria eliminated a substantial
number of 10-watt school stations from consideration but gave them
standards to work toward should they wish to engage in a public radio
service. Operations were to begin in mid-February and interconnections to commence by the summer of 1970. Public radio had made
a substantial leap in self-concept and organization.[79]

The FCC came to the rescue of interconnection. During the
first month of interconnection, December 1968, the AT&T preempted
equipment 39 times for commercial use. It continued to preempt
with regularity equipment that connected some of the 57 points from
which added relays provided service to 150 stations. (AT&T was
building additional equipment to serve the noncommercial stations
and said the interruptions were temporary.) Nonetheless, the FCC
ruled that noncommercial interconnections were to have the same

priority, and the same full service, as commercial interconnections. Agreement still had not been reached as to the level of charges for the service. The temporary rates established for the experimental phase were still in effect. FCC worked with AT&T and CPB on an informal basis to work out an agreement without using the more expensive and time-consuming procedure of formal rule making.[80]

The FCC had been pondering for several years a policy on domestic satellites. COMSAT, Ford Foundation and others submitted plans. Previously, the White House indicated an intention to become involved in the decision. In January 1970, the White House did become involved. Peter Flanigan, assistant to the president, wrote Dean Burch, chairman of the FCC, to say the White House wanted a system developed on a competitive basis rather than as a license to a single monopoly, such as COMSAT, as the FCC was rumored about to do. The memorandum specifically rejected the Ford Foundation idea that the profits from a domestic satellite be reserved as a subsidy for Educational Television and CPB. Burch said for the FCC that "we intend to study carefully these views and other submissions in the proceedings,"[81] but for all practical purposes that option for long-range financing of public broadcasting was no longer possible.[82]

The idea of using a domestic satellite for educational purposes, including interconnection of public broadcasting, was not shelved, however. The FCC asked the Joint Council on Educational Telecommunications to set up a committee of educational and public broadcasters to study education's needs for communications networks of all types. This request was based on a proposal growing out of President Johnson's interest in a Network for Knowledge, which envisioned a national low-cost network for education, using the facilities of existing and proposed interconnection systems and satellite systems.[83]

CPB did not give up the idea of using a domestic satellite for interconnection either, for it announced a joint effort with the Office of Education and National Aeronautic and Space Administration (NASA) to test the feasibility of such an operation. The OE would provide funds to develop programs for Indian children and rural children in isolated areas of the Rocky Mountains. NASA would provide the equipment.[84]

FURTHER FUNDING FOR THE CPB

The corporation's appropriation of $15 million for the 1970 fiscal year was the innocent victim of a conflict between the president and the Congress over control of spending. The CPB funds were part of an omnibus appropriation for the departments of Labor and HEW,

which totaled $1 billion more than President Nixon requested. He
vetoed the appropriation bill in January 1970. In the meantime, the
corporation received funds under a continuing resolution, which
meant that it received the same amount of money as in the previous
year until new legislation was finally passed. The previous appropriation for fiscal year 1969 was $5 million, and the corporation limped
along, drawing against that amount until the president, on March 7,
four months before the end of the fiscal year, signed a bill that provided the full $15 million to CPB. Because of this unfortunate circum-
stance, over which the corporation had no control and which was not
aimed at harassing public broadcasting, CPB had small opportunity
to demonstrate what it could do, since it was operating financially
below the "seed money" level recommended in 1967.

When President Nixon delivered his education reform and budget
message to Congress, [85] he asked for a three-year extension of the
charter of the CPB and a first-year appropriation of $15 million,
plus an additional appropriation of $7.5 million to be matched on a
dollar-for-dollar basis from private sources. The matching feature
was consonant with what Secretary Finch had declared to be a determination to continue to involve private sources in an effort to insulate
the corporation from reliance on government appropriation. The
president still expected to develop a long-range funding proposal and
called for continued discussion at the executive level to develop such
a proposal.

The Senate held hearings on the administration bill on April 1
and 2. [86] Chairman Pastore expressed his hope that the administration would expedite the long-range funding plan and pointed out quite
practically that in the meantime, the corporation must have funds.
A three-year extension would remove all hurdles for the corporation
for a while and would provide much needed continuity and the opportunity to plan ahead. He approved the matching scheme as an incentive
to public broadcasters to pursue private funding. Pastore said since
the committee supported the administration bill, the hearing would
be devoted largely to oversight of public broadcasting, including the
accomplishments and future plans of the industry.

Pace approved the matching idea but expressed some concern
that care be taken not to take money away from local stations. This
was a legitimate concern, which was eventually resolved equitably.
Macy reported on the establishment of minimum standards for public
radio stations in order to receive grants for operating expenses and
the organization of NPR. In regard to television, he reported on
the creation of career fellowships to train personnel, production
grants to a number of stations, general support grants, and the role
of PBS and interconnection.

Officials of NAEB, representing public broadcasters, expressed their complete satisfaction with the corporation during its first year of operation. In their opinion, the work of the corporation was highly beneficial and the corporation was moving in the proper direction. Various plans for funding had been circulated, and while none was entirely satisfactory, the interim plan calling for matching on a dollar-for-dollar basis was quite acceptable. They agreed that at the outset when funds available to the corporation were scant that the needs of interconnection and series production superseded the need for direct grants to stations but expressed the expectation that direct grants would increase as more funds became available. This expectation became a basic assumption in later long-range funding plans.

When the House of Representatives held hearings two weeks later,[87] Congressman Macdonald opposed the three-year extension as a grace period to provide an excuse for no action to be taken on long-range funding. Pace expressed his satisfaction with the administration. He said that the administration had no knowledge of public broadcasting when it came to power, but that, after a year of observing the corporation, the administration wrote a bill that provided substantial support while allowing the corporation to gain experience and build on its record of accomplishment. Macy told of the progress being made to permit a number of local stations to develop and produce programs for interconnection rather than rely on one or two production centers. CPB President Macy discussed his talks during the preceding year with representatives of the executive branch regarding permanent funding. Their views included an excise tax on the sale of television sets (which the administration rejected), a user tax, a tax on gross receipts of commercial broadcasting, and permanent federal funding based on a matching formula. Final recommendations seemed to be centered around matching funds as incorporated in the bill under discussion, except the corporation officials preferred matching funds derived from the whole system rather than from contributions solely to CPB. The corporation did not wish to become competitors with local stations for contributions.

Albert L. Alford, assistant commissioner of education for legislation, talked about the long-range funding also. The Bureau of the Budget, he said, was responsible for working out the funding compromise, which he described as the "best effort at this time to provide a viable base for permanent funding." He thought the matching plan under discussion would provide an "opportunity to see how well it works and measure public response to the support of the Corporation." This "could very well be the long range funding arrangement if it works out,"[88] he declared.

Gunn, 19 years a public broadcaster, testified for the first time in his new position as president of PBS. In explaining how the system worked, he stressed the importance of local stations as participants in decision making and as multiple sources for production of programs distributed through the interconnection. He thought this emphasis would afford a balanced presentation, giving local stations a larger voice and diminishing the role of the eastern establishment, particularly NET, which would no longer distribute programs or be the sole producer. Children's Television Workshop, producers of "Sesame Street," became a separate production center and no longer a quasi-autonomous branch of NET. Gunn expected to be able to provide programs not only in the morning and evening hours for direct transmission but also in off-the-air hours for use anytime.

The Senate in May passed a committee bill without debate providing for a three-year extension and open-ended authorization of fiscal years 1971, 1972, and 1973, with provision for matching funds. The bill included a committee amendment to require stations to keep for three months recordings of programming of public importance to document any attempt at government influence in public broadcasting.[89] In September, the House passed by voice vote a committee bill to extend the corporation for one year and an appropriation authorization of $30 million, plus $5 million to be matched from private sources. It was explained that the one-year extension was based not on a lack of commitment to public broadcasting but rather on a desire to push the administration into providing a long-range funding proposal. There was no provision for record keeping of public interest programs.[90] A Senate-House conference committee worked out a compromise bill to extend the corporation for two years and, with the concurrence of the Bureau of the Budget for the Nixon Administration, to authorize appropriation each year of $30 million, plus $5 million to be available if matched on a dollar-for-dollar basis, thus providing a potential of $50 million in 1971 and 1972. The Senate provision for record keeping was dropped on the grounds that no hearings had been held on this provision.[91] The Senate and House passed the compromise legislation and President Nixon signed the bill into law on October 10, 1970.[92]

When the appropriation committees met, however, they provided only $23 million. The Senate Appropriation Committee report included the sum of $27.5 million for public television, while the House report had nothing, since an authorization bill had not been passed in the House at the time the committee took up appropriations. In December, a Conference Committee of the Senate and House agreed to provide $20 million in outright appropriations and $3 million for matching purposes.[93] Operating on the basis of a continuing resolution at the 1970 level of $15 million until this time, the CPB finally received an appropriation of $23 million, including matching funds, half way into the fiscal year.

The Appropriations Committee did well regarding the funding of educational broadcasting facilities. The administration requested only $4 million of the $15 million authorized, but the committee appropriated $11 million for facilities construction in the 1971 fiscal year. The Congress removed the $250,000 limitation on the size of grants to be awarded.

With the purpose of encouraging private sources to provide more money for public broadcasting, the FCC, at the end of September 1970, revised the standards whereby educational television and radio stations could announce the sources of funds to produce programs or pay operating costs. The new FCC rules authorized stations to announce twice orally and visually the name of a company or foundation furnishing or producing a program. The agency allowed a station to mention three times a day the name of a party that contributed all or a major part of the station's operating costs. No mention of a product or service was permitted.[94] William Lamb, senior vice president and treasurer of Channel 13 in New York City, which had recently merged with NET, felt the rules should have been modified to allow a product or service to be mentioned if the corporation's name was unknown, and David J. Curtin, vice president of Xerox, said his company would have liked to say what his corporation stood for.[95] Nonetheless, the FCC action provided an increasingly important outlet for corporate advertising and made it easier for CPB to obtain contributions that could be used to match federal dollars.

The chairman of General Foods Corporation, C. W. Cook, in announcing a grant of $300,000 to "Sesame Street," said his corporation, manufacturers of breakfast cereal and other food items, had an obligation to sell its product in the marketplace and to assure the firm's economic viability and to return dividends to investors. He also said the firm could not remain indifferent to society or fail to fulfill its enlarging civic responsibility.[96]

Speaking to the NAEB convention in November 1970, Burch, chairman of the FCC said the commission had gone as far as it could go in relaxing the rules on sponsor identification on noncommercial educational broadcasts. "We will not take the route of seeking greater financing for you by making you more commercial—by permitting you to obtain greater backing from commercial sponsors," he declared. The primary responsibility for financing public broadcasting was that of the federal government, not commercial enterprise. "Don't strive to compete with commercial broadcasting for a maximum audience," Burch continued. "Do your own thing. Don't play a number's game."[97]

Federal agencies frequently provided funds for educational programming. Large grants to the Children's Television Workshop have been mentioned. Another example was a grant of $600,000 from the

OE to the CPB to set up a public broadcasting environment center
in which government and private groups could pool their resources
in a coordinated effort to produce pilot television and radio programs,
conduct surveys of environmental information and educational programs, and collect material for a film and reference library.[98]

Another example of close cooperation between the CPB and the
OE was the joint effort of the corporation and the National Center for
Educational Statistics to produce Status Report on Public Broadcasting.
The study reported on the general development of public broadcasting,
finances, employment, broadcasting and production, interconnection
service, and audience.*

Cognizant of the criticism that public broadcasting was too little
concerned with education, the corporation commissioned the Center
for Educational Enquiry, headed by James A. Perkins, president of
Cornell University, to produce recommendations for specific projects
"to make full use of broadcasting in education."[99]

Several developments at the FCC demonstrated the agency's
positive attitude toward noncommercial educational broadcasting.
When H. Rex Lee replaced Robert E. Lee as chairman of the FCC-
sponsored National Committee on Full Development of Instructional
Television Fixed Service, the regulatory agency also named him
educational communications commissioner. As governor of American
Samoa, Lee had established an instructional television system for the
islands. This new post made the incumbent responsible for keeping
the other commissioners informed on developments in the industry
and for recommending changes in policy. The commission also
authorized two new services. It established on a regular basis, after
four years of experiment, a service whereby educational television
stations could transmit "scrambled" program material not suitable
for the general public to specialized audiences, such as police or
physicians, who viewed the material on special receivers that "un-
scrambled" the transmissions. The commission gave temporary
authority for three stations to operate automated tape recordings.
These stations transmitted at nonbroadcast hours during the night
specialized educational programs to schools equipped with videotape
recorders that turned on and off by coded signals. The service established an economic means of providing a greater number of school
programs and permitted maximum flexibility in scheduling and repeat-
ing programs. It also permitted creation of a library of short, single-
concept film and video tapes to be transmitted through regularly
assigned frequencies.[100]

---

*Corporation for Public Broadcasting, Station Report on Public
Broadcasting 1973 (Washington, D.C.: U.S. Government Printing
Office, 1975), is an example.

Public broadcasting seemed to be in a secure position. The
White House was recommending three-year funding. Executive level
managers and planners were coming close to a permanent funding
scheme based on the matching concept. The Senate passed legislation affecting CPB by voice vote after friendly hearings. Senators
Magnuson and Pastore were powerful friends of public broadcasting
in powerful positions. The House passed the most recent legislation,
extending the corporation by an overwhelming margin after a hearing
concluding with no minority views. Congressmen Staggers and
Macdonald were staunch supporters. The FCC contrived to take the
initiative to assist public broadcasting and had done so in assuming
reliable interconnection and in helping to obtain contributions. Progress was being made in meeting the concerns and expectations of
local stations. Program production was being shifted to centers
other than in New York. Direct station grants for operating expenses
were increasing as appropriations to CPB increased. PBS was sharing
decision making. Facilities construction grants were flowing, and
combined with local funds, were resulting in more and better-equipped
stations. OE was helping to fund "Sesame Street," the successful,
instructional, educational program for preschoolers. Progress was
being made on all fronts, yet dissension, disappointment, and disaster
loomed.

NOTES

1. Ford Foundation, Ford Foundation Annual Reports 1959-1966
(New York: Ford Foundation, 1959-66).
2. Federal Register, XXXI, 3507.
3. New York Times, May 15, 1965, June 3, 1965.
4. Federal Register, XXXI, 3507.
5. New York Times, August 2, 1966.
6. Senate, Committee on Commerce, Hearings on Progress in
Space Communication; and the Ford Foundation Proposal for a Broadcasters Non-Profit Satellite Service, 89 Cong., 2 Sess.; New York
Times, August 11, 1966, August 18, 1966, August 19, 1966.
7. New York Times, August 29, 1966.
8. Senate, Committee on Commerce, Subcommittee on Communications, Public Television Act of 1967, Hearings on S1160,
90 Cong., 1 Sess.; John E. Burke, "The Public Broadcasting Act
of 1967: Part I: Historical Origins and the Carnegie Commission,"
Educational Broadcasting Review 6, no. 2 (April 1972): 113-18.
9. New York Times, November 11, 1965.
10. Ibid.
11. Ibid., November 21, 1965.

12. Ibid., January 26, 1967.

13. John E. Burke, "The Public Broadcasting Act of 1967: Part II: The Carnegie Commission Report, Development of Legislation, and the Second National Conference on Long-Range Financing," Educational Broadcasting Review 6, no. 3 (June 1972): 184; Public Papers of the Presidents of the United States. Lyndon B. Johnson, 1967, Book I (Washington, D.C.: U.S. Government Printing Office, 1968), document 3 (hereafter cited as Public Papers. Johnson, 1967, I).

14. Carnegie Commission on Educational Television, Public Television: A Program for Action (New York: Bantam Books, 1967).

15. New York Times, January 26, 1967, January 27, 1967, January 31, 1967.

16. Ibid., January 26, 1967, March 1, 1967.

17. Public Papers. Johnson, 1967, I, document 13.

18. Ibid., document 77.

19. Ibid.

20. New York Times, March 1, 1967.

21. Congressional Record, CXIII, 5225.

22. New York Times, March 12, 1967.

23. Congressional Record, CXIII, 5235.

24. New York Times, March 7, 1967.

25. Congressional Record, CXIII, 6234.

26. New York Times, March 10, 1967.

27. Ibid., April 4, 1967, April 5, 1967.

28. Senate, Bill 90-1160.

29. Senate, Committee on Commerce, Subcommittee on Communications, Public Television Act of 1967, Hearings on S1160, 90 Cong., 1 Sess.

30. Ibid.

31. Ibid.

32. New York Times, April 23, 1967, May 11, 1967.

33. Senate, Report 90-222.

34. Congressional Record, CXIII, 12985-13007.

35. House of Representatives, Bill 90-6736.

36. House of Representatives, Committee on Interstate and Foreign Commerce, Public Television Act of 1967, Hearings on H R 6736 and S 1160 and Similar Bills [and] H R 4140 and Similar Bills, 90 Cong., 1 Sess.

37. New York Times, August 20, 1967.

38. House of Representatives, Report 90-572.

39. Congressional Record, CXIII, 26379-26417.

40. Ibid.

41. House of Representatives, Report 90-794.

42. Congressional Record, CXIII, 29320, 29382, 30198; John E. Burke, "The Public Broadcasting Act of 1967: Part III: Congressional Action and Final Passage," Educational Broadcasting Review 6, no. 4 (August 1972): 264-65.

43. Public Law 90-129.

44. Public Papers of the Presidents of the United States. Lyndon B. Johnson, 1967, Book II (Washington, D.C.: U.S. Government Printing Office, 1968), document 474 (hereafter cited as Public Papers, Johnson, 1967, II).

45. New York Times, November 8, 1967.

46. Ibid., January 22, 1968.

47. Public Papers of the Presidents of the United States. Lyndon B. Johnson, 1968-69, Book I (Washington, D.C.: U.S. Government Printing Office, 1970), document 39.

48. Ibid., document 54.

49. New York Times, February 14, 1968, February 18, 1968.

50. Ibid., February 25, 1968.

51. Senate, Committee on Commerce, Hearings on Nominations, 90 Cong., 1 and 2 Sess.

52. Senate, Report 90-1017; Congressional Record, CXIV, 7357.

53. House of Representatives, Committee on Interstate and Foreign Commerce, Subcommittee on Communications and Power, Amend Communications Act of 1934, Hearings on HR 15986, 90 Cong., 2 Sess.

54. House of Representatives, Report 90-1281.

55. Ibid.

56. New York Times, April 21, 1968.

57. Congressional Record, CXIV, 19425-10436.

58. Public Law 90-294.

59. Congressional Record, CXIV, 30190.

60. Federal Register, XXXIII, 12853.

61. New York Times, November 11, 1968.

62. Ibid., November 25, 1968.

63. Ibid., January 25, 1969.

64. Ibid., February 7, 1969.

65. Ibid., February 23, 1969.

66. Ibid., April 9, 1969.

67. Ibid., April 11, 1969, April 29, 1969.

68. Senate, Committee on Commerce, Subcommittee on Communications, Extension of Authorization under Public Broadcasting Act of 1967, Hearing on S 1242, 91 Cong., 1 Sess.

69. Dick Netzer, Long-Range Financing of Public Broadcasting (New York: National Citizens Committee for Broadcasting, 1969).

70. Senate, Report 91-167; Congressional Record, CXV, 12207; see Richard M. Polsky, Getting to Sesame Street: Origins of the Children's Television Workshop (New York: Praeger, 1974).

71. House of Representatives, Committee on Interstate and
Foreign Commerce, Subcommittee on Communications and Power,
Educational Television and Radio Amendment of 1969, Hearings on
HR 4212, HR 7737, and S 1242, 91 Cong., 1 Sess.

72. Ibid.

73. House of Representatives, Report 91-466.

74. Congressional Record, CXV, 29328-29346.

75. Public Law 91-97.

76. Ibid.

77. New York Times, October 10, 1969, November 5, 1969.

78. Ibid., August 7, 1969.

79. Ibid., December 4, 1969.

80. Federal Communications Commission, vol. 17, Commission
Reports, 2nd Series (Washington, D.C.: U.S. Government Printing
Office, 1970), pp. 155-58.

81. Ibid.

82. New York Times, January 24, 1970.

83. Ibid., February 8, 1970.

84. Ibid., February 3, 1970, February 6, 1972.

85. Public Papers of the Presidents of the United States.
Richard M. Nixon, 1970 (Washington, D.C.: U.S. Government
Printing Office, 1971), documents 22 and 66.

86. Senate, Committee on Commerce, Subcommittee on Communications, Continued Financing for Corporation for Public Broadcasting, Hearings on S 3558, 91 Cong., 2 Sess.

87. House of Representatives, Committee on Interstate and
Foreign Commerce, Subcommittee on Communications and Power,
Public Broadcasting Financing Act of 1970, Hearings on HR 16338
and HR 16580, 91 Cong., 2 Sess.

88. Senate, Subcommittee on Communications, Hearings on
S 3558.

89. Senate, Report 91-869; Congressional Record, CXVI, 15993.

90. House of Representatives, Report 91-1274; Congressional
Record, CXVI, 31199-31203.

91. House of Representatives, Report 91-1466.

92. Public Law 91-437.

93. Congressional Record, CXVI, 41533.

94. Federal Communications Commission, vol. 25, Commission
Reports, 2nd Series (Washington, D.C.: U.S. Government Printing
Office, 1971), p. 779.

95. New York Times, August 30, 1970.

96. Ibid., September 20, 1970.

97. Ibid., November 11, 1970.

98. Ibid., May 26, 1970.

99. New York Times, May 22, 1970.

100. Federal Communications Commission, Annual Report 1970 (Washington, D.C.: U.S. Government Printing Office, 1971), pp. 45-47.

CHAPTER

7

THE CONGRESS AND
THE PRESIDENT—
LONG-RANGE FINANCING

NIXON ADMINISTRATION CAMPAIGN TO
INTERFERE WITH TELEVISION NEWS
AND PUBLIC BROADCASTING

The year 1970 marked the emergence of a Nixon Administration campaign to interfere with television news. The administration felt that it was being treated unfairly and began an intense effort to intimidate and harass broadcasters. Vice President Spiro T. Agnew was the chief spokesman. In speech after speech, he denounced domination of the news by commercial networks centered in New York City. As a result of this badgering, it was expected that network influence would be fragmented and that the power of local stations less critical of the national administration and more devoted to area happenings would be enhanced. The vice president was only one tool of the administration used to create fear and divisiveness. The FBI harassed correspondents of the New York Times and CBS with federal subpoenas regarding sources of articles and programming on the Black Panthers. The Federal Communications Commission set a limit on the number of network hours of evening broadcasting, with the effect of eliminating the possibility of late evening network news programs. Internal Revenue Service agents screened 1969 National Educational Television programming and attempted to interview producers to determine whether any programs advocated legislation, which if they had would have adversely affected the tax status of NET and its principal funder, the Ford Foundation. Sander Vanocur, a network news commentator, lamented, "I have never seen such flagrant pressure put on the United States press as in this Administration." And Vice President Agnew said tongue-in-cheek, "I think I have had a modicum of success." Federal Communications Commissioner Nicholas Johnson remarked

170

on the effect of the administration effort on the fall schedule of programming on commercial television and characterized the public
affairs and special programs as being "little bark and no bite." He
said, however, "The most hopeful aspect [of the new season] is noncommercial public broadcasting."[1]

Public broadcasting was not to be immune from intimidation,
interference, and harassment. In the name of grass roots localism,
the administration attempted to squelch public affairs programming
thought to be anti-Nixon. Because of its newness and dependence on
federal funding, public broadcasting was particularly vulnerable to
attack from administration spokesmen in Congress and from a new
agency in the executive branch—Office of Telecommunication Policy
(OTP).

On September 4, Congress authorized OTP as an executive agency
to oversee the use of broadcasting channels assigned to federal government use and to advise the president on electronic communications,
including cable television and domestic satellites. Clay T. Whitehead,
an electrical engineer with a doctorate in management who had worked
in the Nixon election campaign and had helped plan the organization
of the office, was named director. Whitehead, although much brighter
and more sophisticated, became the Agnew of public broadcasting,
with the important exception that he later left government service
honorably with a record of achievement rather than as a self-confessed
tax evader. It would be several months before Whitehead became
known in public broadcasting circles for his misuse of OTP to intimidate broadcasters.[2]

Since Congress had extended the Corporation for Public Broadcasting for two years and provided authorizations of $35 million for
1971 and 1972, no hearings on public broadcasting were held in 1971,
except for those regarding appropriations for the 1972 fiscal year.
At the House of Representatives appropriations subcommittee hearing
on the Office of Education and related agencies, Representative Daniel
Flood assured John W. Macy that the subcommittee was "prejudiced
in your favor" and the CPB was "one of our favorite programs."[3]
Macy spent more time with this committee than was usual for such
occasions. In the three previous years, no hearings had been held
in the House, and the appropriation to the corporation had been handled
in a conference committee representing the House and Senate. Macy
began by explaining the budgetary procedure. The corporation wrote
out and justified a budget request, which it sent by September 30,
the same as other federal agencies, to the Office of Management
and Budget (OMB, which replaced the Bureau of the Budget). OMB
held hearings and in conjunction with the White House staff cleared
an amount of money to be included in the president's budget message
in January. As an independent agency, CPB was not bound to defend

the president's budget figures. As to educational broadcasting facilities construction, HEW, CPB, and NAEB representatives conferred
before HEW included an amount for this program in its budget request
to OMB. In recent years, OMB had approved less than the amount
Congress authorized, but in the previous year, Congress had appropriated $11 million rather than the $4 million included in the president's budget message. HEW, as an executive agency, was bound to
support the amount requested in the president's budget. Macy stressed
the importance of the grants to build new stations for wider coverage
in the United States and in order to improve facilities and equipment
in existing stations to make better and more flexible uses of CPB
and Public Broadcasting Service (PBS) support. In response to Flood's
questions, Macy assured the chairman that the corporation was placing
greater emphasis on the educational uses of public broadcasting and
planning larger grants to local stations for operating expenses. The
House Committee approved the full $35 million authorized for the
corporation ($30 million direct grant, plus $5 million available for
matching). It approved $11 million for educational broadcasting
facilities grants rather than the $4 million requested by HEW. Macy
presented essentially the same material to the Senate appropriations
subcommittee, 4 which consisted of only Senator Ernest Hollings, who
said he was also "prejudiced" in behalf of public broadcasting. Hollings
had originated legislation authorizing educational television in his home
state of South Carolina and, as governor, had appointed the first television commission. The appropriations committee of the Senate, with
Warren Magnuson as chairman, made the full $35 million available
to the corporation and the full $15 million available for facilities
grants. The House and Senate conference committee approved $35
million for the corporation and split the difference between the two
chambers, to approve $13 million for facilities.5

Increased appropriations made it possible to increase services
in radio and education. The National Public Radio (NPR) network
began operations on May 3, 1971, connecting 90 stations in 32 states.
The FCC had licensed 457 noncommercial educational broadcasting
stations, but most of these were schools and colleges, with low-power
and intermittent schedules, and they did not qualify for network
affiliation or financial grants. The network began by providing news
and interviews for one and a half hours Monday through Friday evenings. The next step was to provide a morning news program and a
full day of cultural programming on Saturdays. Donald R. Quayle,
president of NPR, described how the network operated. He explained
that some new programs would originate from the Washington, D.C.,
headquarters, but that the network would switch live to points throughout the network for segments of news and interviews with newsworthy
personalities. CPB made grants to local stations to participate in

the network radio news program. Macy, speaking to the 1971 Public Television Conference, announced the corporation's intention to use public radio and television for a nationwide system of preparation for high school equivalency testing and certification.[6]

At midyear, the FCC announced that agreement had been reached with AT&T and CPB to establish interconnection on a permanent basis and, thus, end the fear of preemption for commercial use of the lines used by public broadcasting. AT&T guaranteed 71 connection points, providing service to 100 stations by March 1972, and 110 connection points, providing service to the entire network of 225 public broadcasting stations by January 1, 1973. Rates for this service would begin at $2 million for the 1972 fiscal year and increase by $1 million annually to $3 million for 1973, $4 million for 1974, and $4.9 million for 1975.[7]

PBS, despite problems, was making satisfactory progress toward using the interconnection. After 15 months of service, PBS was still plagued, as was its parent CPB, with the uncertainties of annual congressional appropriations, the distrust of politicians, and the indifference of viewers. PBS was held in suspicion by program producers. For example, PBS had been sharply critical of an NET-produced program entitled "Banks and the Poor." Reviewers and Congress, as well as PBS, thought parts of the program lacked objectivity. The controversy pointed out the peculiar position of the broadcast service. Unlike commercial networks, PBS did not produce programs. It allocated time slots to competing producers and recommended which producers were to use production grants; it was, therefore, in a position of strategic control over the types and quality of programs produced. Its administrative headquarters were in Washington, D.C.; its technical facilities for interconnection were in New York City; and its production centers in 1970 included 22 stations throughout the United States. The eight principal production centers were in New York, the site of Children's Television Workshop and NET, which had merged with Channel 13 to form WNET; Pittsburgh (WQED); Boston (WGBH); Chicago (WTTW); San Francisco (KQED); Los Angeles (KCET); and Washington, D.C., where PBS and CPB in conjunction with station WETA and with substantial Ford Foundation funding created the National Public Affairs Broadcasting Center for Public Television (NPACT). It was difficult for PBS to establish a clear image of its role and responsibility among the many public broadcasting entities: CPB, NPR, NET, NPACT, and so forth.[8]

Not everyone was satisfied, however, with the direction in which PBS was going. Arthur L. Singer, Jr., was one of those. Singer, an associate of the Alfred P. Sloan Foundation, had been involved in organizing the Carnegie Commission on Educational Television and, with Stephen White, had written the final report. He charged in a

conference speech that the public broadcasting system had become
a fourth network under the domination of the Ford Foundation, CPB,
and PBS. He felt the Carnegie Commission goal of a pluralistic
system, whereby local stations would have an opportunity and responsibility for substantative communication, had been subverted and a
centralized system, whereby local stations were carriers of decisions
made by a distant administration, substituted. He specifically resented
the power of PBS to rule on specific content and the undue control
that piecemeal funding afforded. The tag "fourth network" and the
call for more local station control and funding would dominate discussions of public broadcasting for several years.[9]

Hartford N. Gunn explained that power would swing back and
forth until a balance was struck. The crucial item was money.
Stations did not have enough money to program for their local audience
or for the interconnection. CPB did not yet have enough money to
provide funds for duplicate efforts.[10]

Meanwhile, a momentous power struggle was developing between
the OTP and the CPB. Soon after the OTP was organized, Whitehead
and representatives of the corporation began a series of meetings
that lasted over a ten-month period. The discussions concerned
long-range financing. Both interests agreed that financing should
come from general taxation. Whitehead, representing the Nixon
Administration, wanted greater emphasis on the local stations, and
Macy, representing the corporation, agreed with this emphasis but
wanted to protect the corporation's interests as well. Whitehead
proposed that a fixed percentage of the federal funds be designated
for the support of local station operations, but Macy, while not
opposed to providing such funds, balked at providing a mandated
amount. Whitehead wanted internal changes in the national organization that would transfer some power and responsibility to the local
level. Again, Whitehead expressed the administration's concern
over the appointment of Vanocur as anchorman for news and public
affairs programs of NPACT. The administration felt that Vanocur,
a former broadcaster for NBC and a close associate of the Kennedy
family, was biased against Richard Nixon. Macy explained that the
corporation provided funds to the production center but did not control
its personnel policies and should not interfere, nor should the executive branch of government, in such policies. The negotiations came
to an impasse, and OTP withdrew its long-range funding proposal
from further consideration in July 1971.[11]

In October, Whitehead spoke to the annual meeting of the National
Association of Educational Broadcasters in Miami Beach. He was
sharply critical of what he called "centralizing of authority in CPB"
and said such centralization was contrary to the Public Broadcasting
Act, which emphasized the need for local production. He said that

long-range funding lay in the distant future if public broadcasting
continued to be structured as it then was. In this and subsequent
speeches, he alleged that the corporation had become a fourth network and suggested that Congress should appropriate funds directly
to the stations to preserve their autonomy from the encroachment
of the corporation. He made it clear that the administration was
opposed to news and public affairs programming, and particularly
to the liberal bias of NPACT. The message was indeed clear: there
would be no permanent funding until public broadcasting became what
the administration wanted it to be.[12]

Despite continued administration efforts to drive a wedge between
the local stations and the corporation through unwarranted and increased interference in the affairs of public broadcasting, the medium
was not torn apart by internal rifts on these external political pressures. There was honest disagreement, which the Nixon Administration attempted to exploit, but public broadcasters worked for a
resolution of these disagreements and eventually emerged stronger
and better financed. The essential elements of debate were over
program control, program content, appropriate audience, and money.
They were concerned with specific policies and with a proper balance
between the corporation and the local stations, and its concerns
centered around the federated, loosely run, station-manager-dominated
PBS. They were still seeking an accommodation to the pre-Carnegie
report concept of educational television tied to instruction and/or the
intellectual elite and the post-Carnegie concept of public television
serving the full needs of the American people.[13] While it can be
argued that the administration's interference goaded public broadcasters into resolving their debate on key issues, it can also be
demonstrated that the administration's actions raised anxieties among
broadcasters, slowed development of public broadcasting, ended the
careers of distinguished government officials, divided on partisan
lines the congressional supporters of public broadcasting, subverted
the purpose of OTP, and cheapened the presidency.

Still reeling from Whitehead's October speech, the corporation
was further rocked when the administration raised questions about
salaries being paid corporation officials and public affairs broadcasters that were larger than those paid congressmen and cabinet
officers. The administration was particularly incensed that the
NPACT paid Vanocur $85,000 and Robert MacNeil $65,000 for weekly
programs and special assignments. Congressional supporter Torbert
Macdonald admitted to being a "little shocked" but urged that the
federal government get on with the real problem, which was long-
range financing. Lionel Van Deerlin, another congressional supporter
and former radio and television news editor and analyst, pointed out
that the salaries were paid by an independent production center funded

by CPB and the Ford Foundation and, while high, were not at the
level of commercial networks. Still, he thought the attempt should
be made to build up public television's own personalities like Julia
Child, the French Chef, rather than attempt to buy personalities
like Vanocur and MacNeil, who had established their identities through
commercial broadcasting.[14]

Public affairs programming included various sources and ap-
proaches to the topic, and they all raised questions as to how much
freedom of the press a government-financed system would permit.
"World Press" from San Francisco analyzed the foreign press. From
Los Angeles, "The Advocates" used a courtroom setting to provide
arguments for and against an issue. "Black Journal" was aimed directly at a black audience. William Buckley's "Firing Line" provided an
articulate, politically conservative moderator for a talk program.
"Bill Moyers' Journal" provided an opportunity for an experienced
newspaper publisher to discuss issues and public concerns. Using
satire as a means of commentary about the passing scene, "The
Great American Dream Machine" was an innovative television program
produced in New York. Documentaries and satire struck sensitive
nerves in government, and some individual programs, such as "The
Banks and the Poor" and "FBI Subsidy of Violence," created considerable controversy.[15]

The damage had been done to the chances of obtaining permanent
funding, and both the administration and congress tacitly agreed to
wait until after the 1972 elections. Gunn said public television would
"mark time until funding was clarified," and the corporation began
cutting expenses because of uncertainties regarding future funding. It
cut program funds to the production centers, including the cancellation
of hit programs, such as the "The Great American Dream Machine,"
and dropped plans for gavel-to-gavel coverage of the upcoming political conventions. It cut 13 percent from its administrative budget and
shelved plans to consolidate its operations into one Washington, D.C.,
headquarters building. John T. Witherspoon, director of television
operations of CPB, was quite disappointed because of these developments and charged the Nixon Administration with trying to shape
public broadcasting to its own designs.[16]

When Congress began consideration of legislation to extend the
Public Broadcasting Act as the election year began, the coalition of
congressional supporters had fragmented.

The president, in his January 1972 budget message, requested
$45 million for the CPB for fiscal year 1972/73. This $10 million
increase was to be disbursed at the local level.[17] His communications advisor, Whitehead, continued his attacks on the corporation.
He told a Senate subcommittee on constitutional rights that national
public affairs programs were "contrary to the spirit" of the legislation,

that legislative restriction on the corporation were "meaningless,"
and that the corporation continued to produce national programs,
even though Congress intended a local emphasis. [18]

Under administration pummeling, the coalition of Republican
and Democratic support of public broadcasting in the congressional
committees fragmented. When the House Subcommittee on Communications and Power began hearings on public broadcasting financing in
early February 1972, Republicans and Democrats had submitted
separate bills and the administration had submitted none. Clarence
J. Brown's bill would extend the educational broadcasting facilities
program for five years and make HEW rather than the corporation
responsible for awarding grants to stations for operating expenses.
The Brown bill would seriously circumscribe the corporation's functions further by prohibiting the use of funds for current news events
or issues of a partisan nature; lobbying; interconnection, advertising,
or promotion; and the corporation from accepting grants from one
source for more than ten percent of the federal appropriation. [19]
Brown said, "By reversing the downward power flow on programming
decisions from the federally well-heeled CPB to a hard-pressed
locally financed station, and by limiting the influence of large outside
sources of income, we can re-establish the balance of instructional
and cultural programming as local communities want it." He claimed
he was acting in his own concern for educational rather than public
television and was not introducing an administration bill. Nonetheless,
it suited the Nixon Administration, and Lyn Nofziger, deputy chairman
of the Republican National Committee, circulated copies of the bill
with the statement, "The Corporation for Public Broadcasting is a
victim of fiscal irresponsibility and partisan non-objectivity in its
hiring practices and programming." [20] The chairman of the House
subcommittee, Congressman Macdonald, submitted his own bill, [21]
which provided for extending the corporation for five years, increasing
funding authorizations significantly, establishing a special fund to
insulate the appropriation, maintaining the matching funding, and
mandating 30 percent of the funds for local stations. After the hearings were completed, the administration submitted a bill to extend
the corporation for one year, [22] to provide $45 million ($40 million
appropriation, plus $5 million matching), and to require that $15
million be distributed to local stations.

At the hearings conducted February 1-3, [23] most of those giving
testimony made a considerable effort to explain away the criticism
or to accommodate themselves to the demands. They appeared conciliatory despite the efforts to split them apart and exuded sufficient
solidarity so that the subcommittee in its private deliberations was
able to bring itself back together with less dissent (when it concluded
its private discussion) than when the public hearings began.

Frank Pace led off the conciliating effort by describing how the corporation had reordered its priorities and, in fact, deferred broadly to the administration's objections. The corporation intended to increase its support to local stations to meet basic operating and programming production costs and to distribute at least 30 percent of its funds in that way rather than 12 percent as it was then doing. It intended to spend more effort on educational aspects of television, including instruction, and particularly adult education, and had no plans for election year coverage. It would give greater emphasis to technological research and development. And finally, the corporation intended to provide programs of increased quality and alternative programs for more choice at the local level.

James B. Killian's letter defended and explained the corporation's position from the standpoint of the board of directors. He felt that the corporation personnel weighted the differing views of all parties to bring balance, fairness, objectivity, and freedom of creativity of expression, as well as honoring the autonomy, independence, and diversity of the local stations. He reiterated that a network was undesirable but that the lack of funds had prevented providing a variety of choice. Instead, with policies shaped by representatives of local stations, PBS had been selective in scheduling programs for the limited number of interconnection programs available. Moreover, he pointed out, many stations did not have recording equipment necessary to record and store programs for later, more convenient broadcast and had to show programs when they arrived on the interconnection or lose them. Killian wrote that the board was acutely aware of the need for balance and objectivity in public affairs programming.

In analyzing disagreement with local stations, Macy discussed funds and programming. There was no intention, he said, on the part of the corporation to deny an increasingly larger share of the funds to local stations; there was only the desire of the local stations to get a larger share sooner. Programs, he pointed out, were selected by the station managers who ran PBS, and all stations were polled four times a year on their attitude to specific programs. In commenting on the high salaries paid in some instances, he believed that high-quality programming required professional talent, which was expensive.

Called up to explain the salary controversy, Pace stated that, previously, program grants were made to stations which hired the talent and determined the compensation, but that in the future, CPB would review any salary using more than $36,000 in federal funds.

When local station personnel testified, they supported the corporation. Ralph B. Rogers, a Texas industrialist and chairman of the board of KERA-TV in Dallas, testified that more money should be provided locally but not at the expense of interconnection or of high-quality nationally produced programs. He went on to describe an

informal meeting ten days previously of the chairmen of the boards
of 11 of the largest public television stations, wherein they agreed
to become active in seeking long-range funding for public television.
NAEB, recognizing the need during a Republican administration to
organize a group of industrialists with economic clout to lobby for
public broadcasting, assembled the group with Ford Foundation funding. Representatives met with the board of directors of CPB and
said they wanted to become more involved, in order to relieve the
economic and political pressures on the system and to assure a stable
future. Rogers and the group he represented were to become powerful figures in public television. David Ives, president of WGBH-TV
in Boston, reported on a recent meeting of Eastern Educational Network representatives who supported the idea of a sliding scale,
whereby as funds appropriated for CPB increased, the percentage
to local stations increased also. He said the local station did not
have disagreement on policies with the corporation and pointed out
there was an elaborate structure for seeing to it that the stations
themselves were heard within the whole system. The problem was
not having enough money in the whole system. Dale K. Ouzts, executive vice president and general manager of KPTS in Wichita, said
the local stations wanted an equitable percentage of the money not
the total amount and that local audiences wanted the quality of programming which was available from national sources and did not
wish to be sustained on local programming.

William Harley, representing the NAEB, spoke out for the need
for increased funding for direct operation support at the local level,
increased funding for the corporation, increased funding for educational broadcasting programs, and grants for instructional television.
He strongly supported the idea of a sliding scale of support to local
stations, whereby the percentage of support, as well as the amount
of support, increased as larger appropriations were made for public
broadcasting. The Reverend William Fore, speaking for the Advisory
Council of National Organizations, which represented 37 national
organizations interested in public television, said that despite the
efforts to create a split, there was no basic distrust or serious problem between the corporation and the stations.

When FCC chairman Dean Burch was also asked about Clay T.
Whitehead, Burch said he and the commission listened to Whitehead
but did not do what he said. Johnson, the gadfly of the FCC, was
more blunt. He said the administration was criticizing CPB because
production centers had hired public affairs commentators who disagreed with the administration. He said the administration criticized
PBS for becoming a fourth network because it represented to the
administration a conspiracy of the eastern media establishment. He
charged that the administration was refusing to come up with a plan

for long-range funding until the corporation agreed to "monitor" public affairs programming.

Whitehead had his chance to speak at the end of the hearing. He opposed the bills before the committee as too expensive in total amounts authorized and too cheap in the percentage provided to stations. He preferred an administrative measure that would extend the life of the corporation for one year rather than five and would provide $45 million, an increase of $10 million, and would mandate a larger percentage of the funds for local stations. Whitehead justified modest annual appropriations on the grounds that the relationship between the central organization and the local stations was still largely unclear and that until the matters were clarified and the directions better defined, it was more sound not to rush forward.

Whitehead testified that his specific concerns were four in number: (1) he thought the independence of local stations suffered because the CPB did not devote sufficient funds to local support and production; (2) he believed local station autonomy was undercut by CPB and PBS efforts to establish a fixed schedule; (3) he also thought program diversity was not enhanced, since the corporation used "in house" production centers and sought mass audiences for news, public affairs, and entertainment; and (4) he further believed that not enough attention was paid to a proper balance between local and national programming and between cultural, entertainment, news, public affairs, educational and instructional programming.

Macy answered Whitehead's charges in a letter to the committee. In response to Whitehead's first point, Macy pointed out that witnesses testified that CPB posed no threat to their independence. He said there was an insufficiency of funds, but that at no foreseeable time would federal funds provide a major share of local costs. In his response to his second point, Macy said there had to be a fixed schedule, because many stations were without recording equipment and because there was not enough money to provide two hours of programming for each hour of broadcasting. In response to the third point, he pointed out that the corporation produced no programs "in house" but that the corporation had expanded to 22 the number of production centers it supported. In response to the last point, Macy answered that, excluding children's programs, about 20 percent of the broadcasting on public television originated with PBS and that the rich selection of programs on public channels could be found nowhere else.

The hearings ended with the administration opposed to long-range funding, the corporation making conciliatory changes, and Congressman Macdonald determined to put a coalition of Democrats and Republicans together again in order to produce a bill that would contain the basic structures for long-range funding to insulate public

broadcasting from the kind of political pressure it was receiving
from the Nixon Administration.

In a further move toward accommodation with the administration,
PBS proposed to its board a revision of its news policies. The board
adopted the proposal and agreed to appoint an experienced newsman
to coordinate the public affairs programs produced by the various
agencies. The coordinator would see that production centers met
their goals, head off problem programs before they were completed,
sensitize the staffs to the type of programs acceptable, and ensure
that standards of fairness and balance were met. The board also
decided to enlarge its membership from 11 to 19 and to provide greater
representation from the local level; public membership on the board
was increased from 2 to 6, and the station managers' membership
increased from 6 to 12.[24] The change in membership was a direct
result of Congressman Macdonald's intercession on behalf of station
managers.

The board of directors of CPB also made changes to reflect the
administration's concerns for localism. On March 18, the board
agreed to consult with a panel of station managers regarding the
formulation of the corporation's annual budget and the distribution
of operating grants. The board members also agreed to invite station
managers to two meetings a year to discuss national concerns and
to other meetings as necessary. They decided to visit more stations
to obtain information and impressions about local operations.[25]

Congressman Macdonald worked very hard with members of his
subcommittee and with members of the full congressional committee
to shape a compromise bill that would receive bipartisan support.
Yet, from his point of view, such a bill had to provide substantially
more money, insulate the industry from government interference,
establish a model for long-range funding, and address the administration's criticism without giving in to administration pressure. After
vociferous discussion, the committee produced a bill that accomplished
these goals, with only one dissenting vote in the subcommittee and
two dissenting votes in the full committee. The compromise bill
extended the corporation for two years to allow the administration
to produce a long-range funding bill. As to funding, the bill contained
a new feature, which provided a breakthrough in the long search for
a method of financing public broadcasting. The bill provided for
federal matching of all nonfederal contributions. Specifically, the
bill stated that in fiscal year 1972/73, the corporation would be
authorized to receive whichever was the lesser amount: $65 million
or $35 million plus a matching grant equal to one-half the nonfederal
contribution in public broadcasting in the previous year. For the
1973/74 fiscal year, the bill authorized CPB to receive whichever
was the lesser amount: $90 million or $50 million plus one-half the

nonfederal contributions. The bill established a Public Broadcasting
Fund in the Treasury, to which the treasurer of the United States
would make a lump sum payment and from which the corporation
could draw as needed. The bill increased the authorization for the
broadcasting facilities program from the currently authorized $15
million to $25 million to meet the needs of existing stations for broad-
casting equipment, as well as to build new stations and enlarge older
ones. The proposed legislation also addressed criticism of the system. It mandated that 30 percent of the appropriation be distributed
to local stations. It stated that five members of the board of directors
of the CPB must be chief executives of noncommercial educational
broadcasting stations, in order to ensure that persons with practical
experience at the local level participated in the decision-making process. It also provided a ceiling of $60,000 on salaries of corporation
employees but did not limit the salaries of on-the-air personnel.

The dissenters felt there ought to be more emphasis on educational instruction and more effort to ensure independent management,
finances, and control at the local level. Representative Hastings
Keith struck the mood of the committee when he declared "on balance
[the bill is] a worthwhile addition to our national educational effort."[26]

Before the House of Representatives took up the proposed legislation, the public broadcasting industry made changes that would insulate
somewhat two major production centers from government interference
and, at the same time, bring them closer to the local level, by asso-
ciating them directly with television broadcasting stations. Ford
Foundation funds made it possible to merge NPACT with WETA in
Washington, D.C., and to move from Howard University to a new
site in Alexandria, Virginia, in December 1972. The merger was
said to provide greater efficiency and one more layer of insulation
from government. Concluding a power struggle that began with the
passage of the Public Broadcasting Act, NET merged with WNET/13
in New York City. The independent production company, the main-
stay with Ford Foundation support of educational broadcasting before
the CPB, had fought to maintain its preeminent position as arbiter
of the educational airwaves; however, large public television stations
wanted a greater role in producing programs, and other local stations
wanted a greater part in deciding what was produced. Public television officials in Washington cut back on grants to NET as the other
production centers expanded. The Nixon Administration's cries
about the dominance of public broadcasting by the eastern establishment and the need for grass roots localism were a factor. Merger
with public television in New York City eliminated NET as a symbol
in the struggle with the administration.[27]

Congressman Macdonald managed on the floor of the House the
bill to extend the CPB for two more years and to provide up to $115

million in financial support. He explained to the House that the bill
was a compromise measure that sought to refine the operations of
the corporation, taking into account its work since 1967. He cited
as an example adding station managers to the board of directors.
Macdonald claimed wide support for the proposed legislation from
the public television industry and from numerous groups that were
members of ACNO. He pointed out that the administration called
for only a one-year extension and $10 million increase in the funding
authorization and decried Whitehead's speeches, which attempted to
divide and conquer public broadcasting, and the desire on the part
of the executive branch to make public broadcasting a second-class
public service.

Other members of the subcommittee spoke in behalf of the bill.
They said their differences had been worked out in committee after
vigorous examination. They believed a two-year extension was
needed in order to give proper consideration to the long-range funding
bill promised by the administration in the coming year, and they
were convinced that the corporation needed larger appropriations
than the administration was willing to sanction.

The House approved an amendment to limit salaries for corporation executives to the level of Congressmen ($42,500) but rejected a
similar limit on the salaries of performers. Nixon supporters moved
to eliminate the bill under consideration and substituted the administration measure, reducing the corporation's authority to one more
year and reducing the funding authorization from $65 million to $45
million. It was argued that the corporation was not doing what it
was supposed to be doing at the local level and was too much involved
in national public affairs. Representative Samuel L. Devine of Ohio
said public broadcasting bears the "political and cultural outlook of
New York City" and argued that "left-leaning" people were producing
public affairs programs and should be eliminated. Supporters of the
bill explained again that the administration promised a long-range
funding bill in June 1973 and that a one-year extension would not provide enough time to give the proposal full consideration. The attempt
of Republicans and Southern Democrats to substitute the administration bill failed by a vote of 188 to 166, and the committee bill then
passed 256 to 69.[28]

Senator John O. Pastore did not hold public hearings on public
broadcasting legislation in 1972. Instead, he took the opportunity of
using a hearing before his committee[29] on June 13 regarding the
renomination of two members of the board of directors of CPB to
ask corporation officials about the legislation that the House of Representatives passed a few days earlier and to give them some advice.
They explained the need for funding as far ahead as possible, to provide them with planning time and stability to deal with local station

allocations, interconnection, and national programming. Macy
expressed his belief that Congress and the corporation had relied
too heavily on Johnson and Nixon Administration promises to take
the initiative in making long-range funding proposals. It was his
belief that the corporation had to take additional responsibility, and
he announced that he had appointed a task force to write a proposal
and to make every effort to get it adopted. Pastore attempted to
explain to the corporation officials the congressional point of view.
He said as long as federal money was involved in corporation activity
to any large extent, there would always be a desire on the part of
Congress to talk about programs, because it was the responsibility
of Congress to determine how federal money is spent. He explained
that many congressmen wanted an annual extension so that they could
guide the direction the programs took. He went on to explain that
many congressmen failed to see the distinction between public television and the commercial networks, because public television was
providing public affairs programs, and its commentaries sounded
just like the ones on commercial networks. They asked, What is
the difference? There was supposed to be a difference. He instructed
them about how Congress felt about high salaries paid from taxpayers
money. He said congressmen compared corporation salaries with
their own salaries and concluded that the appropriations were used
for administrative purposes rather than for the objectives of the
program.

He explained to the officers of the corporation the feelings and
beliefs of members of his own committee and he explained why he
held no public hearings but confined the committee debate to the
committee room rather than frighten the industry further by making
it privy to the dissension within the ranks of his committee, which
had supported public television from the beginning of congressional
involvement with educational broadcasting legislation.

The committee report to the larger body split on party lines in
its views regarding the bill passed in the House of Representatives.[30]
The Democratic majority favored the bill, while Republican Senators
Howard H. Baker, Jr., Norris Cotton, and Robert P. Griffin declined
to support the legislation and issued supplemental views much in line
with what administration spokesman Whitehead had been saying. The
minority senators observed that stations were licensed to serve the
public interest of the local communities and that since the corporation
and local stations were examining their role, it was premature to cut
short this reevaluation by adopting long-range funding schemes and
authorizing the larger sums of money in the House legislation. They
felt PBS had established a 19-hour-a-week fixed schedule network
contrary to the intent of Congress and that the proper balance between
localism and centralism must be struck before more than annual

renewal of the corporation was appropriate. They said the administration had made a commitment to submit long-range-funding legislation in time to take action prior to June 20, 1973, and ought to be taken at its word.

On the floor of the upper house, Senator Baker moved to amend the committee bill, which was exactly like that passed in the House of Representatives, and substitute his own version, which would extend the corporation for one year and authorize an appropriation of $45 million. Baker argued that a one-year extension and limited money would put pressure on the corporation to get its house in order, that is, to give more attention to education, strengthen local stations, and curb its national programming. Senator Lowell P. Weicker, Jr., said bluntly that the one-year extension bill was the work of the administration, which did not like certain public affairs programs and commentators on public television. The Senate rejected the Baker amendment in a vote of 58 to 26 and went on to adopt the House bill by a vote of 82 to 1.[31]

One week after the Senate vote and two days after the Senate appropriations committee included $60 million for the corporation in its HEW-Labor Department appropriations bill, President Richard M. Nixon vetoed the proposed Public Broadcast Act of 1972. The chief executive stated his objections in a veto message to Congress written by Whitehead. Nixon complained that the CPB, which was originally intended only to serve the local stations, had become a center for power and a focal point of control of the entire public broadcasting system. He stated that the question of financing "cannot be resolved until the structure of public broadcasting was more firmly established, and we have a more extensive record of experience on which to evaluate its role in national life." He pointed out that funding had risen from $5 million in 1965 to $35 million in 1972 and that he had requested $45 million for 1973. Funding levels in the vetoed legislation were "unwarranted in light of serious questions yet unanswered by our brief experience with public broadcasting." He requested a "continuation of carefully measured annual funding subject to regular budgetary oversight and review." President Nixon urged Congress to reconsider the bill he had originally recommended for a one-year extension and a $45 million authorization.[32]

The press was quick to point out Whitehead's views expressed earlier that public money should not be spent on controversial views and to quote White House Press Secretary Ronald L. Ziegler's doubts that public television should distribute national public affairs programs in competition with the networks.[33] Congressmen were more direct. Representative Robert O. Tiernan told the House there was no better testimony than the president's veto that the threat to localism came from the White House and no better proof of Douglass

Cater's assertion that the public broadcasting system was capable of
being manipulated by budgetary and appointive pressures from the
White House. He claimed the purpose of the veto was to emasculate
NPACT and prevent aggressive coverage of Nixon's bid for reelection
and to proclaim a victory of the OTP over the Subcommittee on Communications and Power of the House of Representatives. He deplored
this attempt of the White House staff to turn the electronic media to
their own ends. Macdonald, the congressman who had worked the
hardest for the legislation and lost the most in prestige by the veto,
informed the House of Representatives that CPB in five years had
done a great job of upgrading public broadcasting from a gaggle of
weak, disjointed stations with virtually no audience to a viable medium
that offered the American public a choice in their viewing and listening. He claimed that for an illustration of how political pressure
could be applied to reduce public broadcasting to a frightened, unsure,
bland medium, one only need look at the record of the past eight
months. From Whitehead's speaking tour to Nixon's veto, it was a
record of implied or direct threats, promises and divisive tactics.[34]

Deciding not to try to override the veto, Senator Pastore smoothly
introduced, and the Senate passed by voice vote without debate, President Nixon's request for a one-year extension of the corporation and
an authorization of $45 million. Pastore tacked onto the president's
request an increase from $15 million to $25 million in the authorization for broadcasting facilities construction grants. Tongue in cheek,
the senator said this was done in the spirit of the president's veto
message, in which he asked for more funds at the local level.[35]
As PBS officials pointed out, the original legislation would have
provided more money to local stations than the legislation that the
president asked for and the Senate approved on July 21.

In another voice vote, the House Commerce Committee passed
the Senate version of the administration bill in what the committee
regarded as a bare bones solution to the problem of funding CPB,
which had begun the fiscal year without any authorization or appropriation. The committee's report[36] emphasized that the increase
of $10 million in the authorization did not provide any additional
programming, because the corporation had promised to distribute
30 percent of its appropriation to local stations (13 percent more
than fiscal year 1972), because 46 additional stations had been interconnected and needed service, and because of a $1 million increase
in line charges for interconnection.

For Macy, president of the CPB, the political roof fell in with
the veto. His position had been weakened when PBS and Ford Foundation supported NPACT with its politically liberal public affairs
commentators earning high salaries and drawing Republican and
Democratic criticism. His own intention that PBS must be strong

was in sharp contrast to the administration position that funds must
be spent locally. As a prominent Democrat, he was anathema to
the Republican White House. Further criticism over controversial
shows, as well as his own ill health, coupled with the crippling presidential veto, led to his resignation. In a letter to Pace, the board
chairman, Macy said: "You are aware of my growing belief that
current trends in the development of this industry point toward the
desirability of a change in leadership of the corporation. This is
desirable for the future of the corporation and for my own public
service career."[37] The vice president of CPB also resigned, and
Pace, also a prominent Democrat, stepped down from chairman of
the board to member of the board of directors.

On the heels of these announcements, the House took up, on
August 15, the matter of the one-year extension of the corporation
and a $45 million authorization. Commerce Committee Chairman
Harley O. Staggers observed that the majority of CPB board members
were Republicans and that the CPB chairman, president, and vice
president had all resigned, and he asked the House to pass the measure without amendment to give new leadership a chance to see what
it could do without further restriction. Public television's spokesman
in the House—Congressman Macdonald—also asked the House to
refrain from "nitpicking and quibbling," which only served to make
public broadcasters even more insecure and frightened of the vague
and formless threats to their existence. He claimed that OTP had
arrogated to itself a partisan policy and said that a way must be found
to stop the meddling and affirm the corporation as independent and
free from political pressure. Congressman Van Deerlin agreed that
administration spokesmen had a "sinister and chilling" effect on the
industry with remarks like "the message is getting through" and
"we're keepin an eye" on them. He hoped the administration would
make good its long-delayed promise to provide a long-range funding
plan that would assure the independence of the corporation. The
House passed the bill on August 15 by a vote of 377 to 8.[38] The
president signed the bill at the end of the month.[39]

President Nixon soon named his replacement for chairman of
the board and president of the corporation. Nixon selected as the
new chairman Thomas B. Curtis, a former Republican congressman
from the state of Missouri and a vice president and general counsel
for Encyclopaedia Britannica. He selected as the new president
Henry W. Loomis, who had a long career in education and government.
Loomis was a physicist and assistant president of MIT before entering
government service in a number of positions, including deputy U.S.
commissioner of education and deputy director of the U.S. Information
Agency. He headed a group of policy advisors to President Nixon
after his election in 1968.[40] He was seen as an advocate of the White

House position on public broadcasting, and his early statements lived
up to the expectation.

Loomis declared in an early policy statement that the CPB would
take full responsibility for the programs distributed over PBS and
disagreed with the view that PBS should be insulated from the corporation with regard to program content. Loomis said cultural
programs would be stressed and that "instant analysis" after public
affairs events and other such techniques that mimed commercial
television tactics would be dropped. He declared that federal funding
was at a satisfactory level and that long-range funding would not be
attempted for several years. All in all, his views mirrored those
of the White House staff, especially Patrick J. Buchanan, Charles
Colson, and Peter M. Flanigan, as did the fall schedule, which
featured cultural programming and demonstrated that "public funding
and public muckraking" did not go together.[41]

To counter this thrust, Gunn proposed a radical shift in funding.
He proposed that the corporation turn over to the local stations 90
percent of its funds—federal, foundation, and private—and give the
stations autonomy in their use of funds to choose, produce, and buy
programs. Ten percent would be retained for innovation. Such a
move, in his opinion, would go a long way to assuage the criticism
of the Nixon Administration and some segments of Congress that the
system was too centralized. A station cooperative would be formed
to provide each local station the opportunity to decide what programs
it wanted produced and to buy them for local viewing. This move
would have other results. The corporation would be stripped of its
power to decide what was financed and offered on the network; PBS
would be reduced to a distributor of programs. The South, West,
and Midwest would have a greater voice in the system, which had
been slanted toward the East.[42]

Loomis had introduced a similar market plan in the U.S. Information Agency when he was associated with that organization, and he
told NAEB convention delegates in November 1972, that he favored
channeling money directly to the stations and encouraging them to
set their own goals.[43]

Stations were appalled, however, a few days after the NAEB
convention when the corporation informed them that 21 hours of
NASA-produced coverage of Apollo 17 would be available. PBS
had not even been consulted, and the stations saw the move as an
opening wedge in Loomis's announced policy to get more involved
in programming. Critics were aghast at what they saw as a blatant
attempt to take programming prerogatives from PBS, widen exposure
for a government-produced version of a news event, and produce,
potentially, a 21-hour commercial for a NASA product. The corporation backed down, saying that time was too short to obtain the required

staff and technical facilities. The corporation also announced that
the incident was an example of the lack of clear lines of authority
which had been allowed to exist under previous administrators and
that the staff was busy drawing up new policies.[44]

That crisis had barely passed when the Nixon Administration,
newly installed for another four-year term, announced draft legislation to revise the procedure for licensing commercial and noncommercial radio and television broadcasting stations. The proposal
offered licensees two concessions and one measure of increased
accountability. The first concession would allow licenses to be renewed for five years rather than three. The second concession would
allow licenses to be challenged only after a license had been revoked
or had not been renewed rather than at the time of application for
license renewal. The accountability provision was a chiller. Individual licensees would be held accountable at license renewal time for
the content of their programs, including network programs. This
was a strong move on the part of the administration to keep broadcasters in line economically and ideologically.[45]

Whitehead made this point clear in a speech at a Sigma Delta
Chi luncheon in Indianapolis. He charged network news programs
with a "lack of balance and objectivity." He further charged them
with "ideological plugola," or with plugging ideas in accordance with
their own beliefs. Whitehead thought the individual local stations
should be held responsible for network ideology.[46]

Nicholas Johnson responded that "the only national institutions
remotely capable of serving as a check on abuses of Presidential
power are the three networks—and especially their news departments.
It appears that young Clay Whitehead is to provide us with 'four more
years' of Nixon's war on the networks."[47] The effects of the war
would not be limited to the networks, of course, because local public
television stations would be held responsible for programs produced
in national programming centers. These centers had already been
admonished for their public affairs programming and for their public
affairs commentators, such as Sander Vanocur, who, perhaps not
incidentally, left public television when his contract expired on
December 31, 1972.[48]

PBS, it will be recalled, was forced by CPB and public television
licensees to distribute programs, to determine the needs of member
stations, to recommend to the corporation programs that the licensees
wished funded, to select noncorporation-funded programs for distribution, and to prepare an overall program distribution schedule. The
board of directors of PBS prepared a position paper in January 1973
on their commitment to decentralization and an independent distribution system. The board challenged the corporation's announced
intention to have more to do with programming, reflecting, they

thought, pressure from the Nixon administration. Board Chairman Robert F. Schenkkan, president and general manager of KLRN-TV in Austin, described the corporation's intention of moving in a more centralized direction as "contrary to the intent of Congress." Declaring it a "crucial time for noncommercial broadcasting," Schenkkan lamented plans to eliminate numerous public affairs programs. Such programs as "Firing Line," "Black Journal," "Bill Moyers' Journal," "The Advocates," "Wall Street Week," and "Washington Week in Review" were slated for cancellation in what seemed to be a response to administration pressure to control the news and discredit elements of the press not supporting Nixon.[49]

On January 10, CPB reported the results of an extensive study begun eight months earlier on the functions of CPB and PBS. The study concluded that there was duplication in the programming, legal, research, and public awareness areas, that these functions would be better handled in the corporation, and that CPB should take a much stronger role in programming decisions. PBS and its members saw the action as an attempt to remove from their control the selection of non-CPB funded programs and the scheduling of CPB and non-CPB funded programs. Schenkkan said the corporation had never communicated its dissatisfaction to PBS and asserted that the personal judgment of corporation personnel in program selection would not be acceptable to the stations. Curtis stated the action was taken in part to meet the objections raised by the White House and some members of Congress on the objectivity of public affairs programs. Critics were quick to point out the corporation was potentially the maximum pressure point from government and placing programming decisions in the corporation increased the potential for political control and, in fact, raised the very real possibility that a fourth television network under White House control could become a reality.[50]

The PBS board met in emergency session to consider alternative ways to fund the interconnection directly under the control of stations so that they could guarantee to themselves the right to air programs with or without corporation sanction or funding. The Eastern Educational Network made plans to find their own funds to produce controversial programs.[51]

Macy, in a speech to the Alfred I. du Pont-Columbia University Awards in Broadcasting Journalism dinner, surveyed the developing scene from his perspective as former president of CPB. He said the danger for public affairs programming was incipient from the time the Public Broadcasting Act was first passed and proponents failed to get into the law "adequate insulation of journalistic programming from the political interference of the public sponsor, the United States government."[52] In framing the Public Broadcasting Act, the concern was to insulate the stations from Congress. The framers

did not foresee interference from the executive branch of government.
The corporation established itself as a heat shield to insulate PBS
from political fire. And yet, subjects, judgments, interpretation,
and personnel selections came under fire from "special interests,
station representatives, and government spokesmen."[53] The Nixon
Administration began an all-out attack in 1971. "Well aware of the
potency of television, that leadership was unwilling to accept free
video journalism supported by Federal funds." Following the veto,
Nixon appointees took over control of the corporation and began to
question programs previously funded and to drop personalities offering unfavorable assessments of the administration and withdrawing
PBS programming responsibility on behalf of stations. To Macy, the
heat shield had been penetrated and public video badly burned.[54]

Buchanan, a White House assistant, appeared in March on the
"Dick Cavett Show," a late-night ABC television program, and talked
about public television. He said he helped draft the president's veto
message of the Public Television Act of 1972. Buchanan said the
White House staff compared the increased funding measure with
what it saw on public television. It saw Vanocur as "a notorious
Kennedy sycophant," MacNeil as a person "who is definitely anti-
Administration," Elizabeth Drew as "definitely not pro-Administration,"
"Washington Week in Review" as "unbalanced against us," "Black
Journal" as "unbalanced against us," "Bill Moyers' Journal" as
"unbalanced against us," and Buckley, a conservative commentator,
as "a figleaf." President Nixon vetoed the bill and, according to
Buchanan, "now you've got a different situation in public television."[55]

The board of directors of the CPB met in Washington and decided
not to fund public television programs perceived as "too controversial."
Consequently, the board dropped Buckley's "Firing Line," "Bill
Moyers' Journal," "Washington Week in Review," and "America '73."
The board noted that the corporation had been operating on only $35
million instead of the $45 million appropriated. Funds for the cor-
poration were included in an HEW-Labor Department appropriation
bill, which the president vetoed in a running battle with Congress
over government expenditures. Congress had thus far not passed
another bill, and so all the agencies covered in the bill were continued
by resolution at the same budgetary level as the 1972 fiscal year.
The directors asked for relief in the form of a special appropriation.
The board directed the officers to support legislation at upcoming
congressional hearings for two-year funding at the level of $60 million
for 1974 and $80 million for 1975. The body would not push for long-
range funding. Finally, the board voted to cooperate with a new
committee formed to revamp PBS.[56]

The new committee was the result of extraordinary efforts on
the part of Rogers, a Texas industrialist and chairman of the board

of KERA in Dallas. Alarmed at the shift in the balance of power
between PBS and CPB, convinced that the "lay" board chairmen,
representing the public in public television, were being ignored in
the struggle, and hopeful that he and other concerned chairmen could
help in settling the dispute and reestablish the momentum for public
broadcasting, Rogers organized the Coordinating Committee of Governing Board's of Public Television Stations, composed of chairmen of
boards of directors of public television stations in the United States
as a base of operations. The chairmen's committee then proposed
to combine with manager-dominated PBS and Educational Television
Stations (an arm of NAEB) to form one organization. The reorganization was mandated by the fact that neither the chairmen nor the
managers nor the educators could prevail alone against CPB and the
White House. To overcome the threat that jeopardized public broadcasting, a new power center was aggregated from those three entities
to negotiate from a position of strength with the corporation and speak
with a strong voice to the executive and legislative branches of the
government. The combined forces would operate the interconnection
and deliver a national program service. The stations, therefore,
would control access to the interconnection and provide programs
from corporation-funded sources and noncorporation funded sources.[57]

Formal merger took place on March 31. The new organization
called itself by the old name—PBS—but the structure was different.
Licenses elected two boards: the board of governors, composed of
15 lay members of boards of directors of public television stations,
directed the business functions, and the board of managers, composed
of 15 station managers of public television stations, served in an
advisory capacity. Even before formal amalgamation, negotiations
began with the corporation. The Ford Foundation, which had provided
public television with $250 million in funding, made it clear that un-
less the stations had control of programming and scheduling, it would
not support public television to the previous extent. Curtis, chief
negotiator for the corporation, did not believe his organization and
the emerging combination with Ford Foundation support were neces-
sarily on a collision course and opined that an accommodation could
be reached.[58]

At this juncture, Senator Pastore held hearings on a new bill to
extend the corporation for two years, with an authorization of $60
million for fiscal year 1974 and $80 million for fiscal year 1975,
and to extend the educational broadcasting facilities program for
four years, with authorization of $25 million each year.[59] Curtis,
of the corporation, Gunn, of PBS, and the rest of the public television
establishment in a display of unanimity despite the unsettled state of
their relationship supported the legislation in hearings held March 28-
30.

Senator Pastore deplored the president's vetoes of the bill to increase authorizations for the corporation for two years and the HEW appropriations bill, which included funds for the corporation. He said the "suffocation method of cutting down the authorization period and cutting down money that Congress had been willing to appropriate" seriously affected the ability to plan imaginatively and effectively. He quoted the Buchanan interview on commercial television and cited it as evidence of White House interference in public broadcasting. Senator Baker, recently seen as the White House spokesman on the committee, took note of the negotiations between CPB and PBS and hoped the process would result in a new relationship with local stations.60

Curtis described reductions in program plans resulting from reduced expectations in funding and pleaded for more operating funds and more facilities funds so that local stations would be less dependent on the interconnection. He expressed confidence that the current negotiations with PBS would result in a new system to get local opinion on choices and declared that the negotiating parties had about reached an agreement. Killian summed up the board's frustration succinctly when he declared that the prime enemies of localism were one-year appropriations and inadequate funds. Robert S. Benjamin, also a member of the board of directors, described the Buchanan broadcast as an outrage and urged that attention be given to the children's programs and public health programs, on which the corporation was spending $13 million and $1 million respectively that year, as well as the public affairs programs.

Loomis, corporation president, defended actions to reduce the grant to WETA for public affairs programming from $1.2 million to $800,000 and the decision to fund individual programs rather than provide a lump sum as necessitated from a lack of funds rather than for the purpose of censorship. He was justly proud of advances in public radio. In 1969, only 25 stations provided a full broadcast service, while another 73 were offering minimum level service. In 1973, however, 75 stations were providing full service and 145 minimum service.

Burch, representing the FCC, again gave his full support to the legislation. Harley, of the NAEB, believed that the controversy between CPB and PBS over a centrally controlled or station-controlled interconnection and program service would be worked out agreeably in a short time. Rogers echoed these beliefs in his testimony. Rogers said the differences between the local stations and the corporation were basically due to the insufficiency of funds at the national level and that more funds and more diversity would result in less difficulties and less differences.

Whitehead's testimony was pretty much a carbon copy of previous testimony. He claimed that programming over PBS had become a fourth network. "Such a monolithic approach to public broadcasting," he said, "is inimical to the letter and spirit of the Public Broadcasting Act." He recommended doing away with interconnection and the "centralized bureaucracy between stations and CPB," meaning PBS.[61] In regard to public affairs, he declared that "reliance on federal monies to support public affairs programming is inappropriate and potentially dangerous." Until the basic problems with public broadcasting were resolved, the administration would recommend annual appropriations and limited increases in funding. The administration recommended an appropriation of $45 million for 1974. This was an increase of $10 million over the amount CPB would actually receive in 1973 but no increase in the authorization.

In summing up the hearings and making its report to the Senate, the committee agreed that local stations were indeed the bedrock of the system and that, within its resources, the corporation was making every effort to aid the development of those stations. The committee declared that public television was not a fourth network in the sense of a commercial broadcasting network and affirmed that public affairs broadcasting was appropriate for public television so long as it was objective and fair. It expressed satisfaction with the mix of local and national programming, but warned that without color videotape recording equipment made possible by larger appropriations for public broadcasting facilities, the local stations could not have their own schedules. In a peroration, the committee declared:

> Government intrusion into the medium has no more place
> than biased public affairs programming. Whether it is
> the bludgeon of patently inadequate funding or subtle
> innuendoes of government officials, the results are the
> same: A chilling effect on the open and robust exchange
> of ideas, and a diminution of the very special service
> public broadcasting brings to over 40 million people.[62]

The committee passed on to the full Senate a bill authorizing an appropriation to the corporation of $55 million, plus $5 million for matching in fiscal year 1974, and $75 million, plus $5 million for matching in 1975. For educational broadcasting facilities, the committee voted to authorize an appropriation of $25 million in each of the 1974, 1975, 1976, and 1977 fiscal years. The Pastore committee had proved once again its commitment to public broadcasting and had demonstrated that the bipartisan support for this activity had been welded together again despite what seemed to many to be the willingness of the White House to use partisan efforts to undermine it.

Other Senate and House committee supporters of public broadcasting were the appropriations committees and their subcommittees on appropriations for the Department of Labor and the Department of Health, Education and Welfare and related agencies. CPB was a "related agency" and warranted a separate section of the bill, while the facilities program was buried, along with hundreds of other programs, in the HEW portion. Several times, and the spring of 1973 was another example,[63] the committees scheduled testimony on funds for public broadcasting, even though no authorization had yet been voted. Representative Flood summed up the attitude, when he said simply, "this subcommittee has always evidenced special interest in public broadcasting since it was created."[64] Committee members regularly voted appropriations equal to the authorizations for CPB. They had difficulty convincing HEW that it should request appropriations equal to the authorizations for educational broadcasting facilities and consistently appropriated more money than HEW requested but less than the authorization.

The budget procedure in HEW, as it affected the facilities program, was for the secretary's office to gather requests for money from the various divisions of the department and to review and consolidate these into a request to the White House, where the request was to be analyzed and fit into the overall administration budget. The White House, through the Office of Management and Budget, would approve a figure for the department and for specific programs. The departments generally asked for more money than was available, and cuts were made in programs to which the administration gave low priorities.

There were at least three other reasons why HEW requested less than was authorized. Responsibility for the program was shifted several times within divisions of the department. Consequently, with each change, new people had to become acquainted with it and convinced of the value of trying for full funding. HEW was philosophically more interested in software—the development of actual television programs, such as "Sesame Street"—than hardware—the construction of facilities and the acquisition of equipment. HEW officials were also convinced that public broadcasting coverage had been extended to the ultimate practical limits. Public television coverage reached 80 percent of the American people and public radio reached 68 percent, and HEW felt it inexpedient to try to obtain 100 percent coverage because of the high cost involved in trying to extend reception to the rest of the population, which was widely scattered in remote areas.

As previously stated, the appropriations committee provided more funds than HEW (as directed by OMB) requested but less than Congress authorized. For example, in fiscal year 1971, Congress authorized an appropriation of $15 million; the administration requested $4 million; and Congress appropriated $11 million. For fiscal year 1972, Congress authorized $15 million; the administration again requested $4 million; and Congress appropriated $13 million. And finally, for fiscal year 1973, Congress authorized $25 million; the administration requested $4 million; and Congress appropriated $15 million in an omnibus bill that was vetoed as too expensive and cut to $13 million in the final version.[65]

At stake in this exercise in requesting receiving funds were new stations, higher towers, color cameras, and videotape equipment—all vitally needed to provide increased coverage, better reception, and more choice at the local level in programs and schedules.

As these vital hearings concluded, negotiations between PBS and CPB concluded also. Curtis took the pact to his board of directors, believing he had their backing for a compromise agreement that would adjust the relationship between CPB and the stations represented by PBS and end the impasse between them. The agreement would give the corporation greater control over the selection of programs to be aired on the interconnection but not as much as it claimed in January. PBS would be allowed to transmit programs, including politically sensitive public affairs programs, produced without corporation funds.

On April 13, 1973, the board of directors voted 10 to 4 to defer action, appoint a new committee, and conduct further meetings with PBS.[66] Curtis was thunderstruck, and when he learned that a representative of the administration had telephoned four members of the board before the vote, he suspected White House interference in the independence of the board and promptly resigned. Flanigan, assistant to the president, was later identified as the member of the White House staff who made telephone calls to members of the board.[67]

Rogers, chief discussant for PBS, was quite disappointed and suggested that improper political influence had been exerted on CPB board members by Whitehead. Rogers said that he, Curtis, and others had worked for three months to reach an agreement and then something happened. "I suspect it was Mr. Whitehead who happened," he said. The White House acknowledged that Whitehead had been in touch with board members "in a continuing way" but denied that he "tried to coerce anyone."[68]

In an interview with the New York Times, Curtis said he understood it was the intent of Congress and Nixon that the corporation was to be set up in such a way that it would never be a propaganda arm of the administration. Yet, the conservative Republican from Missouri charged, the White House interfered, contrary to what he had understood to be explicit guarantees. The White House, he revealed, "constantly talks to members of the board, calling them privately and interfering with the process" of deliberation. He urged the board to reassert its independence and integrity.[69]

Following these startling developments, the Senate, on May 7, took up Senate Bill 1090 to extend the corporation for two years, authorized $55 million, plus $5 million in matching funds, for fiscal year 1974 and $75 million, plus $5 million, for fiscal year 1975. The bill also authorized $25 million for educational broadcasting facilities in fiscal year 1974 and each succeeding three years. To assure compliance with the requirement that all sides of a controversy receive fair treatment, the bill required stations to make and retain for 60 days audio recording of "programs of public importance," meaning public affairs. Senator Pastore related that corporation officials and all concerned agreed one year was not enough and said he thought two years was a reasonable median between those who wanted one year (the administration) and those who wanted more. Senator Baker talked about the unhealthy influence of the Ford Foundation's withholding its funding awards until after the CPB-PBS negotiations were complete. He urged HEW to give greater priority to purchasing tape equipment, so that more than the current 25 percent could tape and store programs for viewing. He asked that the authorization for 1975 be reduced from $75 million to $65 million and, in a prearranged move, Senator Pastore accepted the amendment without a vote in the spirit of compromise and in an effort to guarantee there would be no administration veto if he acceded to a request from the Republican leadership in the Senate. Senator Jesse Helms, a conservative Republican from North Carolina, moved to amend the bill to provide for a one-year extension with $50 million authorized, as Whitehead had mentioned, but this effort was defeated 62 votes to 12. Quoting Buchanan's remarks on the telecast with Dick Cavett and noting Curtis's resignation, Senator Philip Hart lamented the lack of independence of the board of directors of CPB. After Senators Magnuson and James B. Pearson offered their strong support for the bill and the independence of the board, the Senate passed the measure 66 to 6.[70]

The board wanted desperately to prove its independence of the White House and gave strong assurances to Killian that it would be so when it elected him chairman of its board on May 9. Killian, a figure of strength and integrity and widely recognized as the progenitor of public broadcasting since the publication of the Carnegie Report, accepted the post on several conditions. He insisted that negotiations with PBS be speedily completed, that long-range funding plans be disinterred and given new life in order to remove the corporation activities from the political hazards of annual appropriations, that local stations be strengthened with autonomy and independence, and that public affairs be reaffirmed as an essential responsibility of public broadcasting. The board provided assurance on all points, and negotiations were renewed in earnest.[71]

Killian, in an interview with the New York Times, commented
on the board's renewed determination to operate independently of
the administration. He pointed out that the Watergate scandals,
which were rocking the country, had resulted in diminished antagon-
ism toward the press on the part of the Nixon Administration. He
felt that this apparent aftermath of Watergate would help assure that
public broadcasting would not be interfered with. Killian declared,
"I think we may have gone through a period where there will be a
new affirmation, a new understanding, that this board is going to be
free of political control."[72]

In two weeks, the negotiating committee for PBS and CPB,
essentially Killian and Rogers, hammered out an agreement that
both parent groups speedily approved. The following points were
agreed to. CPB would provide production funds for programs it
considered appropriate. CPB would pay PBS only for costs of interconnection. PBS would interconnect whatever programs it chose to
distribute, including those produced from funds other than the corporation's. PBS and CPB would both agree on a yearly schedule, which
PBS would draw up. Questions of balance and objectivity would be
settled by a monitoring committee of three representatives from
each organization, and it would take four votes to disconnect a program. Both reaffirmed that public affairs programming was an essential responsibility of public television. Both would work together for
long-range funding.[73]

The agreement was met with satisfaction and relief and a feeling
that peace had been restored. Killian described the pact as "a partnership to broaden the base, strengthen the independence and quicken
the promise of public television." Rogers felt that the five months
of negotiations might have been the most productive months in public
broadcasting. Meeting with the ACNO, Loomis said he had talked
to Whitehead concerning the merits of the compromise and had assured
him that it went a long way toward the desire to decentralize public
broadcasting.[74]

It was with a great deal of relief and unfeigned enthusiasm that
spokesmen for public broadcasting testified before Macdonald's
Subcommittee on Commerce and Power regarding proposed legislation
to extend the corporation and authorize funds for two years.[75] Macdonald reviewed happenings of the previous year and expressed satisfaction that an agreement had been signed. Killian, too, expressed
satisfaction that the board had declared its intention to be independent
and paid tribute to Representative Macdonald for significant efforts
in bringing the corporation and PBS together in an agreement. He
reported that the board had taken the initiative and established a
committee chaired by board member Joseph Hughes to draw up funding
plans and hinted that an ingenious matching plan was under considera-

tion. In his testimony, Loomis described the industry as having worked itself together again. Rogers received a warm welcome because of his work in organizing the local stations for a more prominent role in public broadcasting. It was his opinion that the new agreement provided for a significant degree of localism, and he hoped the president would recognize this and support legislation for more than one year funding.

OTP's Whitehead testified that while "real progress" had been made toward providing for decentralization, it would still take time to see how the arrangement worked out. "Until there is wholehearted compliance," he said, "with the policies of the 1967 act and the future directions for public broadcasting are clear, Congress should not be expected to adopt a plan of long range insulated funding." Unresolved "is the question of journalistic public affairs programming on a taxpayer-supported broadcasting system." He urged the adoption of funding one year at a time to allow for a period of waiting and watching. He was also opposed to the amounts of money being considered.[76]

The threat of another veto hung in the air of the committee room. Whitehead would give no assurance that Nixon would not veto another two-year bill, but he did say "the reasons are less than they were a year ago." Congressman Van Deerlin was impatient. He told Whitehead that if PBS, with its great concern for localism, was satisfied, and if CPB, with a majority of Nixon appointees, was satisfied, and if Congress passed a modest funding increase for two years, he could not conceive of how the president could be dissatisfied or justify a veto.[77]

The last two days of the mid-June hearings featured reports on the Ford Foundation, the educational broadcasting facilities program, and substantial advances in public radio.

Ford Foundation President McGeorge Bundy talked about the foundation's role in television over the years and explained its position regarding access to the interconnection. Ford began making grants in the 1950s to commercial television for outstanding programs, such as "Omnibus." In the 1960s, it began making grants to noncommercial television. It gave about $6 million a year to NET for quality, high-cost programming. The foundation supported the work of the Carnegie Commission and helped establish low-cost interconnection. It measured its actions and funding to the stated needs of CPB and the licensees, primarily in funding a number of production centers. The foundation consistently gave its support to long-range funding and backed the agreement between CPB and PBS. Bundy noted the criticism received for withholding financial backing for public television until after an agreement had been reached as to whether nonfederally funded programs at production centers would have access to the interconnection. He explained that the foundation could not make grants for programs unless there was some certainty that the program would be distributed. He emphasized that the foundation supported the production centers, not specific programs or series.

Commissioner of Education designate John R. Ottina reviewed the awarding of 429 grants, totaling $77 million, since the educational broadcasting facilities program had begun. He noted with satisfaction that the programming had helped make it possible for 79 percent of the American people to receive public television and 65 percent to receive public radio. In his opinion, the task of assisting in the construction of noncommercial educational broadcasting facilities was almost completed, and the primary task for the future was to expand existing facilities and provide equipment. Ottina observed that 70 percent of the funds provided in the previous two years were for that purpose. He urged the committee to consider legislation that would provide funds to explore new technologies and their application to education and broadcasting. He spoke also about HEW's interest and role in funding educational programs, primarily in the areas of early childhood education, including the two highly regarded programs "Sesame Street" and "Electric Company."

Public radio received considerable attention from Hugh V. Cordier, chairman of the Association of Public Radio Stations, an outgrowth of a reorganization of NAEB, and Richard Estell, chairman of National Public Radio, the programming agency for the public radio service. Before passage of the Public Broadcasting Act, noncommercial radio was a training ground for future broadcasters, and an aid to formal instruction in radio broadcasting. Very few stations provided a radio service to the public. Afterwards, however, public radio received a new mission and began broadcasting a strong national program service with new stations, new audiences, and new staff with greater competence. Full-time stations increased from 73 to 143, audience potential expanded from 72 to 137 million, and broadcasting time increased 300 percent. Matching grants from the educational broadcasting facilities program were a key factor in this growth. HEW grants made it possible to establish 36 new stations and expand or bring up to standards 56 others. Educational radio, it was explained, was not just a companion but an educator and stimulator of new ideas as well. Because public radio was almost exclusively FM, spokesmen asked the legislators to begin considering regulations that would require makers to manufacture only sets which received both AM and FM stations. Congress had previously passed legislation requiring manufacturers of television receivers to produce sets that received both VHF and UHF.

ACNO, representing 35 organizations, testified on behalf of public broadcasting, and Representative Macdonald urged other

national organizations to affiliate with the group. A spokesman for
National Friends of Public Broadcasting also testified favoring the
pending legislation. This new organization represented primarily
women volunteers who raised money for local stations through auc-
tions and other types of fund drives.

When the Commerce Committee met to consider the legislation,
the Democratic members favored the Senate bill, authorizing a total
of $230 million ($60 million in 1974 and $70 million in 1975 for CPB
and $25 million in 1974, 1975, 1976, and 1977 for facilities), while
the Republican members favored $175 million ($55 million in 1974
and $65 million in 1975 for the corporation and $25 million in 1974
and $30 million in 1975 for facilities). The Democrats accepted
the Republican version to avoid another veto.

The committee's report to the House[78] stressed the need for
planning time in explaining why a two-year authorization was appropriate. The report said it took time to develop series of original,
quality programs for the aged and the consumer and regarding nutri-
tion and public health. Strong local programming needed to be based
on a predictable level of grants. High-quality facilities and talent
go to waste, the report cautioned, without adequate planning. The
government process was a handicap to public broadcasting. The
annual authorization process and the corporation's funding tied to
the annual labor-HEW appropriations bill meant that the corporation
did not receive its funding until well into the fiscal year. This wasteful and unnecessary handicap would be eliminated by two-year and
longer funding.

Public television in the meanwhile was enjoying phenomenal
success. Viewers doubled in New York and other major cities and
public contributions soared. Public television was airing the most
successful public affairs shows in its history. It was providing
gavel-to-gavel coverage of the hearings before the Senate Watergate
Committee. NPACT videotaped the hearings during the daytime
and showed them in the evening, complete with summaries and
commentaries, over the interconnection through 234 local stations.[79]
Public broadcasters could but savor the irony of their success at
the expense of the administration that had sought to cripple its public
affairs broadcasting.

When the bill reached the House floor on July 20, 1973, members
of the House of Representatives were in an optimistic mood about
public broadcasting. The veto of the authorization bill and the subsequent resignation of Macy and Pace, the dissension between CPB
and PBS and the resignation of Curtis, and the veto of the appropriation bill were in the past. Now CPB and PBS had reached agreement,
the corporation promised a long-range funding proposal later in the
year, substantial portions of the federal funds would be going to local

stations as a result of the truce, Vanocur and his $85,000 salary had
been sacrificed, public broadcasting had public confidence, and the
authorization for two more years at increased rates had solid bipartisan support. The House passed the measure 363 to 14.[80] Credit
for these developments and the renewed spirit of courage and optimism
was due in large measure to Killian, Macdonald, Rogers, and Pastore.

The Senate agreed to the House version by voice vote in less
than a week.[81] President Nixon signed the measure into law.[82]
It was a major victory for public broadcasting, and other encouraging
events followed.

Senator Weicker, a member of the Watergate Committee, re-
leased documents that showed how the White House staff engaged in
an orchestrated effort to pressure television into taking a sympathetic
view of Nixon. A memorandum from Colson, White House special
counsel, to H. R. Haldeman, chief of staff, dated September 25,
1970, said network officials are "very much afraid of us" and anxious
"to prove they are 'good guys'." Other memoranda spoke of efforts
to "get the networks" and use the Internal Revenue Service, Justice
Department, FCC, and other federal agencies against them.[83] These
documents confirmed what public broadcasters believed to be the
source and reason for their torment. After the documents became
public, government offices became defensive and wary of new actions.

The power of the OTP receded in proportion to Watergate's
diminution of presidential power. Senator Weicker and his fellow
senator from Connecticut, Abraham Ribicoff, introduced legislation
to dissolve the office. Representative Macdonald noted that OTP
was created in February 1970, when presidential aides were working
on their media strategy and four weeks after Vice President Agnew
led off an attack on the press from Des Moines, Iowa. Macdonald
said OTP never entered into any discussions of policy with Congress
as promised but "did enable the executive branch to speak with a
harsher voice."[84] He supported the Weicker-Ribicoff bill and said,
"If the bill becomes law, the Nixon administration may have learned
one more lesson: the instruments of government are not to be used
for political purposes."[85] Whitehead made no more significant
speeches and dropped from prominence. At the end of the year, he
announced he would resign but that he would first complete work on
several reports and recommendations, including the long-range
funding of public broadcasting.[86]

The resignation of two FCC commissioners, not connected in
any way with Watergate, affected public broadcasting. H. Rex Lee
resigned after serving five years of his seven-year term "to try
something new." His public speeches and public service had been
largely devoted to the support of educational television. Johnson,
a consumer advocate and thorn in the side to the Nixon Administration,

resigned just before his appointment expired to fight the nomination
of the person the president named to replace him. Johnson then
reorganized, and became chairman of, the National Citizens Committee on Broadcasting, which had not been active since 1969. The
organization hoped to restore its leadership in the broadcast consumer movement and play an active role in support of public broadcasting.[87]

When President Nixon, on December 19, signed a Labor
Department-HEW appropriation bill, including $50 million for the
corporation, for fiscal year 1974, CPB received the first increase
in funding since receiving $35 million in fiscal year 1972. The
corporation had been severely restricted in its already limited
operating funds by being caught, through no fault of its own, in a
struggle between the executive branch and the legislative branch
over federal spending. Nixon had vetoed the appropriation bill for
fiscal year 1973, in which the corporation was to receive $45 million.
Congress could not override the veto and enacted continuing resolutions to provide funds to all the programs in the Labor-HEW-related
agencies appropriations bill at the current rate—including $35 million
for CPB. Congress passed additional continuing resolutions at the
beginning of fiscal year 1974 in the extended battle with the White
House, with the result that the corporation received money at the
rate of $35 million for the first half of the fiscal year. The increase
of $15 million for the remainder of the year was earmarked for dis-
tribution almost entirely to the 400 local public television and radio
stations. President Nixon was said to be anxious to end the dispute
with Congress and the uncertainty of federal agencies about funding.
This apparently was not the case, however, because at the president's
direction, OMB proceeded to hold back or impound millions of dollars
of appropriated funds, including $2,250,000 from CPB. Lawsuits
challenging the president's right to withhold funds from other programs had been won in federal court, but the president had appealed.
In the meantime, the corporation did not receive all the funds to
which it was entitled, and the local stations, for which the administration was so concerned, did not receive the amount of money on which
they had planned.[88]

At their annual meeting in Washington, D.C., in January 1974,
operators of public television stations established the "marketplace
cooperative" as a democratic means of creating a program schedule
for the interconnection. PBS would no longer decide what programs
were produced and scheduled; PBS would administer the corporation
and distribute programs bought and sold to each other through the
marketplace cooperative. Buying and selling was the key to the
system. Sellers would prepare prospectuses for the programs they
wished to produce. Buyers would use local funds and operating grant

funds distributed from CPB to purchase. If enough buyers put up
enough money to cover the costs of production, a seller would produce a program, and it would be transmitted to the buyers through
the interconnection.

Loomis described the system as "an entirely new ball game,
very different from what we've ever had before in this country, in
that it puts the entire program responsibility squarely with the licensed
stations, localizing the system. The station that selects poorly, that
does not program according to the needs of the community, will have
to answer to its own public for it."[89]

The first time the marketplace cooperative was used, it took
five months to make the final selections. In February, 100 programs
were offered for sale, at a total cost of $41 million. The stations
had $13.5 million to spend ($9.4 million in grants from the Ford
Foundation and CPB and $4.1 million from themselves). The stations
first chose children's programs, including "Sesame Street," "Electric Company," "Misterogers Neighborhood," and "Zoom." Following
the principle of buying as much as possible and spending as little as
possible, the stations chose next those programs with low budgets
or highly subsidized from other sources. They preferred cheap,
proven programs to expensive, experimental ones. After six rounds
of trading, 153 licensees, controlling 246 stations, bought 26
programs—4 children's, 11 public affairs, and 11 cultural. These
programs represented about 25 percent of the schedule. The remainder were locally produced or major series in prime time evening
hours completely underwritten by foundations, private industry, or
federal agencies, such as the CPB, National Endowment for the
Humanities (NEH), or National Endowment for the Arts (NEA), or a
combination of these sources. Although thought cumbersome by
some and conducive to pedestrian programming by others, the
marketplace cooperative seemed to work well administratively and
to allow a measure of decision making hitherto not enjoyed at the
local level.[90]

Programming was discussed extensively in 1974 when Walter
Bogan, head of the educational broadcasting facilities program in
HEW, testified to the House appropriations subcommittee for the
Department of Labor and HEW.[91] Representative Flood again emphasized his committee's intense interest in public broadcasting and
wanted to know why HEW was proposing to cut the appropriation for
facilities from $15.7 million in 1974 to $7 million in 1975 and increase
the appropriation for programs from $3 million to $7 million in the
same years. Bogan explained that the department believed that the
most pressing need was in the area of programming and that technology
such as a domestic satellite and cable rather than traditional broadcast technology would be necessary to reach the department's goal of

providing public broadcasting to 100 percent of the American people by 1980. At the expiration of the current enabling legislation, the department would propose a much broader authorization, to provide funds to engage in study and application of advanced telecommunications technology to public broadcasting. While arguing that these needs existed, the committee thought it significant that in 1972/73, the department had received 161 applications for $36.1 million for the existing program and that the department had made only 78 grants for $13 million. The committee did not receive an answer as to why HEW was not requesting funds to the limit of the authorization when there seemed to be a backlog of need.

HEW, with its larger contributions to the Children's Television Workshop for the production of "Sesame Street" and "Electric Company," was but one of several federal agencies providing funds for public broadcasting programs. The NEH and the NEA were substantial underwriters as well. The budget of the NEH had grown from $2 million in the first year of its funding in 1966 to $40 million in 1973. Ronald S. Berman, chairman of the endowment, said public television had been the most successful means of bringing the humanities to the population at large. From the endowment's standpoint, it was an "extremely efficient use of public funds." Humanities Film Forum, a series of classic films followed by discussions and sponsored by NEH, had the fourth-largest audience on public television. The endowment shared the cost of other series with the Mobil Oil Corporation. In 1974, the endowment announced its largest grant to public television for a single series—$4 million to produce the "Adams Chronicles." Of the sum, $2.5 million was from appropriated funds and $1.5 million was from matching funds to complement a grant from the Mellon Foundation.[92] The NEA joined with the Ford Foundation and CPB in 1974 to create a new body of American literature through television. The New American Television Drama Project was created to produce 12 original plays for television the first year, 24 the second, and would seek funds to continue indefinitely. The plays would be produced at a number of stations, but chiefly at KCET in Los Angeles.[93]

The FCC's allowing underwriters of public television programs to receive a presentor's credit fostered an increase in the number of grants from private industry. Before and after each program sponsored by a corporation or foundation, a slide with the name of the underwriter was shown and a voice saying "Made possible by a grant from . . . " was heard. In 1974, petroleum companies, such as Exxon, Atlantic-Richfield, and Mobil, were substantial backers of public television programs reaching influential audiences in evening hours. They often bought newspaper advertising for programs they underwrote.[94]

In announcing that the Ford Foundation was withdrawing its
support of public television over a four- to five-year period, David
M. Davis, the foundation's program officer for public broadcasting,
said, "The business of a foundation is to try to start new things in
the high risk business. No foundation is doing its job if it stays with
one project forever." The foundation had given more than $200 million
to public broadcasting since 1951, and it was a measure of the maturity
and growth in public television that the Ford Foundation felt comfortable
in gradually withdrawing its support from a medium it had nurtured
so successfully. Six years before, the foundation provided 20 percent of the funds to support the industry; in 1974, the foundation
provided 5 percent of the funds, but it was the same amount of money.
The farewell grants of $40 million would bring the total funding to
$285 million. The grants were intended to build up private support
through matching, to fund such mechanisms as the "marketplace
cooperative" and PBS, to insulate the system from the federal government, and to strengthen principal production centers at WNET, KCET,
WGBH, and WETA.[95]

The general public was also an important contributor to public
broadcasting. The subscription fund drive was an important aspect
of each station's annual activities. A 1974 survey of such drives
showed increases over 1973, when the Watergate hearings opened a
flood of contributions. This was most encouraging to local stations,
who had thought the contributions in the previous years had been anti-
Nixon rather than propublic television. More than 1 million families
contributed an average of $20. With financial assistance from the
Ford Foundation and administrative assistance from PBS, the Stations
Independence Program was launched in an attempt to triple the number of supporters in three years. This effort would be important in
trying to make the stations more self-reliant and would prove a
significant source of income in matching federal dollars in a long-
range funding scheme being discussed (and given a good chance of
passage after the collapse of presidential power as an aftermath of
Watergate).[96]

The fundamental components to be included in permanent-funding
legislation grew out of recommendations of CPB's Task Force on
Long-Range Funding of Public Broadcasting. The idea of a task force
was first endorsed by CPB in April 1972, and subsequently endorsed
by PBS, NPR, and ETS. A task force of 19 professionally competent
members and administrators broadly representative of the public
broadcasting industry was selected in May, June, and July and held
its first meeting in August. In the spring of 1973, a nine-member
group began to design a five-year plan, based on the discussions of
the larger body, and issued a report at the end of the year. The
report[97] contained six fundamental principles.

1. Federal support of public broadcasting from general tax revenues should be authorized by Congress for a period of no less than five years, and a schedule of appropriations for the same period of time should be made part of the authorization.

2. The level of federal support in any fiscal year should match nonfederal support for public broadcasting activities for the second preceding fiscal year on a one to two ratio up to reasonable, established ceilings. Appropriation ceilings would be $100 million in 1975, $125 million in 1976, $150 million in 1977, $175 million in 1978, and $200 million in 1979.

3. Federal support available for any fiscal year should remain available throughout succeeding fiscal years until expended.

4. The distribution of matching funds should be made by CPB in accordance with procedures promulgated by the corporation and agreed upon by representatives of noncommercial educational radio and television licensees.

5. Beyond the funds provided in the matching plan, federal funds for broadcasting facilities should be provided by Congress. Appropriation levels would be $40 million in 1975, $45 million in 1976, $50 million in 1977, $55 million in 1978, and $60 million in 1979.

6. Operations and facilities funds should be available for disbursement at the beginning of each fiscal year.[98]

Using the task force report as a base, OTP drafted legislation and sent it to the White House. The draft legislation followed the task force report closely, except that it provided for less money, required more nonfederal dollars in the matching formula, and left out the facilities program. The proposal provided for five-year funding in graduated increments from $10 million in 1976 to $100 million in 1980 and required $2.5 in nonfederal contributions to acquire $1 in federal funds. It required that federal funds be distributed to local stations, production centers, and radio and television interconnections.

Whitehead apparently felt satisfied that the changes in public broadcasting called for in his October 21, 1971, speech to the NAEB in Miami had been made and the time for long-range funding had come, as he had promised. After all, Nixon had appointed the president of CPB and a majority of the members of the board of directors, PBS had been reduced to a distribution mechanism, local stations were determining the national schedule by ballot, more money was being distributed to local stations, liberal commentators were off the air and conservatives had been added for balance, the number of public affairs programs had been reduced, and program production had been decentralized from the New York–Washington axis.

The draft legislation lay unattended at the White House for two
months. Before leaving the country for a Middle Eastern trip in
June, the president rejected the legislation in a four-line memorandum
to Whitehead. The rejection was attributed to public television's
broadcasting the Senate Watergate hearings in prime time and their
announced intention to carry any impeachment hearings if the president came to trial.[99]

Senator Magnuson was unhappy with the turn of events. He suggested that Congress ought to take the initiative on the legislation
and let the administration endorse what Congress was doing or send
suggestions. Senator Pastore and Representative Macdonald agreed.
On June 25, Magnuson wrote to the president, giving him one last
chance:

> I have been deeply disturbed about the various reports
> to the effect that you have rejected and will not submit
> long range funding legislation for public broadcasting.
> I hope this is not so. If there is to be meaningful action
> in the current Congress, such legislation should be sub-
> mitted in the next 30 days. In the event you are not going
> to submit legislation relating to the long range financing
> of public broadcasting, I would appreciate it if you would
> let me know so that I can take appropriate legislative
> steps.[100]

Whitehead wrote a "strong letter of appeal," and Alexander M.
Haig, Jr., White House chief of staff, and other aides urged the
president to reconsider, arguing that the president's action might
seem vindictive. President Nixon relented and announced in July
he would support long-range funding legislation drawn up by OTP.[101]

LONG-RANGE FUNDING OF PUBLIC
BROADCASTING

In a letter dated July 16, 1974, accompanying the draft legislation,
Whitehead said the problems in public broadcasting had been solved
and the industry was ready for long-range funding. He endorsed the
matching fund principle because it would "assure that federal assistance does not become a dominant force in the system" and provides
incentives to increase nonfederal support. He endorsed the principle
of five-year funding, because it would enable the corporation and
local stations to undertake advance program planning with assurance
as to the level of federal funding available in the foreseeable future.
The legislation if enacted would enhance the commitment to localism

through a distribution of 40 to 50 percent of federal funds on a sliding
scale to local stations. Each television station and each eligible
radio station would receive a basic grant, and the rest of the money
would be used for programming, facilities, and the procurement of
interconnection services. The corporation would be fully accountable,
because officials would be available for annual oversight hearings
and because the Government Accounting Office would audit the financial records. The legislation would permit the use of cable and
satellite technology to disseminate educational radio and television
programming.[102]

Specifically, the proposed legislation provided that there be
established in the Treasury a Public Broadcasting Fund administered
by the secretary of the Treasury. To the fund, Congress would
appropriate for each of the fiscal years 1976 to 1980 an amount equal
to 40 percent ($1 for each $2.50) of the amount of nonfederal support
received by all public broadcasting entities during the fiscal year
second preceding provided the sum did not exceed $70 million for
1976, $80 million for 1977, $90 million for 1978, $95 million for
1979, and $100 million for 1980. The corporation would provide to
local stations 40 percent of the money when the amount was between
$70 million and $90 million, 45 percent when the amount was between
$90 million and $100 million, and 50 percent when the amount was
$100 million.

In a preamble to the proposed Public Broadcasting Financing Act
of 1974, it was declared to be the policy of the federal government:

1. that it is in the public interest to encourage the growth and
development of noncommercial educational radio and television
broadcasting, including the use of such media for instructional purposes.

2. that expansion and development of noncommercial educational
radio and television broadcasting and of diversity of its programming
depend on freedom, imagination, and initiative on both the local and
national levels.

3. that the encouragement and support of noncommercial educational radio and television broadcasting, while matters of importance
for private and local development, are also of appropriate and important concern to federal government.

4. that it furthers the general welfare to encourage noncommercial educational radio and television broadcasting programming which
will be responsive to the interests of the people, both in particular
localities and throughout the United States, and which will constitute
an expression of diversity and excellence.

5. that it is necessary and appropriate for the federal government to complement, assist, and support a national policy that will

most effectively make noncommercial radio and television services
available to all the citizens of the United States.

6. that a private corporation should be created to facilitate the
development of educational radio and television broadcasting and to
afford maximum protection to such broadcasting from extraneous
interference and control.[103]

It was a declaration of independence, a declaration of rights; it
was the most comprehensive statement of federal policy toward public
broadcasting ever written.

Senator Pastore wasted no time scheduling hearings[104] before
his Subcommittee on Communications. He assured the gathering of
public broadcasting representatives, on August 6, 1974, that he
favored the legislation but warned them the bill would face difficulties
in the House of Representatives. The other legislative body, he
pointed out, was reluctant to appropriate beyond one year. Representatives had a tenure of one or two years when any particular
appropriation bill passed, and they had a tradition of not telling future
Congresses what to do. It would be difficult legislation to put over,
but he declared his willingness to try.

Republican spokesman Baker said his concerns about the relationship between the corporation and the local stations had been substantially met with the adoption of the partnership agreement, the
establishment of the National Station Cooperative ("marketplace
cooperative"), and the promise of enlarged local grants. He con-
gratulated Whitehead for his role in bringing the legislation to the
committee.

Whitehead basked in the unaccustomed glow of committee
approval. He urged adoption of the legislation drafted by OTP's
general counsel, Henry Goldberg, as establishing the principle of
local station autonomy from centralized control and insulation of
programming from government control arising from the use of federal
funds. He explained that the Carnegie Commission's recommendations that financing be completely free of the budgetary process was
unacceptable to Lyndon B. Johnson, the committees of Congress,
and the OTP on the grounds that Congress had an inescapable responsibility to hold recipients of tax dollars accountable for their use.
Annual appropriations were just as unacceptable as a permanent
basis for funding because there was insufficient insulation between
the budgetary/appropriation process and sensitive programming
judgments. Multiyear appropriation struck a sensible balance.
Both the executive and legislative branches had to give up some
control of the public broadcasting purse strings and had to trust the
people who ran the local stations.

Senator Pastore lauded Killian, introducing him as a "great advocate of the concept of public broadcasting and a forceful protagonist in getting the job done." Killian saw the pending bill as the "remaining legislative stone in the structure of public broadcasting." He introduced Joseph D. Hughes as the chairman of the corporation's task force and architect of the compromise. He praised Hughes for assembling representatives of all segments of the industry, welding them together, bringing them to consensus, and producing in 14 months a report representing the best judgment of the whole system.[105]

Hughes expressed satisfaction with the legislation but pointed out that his task force plan called for more money; he also addressed the need for more equipment. He said the ceilings in the bill provided no incentives, since the industry had already reached the prescribed mark for nonfederal contributions. Senator Pastore realized the need for more money and said he would fight to raise the limit if possible. The matter of educational broadcasting facilities and equipment would be handled in separate legislation.

Twenty witnesses representing the administration, Congress, FCC, CPB, PBS, NPR, and the Association of Public Radio Stations (the 107 stations eligible for corporation support) testified for the legislation. They stressed the need of long-range funding for planning, insulation, and incentive.

The Commerce Committee reported the bill to the Senate on August 20 with unanimous support, saying "it goes as far as legislation can go in insulating public broadcasting against government interference and providing it with financial stability." The committee raised the authorization to provide more adequate funding levels and to provide incentives for matching. The report stated "the commitment to public broadcasting for long range funding is long overdue and the listening and viewing public has suffered as a consequence."[106]

Senator Magnuson, at the request of HEW and with the approval of the president, introduced a bill[107] to extend the educational broadcasting facilities program for five years and to authorize such funds as needed, estimated to be $35 million. Called the Telecommunications Facilities Act, the bill also authorized demonstrations of health, education, and social services programs transmitted by cable and domestic satellite.

Neither of these bills received further notice, as the attention of Congress and the American people was focused on the drama that resulted in the resignation of Nixon and the swearing in of Gerald R. Ford as president of the United States on August 9, 1974.

Whitehead assured public broadcasters that the White House continued to support long-range funding legislation and that President Ford would place the bill on a list of priority legislation when Congress reconvened on November 18. The president reassured the industry

himself when he sent a message to the annual convention of the NAEB
meeting in Las Vegas in mid-November. The message declared his
support of the Public Broadcasting Financing Act and the Telecommunications Facilities Act and concluded, "I know you share my
hope that the Congress will enact both of these important bills at the
earliest possible date."[108]

Believing that his goals for public broadcasting would at last be
met, Killian resigned as chairman of the board of directors of CPB,
effective December 20, 1974. As he concluded nine years of dedication to the cause of public broadcasting, he recalled a portion of a
letter to the Carnegie Commission from essayist E. B. White regarding the fundamental idea of public broadcasting: "noncommercial
television should address itself to the ideal of excellence, not the
idea of acceptability. . . . It should restate and clarify the social
dilemma and the political pickle. Once in a while it does."[109]

On February 28, 1975, President Ford resubmitted to the new
Congress the White House bill on financing public broadcasting. In
so doing, he stated his conviction that the legislation would assure
that federal support would not dominate the system and encourage
nonfederal contributions. He felt that the need to evaluate the use
of federal funds and the need to operate without restriction were
appropriately reconciled in the five-year funding plan and the annual
oversight hearings in Congress.[110]

An example of the yearly review planned under the proposed
legislation was the hearing before the House of Representatives
Subcommittee on Communications on March 19. Robert S. Benjamin,
chairman of the board of CPB, succinctly traced the development of
the industry. He said educational radio and television began as an
electronic extension of the classroom and in passing the Public Broadcasting Act, Congress had pulled the loosely allied educational stations
together and launched public broadcasting. Benjamin went on to say,
"Solid progress [has been made since then] in sorting out responsibilities and appropriate roles of its constituent organizations, in
planning for the future, in working together to use its limited resource
and staff to achieve one basic purpose today—to provide high quality
public television and radio for the American people." Rogers spoke
concerning the development of the long-range funding proposals and
declared that Congressman Macdonald stood virtually alone in the
House of Representatives during the time of controversy with the
Nixon Administration to carry on the fight for permanent financing
of public broadcasting.[111]

That crisis having passed, there were still two major stumbling
blocks to congressional passage and presidential approval. The
most serious was the determination on the part of the House Appropriations Committee, as Senator Pastore had warned, to pass appro-

priations bills one year at a time. The other was to establish an
authorization/appropriation level that was high enough to provide the
needed funds and to challenge sufficiently the public broadcasting
personnel who must raise matching funds yet low enough to gain the
signature of a president concerned about high government spending.
The friends of public broadcasting in Congress would be called upon
to use their most consummate skills in developing a federal policy
on insulated, long–range funding.

The onus of the task really lay in the House of Representatives,
for in the upper house, public broadcasting's staunch supporters,
Senators Magnuson and Pastore, had the situation well in hand. They
had already held hearings in the previous session and received approval for higher ceilings from Pastore's Subcommittee on Power
and Communications, Magnuson's Committee on Commerce, and the
full Senate. The Appropriations Committee, chaired by Senator
Magnuson, had no strong aversion to multiyear funding.

The Commerce Committee, therefore, reported a bill to the
Senate,[112] based on the previous year's hearings. The bill was
identical to the 1974 legislation, except for a technical change in the
amount of authorization/appropriation to accommodate a change in
the federal fiscal year. The bill authorized more money than the
administration bill. It provided for $88 million in 1976; $22 million
for the 3–month extension of the 1976 fiscal year; $103 million for
1977; $121 million for 1978; $140 million for 1979; and $160 million
for 1980. The administration measure called for $452 million in
federal funds for the period, whereas the Senate bill authorized $634
million. The report pointed out that Congress never intended for
public broadcasting to be permanently funded through annual appropriations and that after considering all the alternatives, the proposed
procedure for matching provided the best solution. It went on to
explain that the growth of the system to 405 radio and television
stations and the substantial audience of 27.8 million households
justified the need for funds and that five-year funding assured stability
in the system and made advanced planning possible. The Senate
report recalled the principle established in 1967, that is, that federal
funds not be used as a vehicle for extraneous government control, and
declared that the proposed legislation reaffirmed and assured that
principle without violating the further principle that Congress was
responsible for designating and disbursing federal funds. CPB would
be held accountable, since its officials would be required to be available to testify, and Congress could take remedial action, if necessary,
by reducing or eliminating advanced funding through amendment.
The matching feature of $1 of federal money for $250 of nonfederal
money assured that the system would not be dominated by the federal
government. Maximum authorizations were a fiscal safeguard against

uncontrolled spending. Finally, the report addressed the question
of localism. Because of the Partnership Agreement between PBS
and CPB and the National Station Agreement to establish the Station
Program Cooperative for the selection of programs, the local stations
were playing a substantial role in decision making. From 40 to 50
percent of the federal appropriations would be provided to local
stations, but the federal share could not exceed 50 percent of the
total nonfederal funds at any one station in order to assure independence. The committee felt that it had at last reached a solution to
long-range financing, if only the appropriations committee would
accept the unusual feature of five-year funding.

The Senate received the report on the proposed law and referred
it to the Senate Appropriations Committee. Senator Pastore, although
not a member of the subcommittee, held a hearing for his public
broadcasting ally Senator Magnuson, chairman of the subcommittee.[11]
Pastore explained that the matter of five-year funding would be worked
out with representatives of the House Appropriations Committee and
that he wanted those invited to testify to build a strong consensus for
the higher ceilings and for five-year funding. A positive record at
the hearing would strengthen the hand of the Senate if they were
required to negotiate in a conference committee with members of
the House of Representatives.

The arguments were well rehearsed and familiar by this time.
The administration ceiling would not provide enough money and would
be not a challenge or incentive, since the system was already generating more than enough nonfederal money to match the maximum
amounts in the administration bill for the first few years. Five-year
funding was necessary to provide stability to the system, time for
advanced planning, and freedom from government interference because
of a program or personality that offended a sensitive government
official.

Other testimony was unfamiliar. Loomis, CPB president, talked
about how public broadcasting had been more closely related to the
interests and consensus of the American people. An Advisory Panel
on Essentials for Effective Minority Programs had produced a study
in 1974 entitled Essentials for Effective Minority Programming (in
Public Broadcasting). In 1975, ACNO conducted a study and wrote
a report Public Broadcasting and Education. A Task Force on
Women in Public Broadcasting had been authorized in October 1974,
and Caroline Isber and Muriel Cartor published a report of the task
force the following year. CPB invited the general public to attend
a board meeting on November 8, 1973, to participate in a discussion
of the role and performance of the corporation; it had expanded its
board of directors to share equally its decision making between
public members and professional manager members. The reorgani-

zation of PBS and the organization of the Association of Public Radio
Stations in 1974 were also cited.

Congressman Macdonald opened five days of hearings[114] before
his Subcommittee on Communications on the administration bill for
$453 million and the Senate bill for $634 million with the statement
that attempts to justify the higher ceiling in the Senate bill would be
an important part of the hearing, as would the need for stable funding.

Benjamin summarized the corporation's funding problems. He
observed that in seven years, the corporation had had to go to Congress six times for authorization and seven times for appropriations.
Even so, the corporation had been funded under continuing resolution
for 39 of its 84 months of existence. It had weathered four presidential vetoes—one of its authorizations and three of its funding through
Labor Department-HEW appropriations. These circumstances of
unpredictable and delayed funding had made planning risky or impossible. Stable funding would enhance the corporation's ability to
mount personnel training programs and engineering studies and to
exploit the potential of a satellite for the distribution of programs.

Benjamin identified Whitehead as the person the corporation had
battled for so many years to get a bill out of the White House. Eleven
alternatives were debated before settling on the matching scheme.
These included a dedicated excise on the sale of radio and television
receivers; a tax on commercial radio and television station gross
revenues, net revenues, or advertising revenues; a tax on cable
television subscription revenues or net revenues; a charge for access
to the spectrum (a license fee); setting aside a portion of income tax
paid by commercial radio and television stations and cable operations;
a dedicated excise tax on residential electric and telephone bills;
proceeds from the profits of operating a domestic satellite system;
a "user charge" paid by families owning radio and television sets;
a Public Broadcasting Development Board financed by the sale of
bonds; federal loan guarantees; and, finally, general tax revenues.
The corporation decided to develop its own plan. The final product
was developed and honed by all interested parties, including broadcasters, educators, administrators, and congressional staff members.
The end product was encompassed in the legislation that Whitehead
and the OTP wrote and for which they gained White House approval.
John Egen, acting director of OTP, stressed administration approval
and quoted President Ford as saying, "this bill is a constructive
approach to the sensitive relationship between federal funding and
freedom of expression. . . . I believe that it will assure the independence of noncommercial radio and television programming for our
nation." Macdonald expressed his pleasure in "working in tandem
with OTP rather than at loggerheads." In a personal reflection, he
described Whitehead as amiable and understanding in private conversation but as adopting a different position and attitude in public.[115]

Representatives of numerous public interest groups spoke on behalf of the Senate version of the bill, which provided higher authorization/appropriation. Macdonald told them that when the bill was scheduled for debate in the House, his staff would contact them to say, "The signal is on to get the people to contact their local representatives, because, obviously you are average citizens but you form a voting bloc, within each constituency." He made it clear that he expected ACNO and other supporting groups to be advocates, as well as advisors.[116]

A report of an organization of business executives, most of whom were chairmen or presidents of major corporations, was thought to be so supportive and so prestigious that it was made part of the record of the hearing. The Committee on Economic Development, through a panel of business executives, educators, and communication experts, published a report after two years of study. Entitled Broadcasting and Cable Television: Policies for Diversity and Change, it supported long-range funding for public television from general tax revenues for periods of five years.

Macdonald applauded this and other demonstrations of support. His final advice, after more than 500 pages of testimony, was "keep on harping. Let Congressmen know they are not the only ones watching and listening to public broadcasting."[117]

The Committee on Commerce adopted the Senate bill with the $634 million spending level and made three changes reflecting a long-standing concern of Brown and others—the bill directed that a significant portion of its funds distributed to licensees be utilized for the development and dissemination of instructional programs. The House version set no limit on the number of times CPB officials would be available for congressional hearings, while the Senate version specified annual appearances. The House bill also called for matching at $1 in tax money for $3 in citizen contributions in fiscal years 1979 and 1980.[118]

The House referred the bill to the Appropriations Committee with respect to its five-year appropriation. The committee reported that it believed the practice of annual review of appropriations was a fundamental responsibility of Congress and should not be abandoned except under the most unusual circumstances. The committee was not persuaded that the budgetary problems of CPB were sufficiently different to justify such a radical consequence of "uncontrolled and back door spending which would be exempt from competition with other programs for federal dollars." A large portion of the budget was already uncontrolled, and the members did not wish to increase the percentage. However, in a compromise engineered by Representative Flood, the committee agreed to approve advance funding in separate legislation in a regular appropriation bill not tied to the authorization bill under consideration. It agreed to an advance appropriation for three years and then annual appropriations for the fiscal year three years ahead. Such an arrangement had been made for a number of health and training programs administered by HEW. Committee members felt they would know the financial outlook three years in advance and still preserve the principal of annual appropriations. The Appropriations Committee said it favored increased appropriations for public broadcasting from other sources. While broadcasters were disappointed, always knowing what the funding would be for three years ahead was preferable to annual appropriation. They would have a substantial period of time to plan and develop high-quality programs.[119]

On the eve of House debate, the Senate Committee on Commerce reported changes in the original bill to reflect the elimination of the appropriation provision and justified the increase in authorization levels from the administration recommendation. The report explained that the increases reflected the projected effects of inflation and also projected the historical growth of the existing public broadcasting entities. The increase also allowed for growth in the number of public radio and television stations. It was also argued that the ceilings had to be raised to provide adequate incentive to seek the maximum practical nonfederal financial support.[120]

The House of Representatives debated the long-range funding bill on November 10. Congressmen Macdonald, Louis Frey, Samuel L. Devine, Brown, and Staggers of the Commerce Committee explained the bill and expressed their enthusiasm for it as a solution to the financing problems that had plagued public broadcasting. Congressmen Flood and Silvio O. Conte of the Appropriations Committee explained their opposition to the joint authorization and appropriation for five years and expressed their willingness to approve advance funding for three years. In a prearranged move, Flood moved on a point of order to strike the appropriation and Macdonald accepted. The bill then passed 336 to 26[121] and was sent to a Senate-House Conference Committee to work out the differences.

The Conference Committee reached agreement and published its report on December 1.[122] The committee agreed to the Senate provision that the matching ratio be one federal dollar for each two and one-half nonfederal dollars in each of the five years. It agreed to drop the House provision that a substantial percentage of the funds be spent on instructional broadcasting, pointing out that the Public Broadcasting Act already covered that subject and that they expected CPB to ensure that the provisions of the act would be carried out. An amendment to the House bill making the corporation subject to certain provisions of the Civil Rights Act of 1967 was dropped, because the corporation was a private corporation not a federal agency.

The corporation had demonstrated that it had a proper concern for the recruitment of women and minorities, however. Finally, it was agreed to adopt the House language on the responsibility of corporation officials to be available for legislative hearings at any time rather than just annually, as it was worded in the Senate version.

The Senate passed the Public Broadcasting Financing Act on December 10, 1975, by voice vote, and the House passed it on December 17 by a vote of 313 to 72.[123]

President Ford signed the bill into law on New Year's Eve and hailed it as a firm basis for the long-term planning of programming and for the development of communications technology for the improved dissemination of educational television and radio. He declared the act would provide "more spine to the stations to produce daring and controversial programs to match the tough problems of the nation."[124]

By the time the legislation passed, the fiscal year was too far advanced to follow through with the three-year advance funding starting with 1976; therefore, Congress appropriated $78 million for that period, with the understanding it would provide three-year funding for 1977, 1978, and 1979. The authorizing legislation set maximum appropriations of $103 million, $121 million, and $140 million in those years. The administration requested only $70 million, $90 million, and $90 million in 1977, 1978, and 1979, respectively. The House Appropriations Committee voted for $96,750,000, $107,150,000, and $120,200,000. The Senate Appropriations Committee, however, approved the same amounts as provided for in the authorizing legislation. A Senate-House Conference Committee reached agreement on the compromise figure of $103 million in fiscal year 1977, $107,150,000 in fiscal year 1978; and $120.2 million in fiscal year 1979.[125] The Appropriations Committee affirmed their determination to honor their part of the agreement and provide appropriations in advance for CPB.

It had taken longer than anyone in 1967 would have anticipated, but public broadcasting at last had long-range financing. Curtailment of domestic spending and preoccupation with the Vietnam War during the Johnson Administration and executive branch interference with public broadcasting for political reasons during the Nixon Administration were the major causes of the delay. Working out the relationship among the constituent parts of the industry was protracted because of the political interference and the slowness in establishing a permanent funding method, of whatever type, for public broadcasting. Nonetheless, without the consummate political skill of a few members of Congress and the absolute conviction that public broadcasting was in the best interest of the American people, the legislation would never have passed. Pastore and Magnuson led in the Senate. Macdonald,

particularly, and Staggers and Flood led in the House of Representatives. Behind the scenes, they threatened and cajoled the recalcitrant—
both in the Congress and the industry. On the stage of public hearings,
they corralled meandering broadcasters long enough to be counted
and contained the quicksilver of CPB, PBS, and the other broadcasting
entities long enough to gauge the warmth of their commitment. They
taught the broadcasters how to perform; they coached broadcasters
in how to obtain funds from their government for the public.

FUNDING OF EDUCATIONAL BROADCASTING FACILITIES

These congressmen taught broadcasters something about dealing
with other parts of the government, for example, HEW, concerning
educational broadcasting facilities. The educational broadcasting
facilities program was a favorite of Congress. Every state and terri-
tory had television receiver grants, and nobody complained except
to say that there was never enough money to satisfy all the needs.
HEW administered the program, which, by 1976, had made 556
grants and helped activate 60 percent of the educational television
stations and 65 percent of the educational radio stations. The number
of noncommercial educational television stations grew from 76, when
the program began in 1962, to 263 in 1976. The number of full service
stations grew from 67, when Congress made noncommercial educational radio stations eligible to receive grants in 1967, to 166 nine
years later. Congress spent $117 million on facilities during the
period, but because of matching provisions and scarcity of federal
funds, the private sector spent over $900 million for educational
broadcasting facilities. Congress felt the extent of nonfederal support
was the best indication of the worth of the facilities program. Despite
the successes, Congress believed HEW failed to give proper attention
to the program. HEW was opposed to hardware programs when Congress first passed the legislation in 1962. Although the department
administrators had changed their minds, this change was not reflected
in the department's budgetary requests, and Congress consistently
authorized more money than asked for by HEW. It was not the case
that the branch chief responsible for long-range funding failed to
appreciate the need. It was the case, however, that with an
administration-imposed budget level for the whole department of
HEW and a vast number of programs competing for full funding within
that limitation, some programs received less than they could use.
When one considers the route a budget request takes through the
federal administration, it is not surprising that what seems crucial
at one layer does not seem so at another. For this program, the

route was Broadcasting Facilities Branch to Bureau of School Systems to Office of Education to secretary's office to Office of Management and Budget and then back down again.

In 1975, when the authorization for the program was in its last year, Secretary Caspar W. Weinberger sent draft legislation to the Senate and House[126] and requested enactment of the Telecommunications Facilities and Demonstration Act of 1975. The proposed legislation would extend the educational broadcasting facilities program for five years, to strengthen the capabilities of existing broadcasting stations, to adapt such stations for additional educational uses, and to build a few more stations to provide equitable coverage. The legislation would authorize demonstrations of nonbroadcast telecommunications technology, such as domestic satellite and cable, to provide health, education, and social services more economically and more efficiently. It was requested that $35 million be authorized over a five-year period for fiscal years 1976 to 1980.

The CPB completed a study in May 1975 at the request of the educational broadcasting facilities program, which concluded that $100 million was needed to improve public television facilities. The CPB's Office of Engineering Research conducted the most extensive study of public television facilities ever made and found that this large sum was needed to provide color transmission and to build new transmission plants and thus solve problems of poor reception.[127]

At hearings conducted in early June,[128] Congressman Macdonald said the subject of the hearings was how much money was needed, not whether the program would be extended. His goal for the program was to make every American accessible to public radio and television and that would require establishing new stations where justified and upgrading existing facilities. Macdonald wanted to know what it would cost.

William A. Morrill, of HEW, argued that there had never been enough money to meet the demands and that his department had not asked for appropriations to equal the amounts Congress authorized because department administration had higher priorities for other programs. Loomis said the program needed $35 million a year just to stand still, not $35 million over five years, as HEW had requested. To increase coverage to 90 percent of the American people, the practical and feasible number, would require upgrading 355 stations, building 40 new ones, and spending $180 million. Gunn, of PBS, said $31 million was needed for a dependable signal for existing stations and $100 million was needed for color cameras and videotape equipment to bring all stations to the best standards. He said $180 million was needed to expand coverage to 90 percent of the country. To expand coverage, 34 stations had their matching funding on hand and needed $68 million, while 48 stations were getting ready and would need $112 million. It was his opinion that facilities were needed and that it was not the proper time to shift to demonstration projects.

Macdonald told the public broadcasters to get together and to agree on a figure. "Get cracking if you want anything to happen," he advised.[129]

Congressmen concerned with public broadcasting wanted facilities; HEW was more interested in demonstrations; and the broadcasters did not have a consensus on how much was needed. To give Congressman Macdonald time to rewrite the legislation, the House continued the existing program for one year, with an appropriation of $12.5 million, rather than the $7 million the administration requested.[130]

Senate hearings on the HEW bill and the House bill in March 1976,[131] brought out OTP's belief on behalf of the White House that more than $7 million a year was excessive, HEW's enthusiasm for demonstrations and complete discretion on their part as to whether the money would be spent on facilities or projects, and public broadcasters' need for funds.

In May, the Senate passed the House version of the legislation.[132] The title—Educational Broadcasting Facilities and Telecommunications Demonstration Act of 1976—reflected the intent of Congress to emphasize the successful broadcasting facilities program. The authorization made the point even clearer. Congress authorized $30 million in 1977 for the broadcasting facilities matching program and $1 million for the nonbroadcast demonstration program. Passage represented, as a report stated, "continuing Congressional commitment," to public broadcasting[133] and showed HEW quite clearly what its priorities ought to be also.

With long-range funding assured and a continuing commitment to facilities funding demonstrated,[134] public broadcasters in 1976 turned their attention to other goals to be achieved and other government assistance to be won.

OTHER GOALS TO BE ACHIEVED

Public broadcasting wanted a less costly and more dependable way to interconnect its stations, and it looked to HEW and the FCC to assist in utilizing a domestic satellite system for this purpose. Harking back to the dreams and plans of the Ford Foundation in 1965, building on experience gained through a NASA-National Institute for Education project in using a communications satellite system to transmit educational programs to remote Rocky Mountain, Alaska, and Appalachian ground terminal, utilizing the leadership of former FCC Commissioner Lee as chairman of a steering committee of the

Public Service Satellite Consortium, spending a $475,000 grant from HEW, and depending on a report of a two-year study that the Ford Foundation paid for in part, PBS told the FCC it planned to link all its stations through three channels of Westar, the domestic satellite system of Western Union, rather than the long lines of AT&T. PBS expected to save $1 million a year. It would borrow $38 million for ten years from lending institutions and assess $25,000 from each station and build 155 to 165 earth stations to receive transmissions and, thus, interconnect every public radio and television station by 1978.[135]

Public broadcasting wanted to make UHF television stations as accessible to viewers as VHF stations, and it asked the FCC to require that all television sets have integrated tuners to make it as easy to dial UHF stations as VHF stations. PBS, CPB, Association of Maximum Service Telecasters, Council of UHF Broadcasting, and the NAB joined forces to ask for this ruling. In 1963, the federal government required that sets manufactured for interstate commerce be capable of receiving both VHF and UHF; however, separate antennae were required for UHF signals, and most sets had separate dials. VHF clicked to each channel, but UHF, like stations on a radio, had to be searched for. Public broadcasters were particularly anxious to join the request to the FCC because 60 percent of the public television stations were on UHF, which because one had to have the fingers of a safecracker to tune in, were not realizing their viewing potential. On January 28, 1970, the FCC ordered that all television receivers with pictures larger than nine inches manufactured after May 1, 1971, have comparable tuning capability for both VHF and UHF channels and that all others be so made after May 1, 1973. The commission later modified its order to require that 10 percent of all models be so manufactured by July 1, 1971, and that all models be so made after July 1, 1974. Since consumers do not replace television receivers as rapidly as they do automobiles, it would take ten years for the ruling to have its intended effect. For the interim, PBS published in 1976 a 16-page booklet, "The PBS/UHF Guide," to instruct viewers in the art of dialing UHF channels and to advise them on the appropriate antenna for each situation.[136]

Public broadcasting wanted to improve VHF penetration in metropolitan areas, and it asked the FCC to add 200 VHF low-power stations to the table of assignments. Computer-assisted engineering studies showed that low-power stations transmitting 20 to 30 miles could be dropped into the existing table of assignments, significantly increasing opportunities for diversified programming and minority ownership. PBS wanted these saved for licensing to public broadcasting.[137]

Public broadcasting wanted to provide better coverage for full-service public radio, and it expected the FCC to develop a new table of assignments for the FM channels reserved and assigned to non-commercial educational radio. The FCC was so anxious over the years for educators to make use of the reserved channels that it encouraged educational institutions to establish their 10-watt stations anywhere on the reserved spectrum that suited their fancy and which did not interfere with another station. As the full-service public radio stations came into existence, they kept banging into the 10-watt limited service stations and also caused some potential interference with television channel 6 and some Canadian frequency assignments. As full-service public radio broadcasting became more widespread, the problem first identified in FCC Docket 14185 in 1968 became increasingly more acute but the solution more elusive.[138] The FCC was in an analogous position with the Federal Radio Commission about 50 years earlier. Anything it did to bring about a more orderly development for the full-service stations with their larger audience, better financing, and broader programming threatened the 10-watt stations, which were on the air first, served a useful educational function, were in a precarious financial situation, and often operated with obsolete equipment. But the FCC had so carefully and faithfully nurtured the 10-watt stations that there was little danger that the regulatory agency would take action which would destroy its offspring.

Finally, public broadcasting wanted to make FM public radio as easy to receive as AM commercial radio, and it looked to Congress in this instance for assistance in passing legislation that would require all radio receivers manufactured for interstate trade to be capable of receiving both AM and FM radio signals. Congressmen Van Deerlin and Brown, ranking members of the House Subcommittee on Communications, introduced the bill for the broadcasters in 1976.[139]

These were the specific matters being considered and yet to be resolved. There were other concerns as well.

Senator Pastore announced in 1976 that he would not seek reelection. Congressman Macdonald died in May 1976. They would be greatly missed, but there would be other leaders, and there were already many other friends and supporters in the federal government.

Killian's prestige and experience saved the Corporation for Public Broadcasting and Rogers's initiative revamped the Public Broadcasting Service. In establishing the dual leadership roles of CPB and PBS, those responsible also created redundant and wasteful bureaucracies, which duplicated efforts and absorbed funds that could be better used for creative programming. They failed to settle the question of ultimate jurisdiction over national programming for public television. Those problems required solution. Other organizational crises would occur and other leaders would arrive.

SUMMARY

Still, the basic policy commitment has been made. Public broadcasting is a product of the federal government. One cannot gainsay,
however, in considering the making of public broadcasting, the
enormous financial and spiritual contributions of the Ford Foundation
or the dedication of a spartan group of educators hanging on over a
period of 50 years in schools, colleges, and universities, or the
dedication of a new tribe of professional public broadcasters spawned
in the last decade.

In looking back over more than 65 years of development from
primitive college laboratories to a sophisticated industry, it has
been federal officials—some elected, some appointed, some hired—
who time after time welded disparate, inarticulate, politically naive
forces together in a consensus of support for federal policies and
programs that are providing the American public a noncommercial
educational broadcasting service.

As a result of the federal impetus and the federal leaders who
have shaped the system, the industry has advanced to the point that
it builds its own consensus, speaks its own mind, and maintains its
own political conscience and integrity.

It is a product of the federal government, but it is no longer
solely dependent on the federal impetus.

NOTES

1. New York Times, May 3, 1970, September 28, 1970.

2. Ibid., December 20, 1972, January 16, 1975.

3. House of Representatives, Committee on Appropriations,
Subcommittee, Office of Education and Related Agencies Appropriations for 1972, Hearings, 92 Cong., 1 Sess.

4. Senate, Committee on Appropriations, Subcommittee, Office
of Education and Related Agencies Appropriations for 1972, Hearings,
92 Cong., 1 Sess.

5. New York Times, June 16, 1971.

6. Ibid., April 3, 1971, April 15, 1971.

7. Federal Communications Commission, Commission Reports,
2nd Series, vol. 31 (Washington, D.C.: U.S. Government Printing
Office, 1972), pp. 496-506.

8. New York Times, June 16, 1971.

9. Ibid., July 5, 1971, July 11, 1971; Albert L. Singer, Jr.,
"The Carnegie Report Revisited," Educational Broadcasting Review 5,
no. 4 (August 1971): 3-10.

10. New York Times, August 22, 1971.

11. John W. Macy, Jr., To Irrigate a Wasteland: The Struggle to Shape a Public Television System in the United States (Berkeley: University of California Press, 1974), pp. 96-98 (hereafter cited as Macy, To Irrigate a Wasteland); New York Times, October 13, 1971.

12. Clay T. Whitehead, "Local Autonomy and the Fourth Network: Striking a Balance," Educational Broadcasting Review 5, no. 6 (December 1971); New York Times, October 21, 1971.

13. Steve Millard, "The Story of Public Broadcasting," Broadcasting (November 8, 1971); Congressional Record, CXVII, 40516; "Public Broadcasting: Controversy over Federal Role," Congressional Quarterly, December 11, 1971.

14. Congressional Record, CXVI, 44371; New York Times, December 2, 1971, December 3, 1971.

15. Macy, To Irrigate a Wasteland, pp. 69-71.

16. New York Times, December 23, 1971; Alfred I. du Pont-Columbia University, Survey of Broadcast Journalism, 1970-71 (New York: Grosset and Dunlop, 1971), chap. 4.

17. Public Papers of the Presidents of the United States. Richard M. Nixon, 1972 (Washington, D.C.: U.S. Government Printing Office, 1973), document 15.

18. Senate, Committee on Judiciary, Subcommittee on Constitutional Rights, Freedom of the Press, 92 Cong., 1 Sess.

19. House of Representatives, Hearings on Bill 92-12808.

20. New York Times, February 2, 1972, February 7, 1972.

21. House of Representatives, Bill 92-11807.

22. House of Representatives, Bill 92-13007.

23. House of Representatives, Committee on Interstate and Foreign Commerce, Subcommittee on Communications and Power, Financing for Public Broadcasting, 1972, Hearings on HR 11807, HR 7443, and HR 12808, 92 Cong., 2 Sess.; see also Fred Powledge, Public Television: A Question of Survival (New York: American Civil Liberties Union, 1972).

24. New York Times, February 23, 1972, March 8, 1972.

25. House of Representatives, Report 92-979.

26. Ibid.

27. New York Times, April 5, 1972, May 25, 1972, June 1, 1972.

28. Congressional Record, CXVIII, 19344-19456, 19478-19485.

29. Senate, Committee on Commerce, Hearings on Nominations, 92 Cong., 2 Sess.

30. Senate, Report 92-892.

31. Congressional Record, CXVIII, 21992-22010.

32. House of Representatives, Document 92-320.

33. New York Times, July 1, 1972.

34. Congressional Record, CXVIII, 24300, 28611, 26572.

35. Ibid., 24805.

36. House of Representatives, Report 92-1292.

37. New York Times, August 11, 1972 .

38. Congressional Record, CXVIII, 28279-28285.

39. Public Law 92-411.

40. New York Times, September 19, 1972, September 22, 1972.

41. Congressional Record, CXVIII, 31924; Chicago Sun-Times, October 11, 1972.

42. New York Times, October 13, 1972.

43. Ibid., November 2, 1972.

44. Ibid., November 11, 1972, November 14, 1972, November 22, 1972.

45. Ibid., December 19, 1972, December 20, 1972.

46. Ibid., December 19, 1972.

47. Ibid., December 20, 1972.

48. Ibid., December 21, 1972.

49. Ibid., January 6, 1973.

50. Ibid., January 12, 1973, January 21, 1973.

51. Ibid., January 24, 1973.

52. Ibid., January 31, 1973.

53. Ibid.

54. Ibid.

55. Ibid., May 28, 1973.

56. Ibid., March 8, 1973.

57. Ibid., March 27, 1973.

58. Ibid., March 31, 1973.

59. Senate, Committee on Commerce, Subcommittee on Communications, Public Broadcasting, Hearings on S 1090 and S 1228, 93 Cong., 1 Sess.

60. Ibid.

61. Ibid.

62. Senate, Report 93-123.

63. House of Representatives, Committee on Appropriations, Subcommittee on Departments of Labor and Health, Education and Welfare, Hearings on Appropriations for 1974, 93 Cong., 1 Sess.

64. Senate, Report 93-123.

65. Senate, Committee on Appropriations, Subcommittee on Departments of Labor and Health, Education and Welfare and Related Agencies, Hearings on HR 8877, 93 Cong.,1 Sess.

66. New York Times, April 14, 1973, April 19, 1973.

67. Columbia Broadcasting System, "Inside Public Television," a television program transmitted April 20, 1976.

68. New York Times, April 20, 1973.

69. Ibid., April 23, 1973.

70. Congressional Record, CXIX, 8401-8415.

71. New York Times, May 9, 1973.

72. Ibid., May 28, 1973.

73. Ibid., May 10, 1973 (CPB proposal), May 18, 1973 (PBS proposal), June 1, 1973 (compromise agreement).

74. Ibid., June 1, 1973, June 3, 1973, June 8, 1973.

75. House of Representatives, Committee on Interstate and Foreign Commerce, Subcommittee on Communications and Power, Public Broadcasting, 1973, Hearings on HR 4560, HR 6872, HR 8538, and S 1090, 93 Cong., 1 Sess.

76. Ibid.

77. Ibid.

78. House of Representatives, Report 93-324.

79. New York Times, June 14, 1973.

80. Congressional Record, CXIX, H 6423-H 6452.

81. Ibid., S 14546.

82. Public Law 93-84.

83. New York Times, December 17, 1973.

84. Ibid., December 30, 1973.

85. Ibid., November 16, 1973.

86. Ibid., November 16, 1973.

87. Ibid., December 14, 1973, December 28, 1973, December 30, 1973.

88. Ibid., December 20, 1973; Senate, Committee on Appropriations, Subcommittee on Departments of Labor and Health, Education and Welfare and Related Agencies, Hearings on HR 15580, 93 Cong., 2 Sess.

89. New York Times, January 24, 1974, February 14, 1974, March 15, 1974, June 15, 1974, July 21, 1974, September 29, 1974.

90. Ibid.

91. House of Representatives, Committee on Appropriations, Subcommittee on Departments of Labor and Health, Education and Welfare, Hearings on Appropriations for 1975, 93 Cong., 2 Sess.

92. "How Fares the NEH?" Change 6 (April 1974): 49; New York Times, June 13, 1974, June 27, 1974.

93. New York Times, June 24, 1974.

94. Ibid., April 16, 1974, July 11, 1974.

95. Ibid., January 24, 1974, May 31, 1974.

96. Ibid., September 16, 1974, November 7, 1974.

97. Corporation for Public Broadcasting, Report of the Task Force on Long-Range Financing of Public Broadcasting (Washington, D.C.: 1973); see Macy, To Irrigate a Wasteland, pp. 109-14.

98. Ibid.

99. New York Times, January 10, 1974, January 16, 1974.

100. Congressional Record, CXX, 13552.

101. New York Times, July 17, 1974, July 21, 1974. See also Les Brown, "Reprieve for Public Television," Change (September 1974): 43-44.

102. Congressional Record, CXX, 13553.

103. Senate, Bill 93-3825.

104. Senate, Committee on Commerce, Subcommittee on Communications, Public Broadcasting Financing Act of 1974, Hearings on S 3825, 93 Cong., 2 Sess.

105. Ibid.

106. Senate, Report 93-1113.

107. Senate, Bill 93-4223.

108. New York Times, November 2, 1974, November 19, 1974.

109. Ibid., December 20, 1974.

110. Senate, Bill 94-893; Congressional Record, CXXI, S 2817.

111. House of Representatives, Committee on Interstate and Foreign Commerce, Subcommittee on Communications, Public Broadcasting Overview, Hearings on Activities in the Field of Public Broadcasting, 94 Cong., 1 Sess.

112. Senate, Report 94-55.

113. Senate, Committee on Appropriations, Subcommittee on Departments of Labor and Health, Education and Welfare and Related Agencies, Hearings on HR 8069, 94 Cong., 1 Sess.

114. House of Representatives, Committee on Interstate and Foreign Commerce, Subcommittee on Communications, Long-Range Financing for Public Broadcasting, Hearings on HR 4563, 94 Cong., 1 Sess.

115. Ibid.

116. Ibid.

117. Ibid.

118. House of Representatives, Report 94-245, part I.

119. Ibid., part II.

120. Senate, Report 94-447.

121. Congressional Record, CXXI H 10866-H 10884.

122. House of Representatives, Report 94-713.

123. Congressional Record, CXXI, S 20863, H 12335, H 12859.

124. Public Law 94-192; New York Times, January 6, 1976.

125. House of Representatives, Report 94-1219; Senate, Report 94-997; House of Representatives, Report 94-1384.

126. Senate, Bill 94-1257.

127. New York Times, May 8, 1975.

128. House of Representatives, Committee on Interstate and Foreign Commerce, Subcommittee on Communications, Telecommunications Facilities and Demonstration Act of 1975, Hearings on HR 4564, 94 Cong., 1 Sess.

129. House of Representatives, Report 94-245.

130. Congressional Record, CXXII, H 82.

131. Senate, Committee on Commerce, Subcommittee on Communications, Educational Broadcasting Facilities, Hearings on HR 4564, HR 9630, and S 1257, 94 Cong., 1 Sess.

132. Congressional Record, CXXII, S 7109.

133. House of Representatives, Report 94-772.

134. Public Law 94-309.

135. New York Times, January 6, 1975, January 22, 1975, February 9, 1976, February 12, 1976.

136. Ibid., July 22, 1975, November 13, 1976; Federal Communications Commission, Annual Report, 1971 (Washington, D.C.: U.S. Government Printing Office, 1972), p. 37.

137. New York Times, January 15, 1976, January 28, 1976.

138. Federal Communications Commission, Annual Report 1968 (Washington, D.C.: U.S. Government Printing Office, 1969), p. 36.

139. House of Representatives, Bill 94-11888.

ABOUT THE AUTHOR

GEORGE H. GIBSON is Vice President and Dean of the College and Professor of History at St. Lawrence University, Canton, New York. Before August 1977, he was Assistant Provost and Associate Professor of History at the University of Delaware, Newark, Delaware. Until 1969, he was coordinator of the Hagley Graduate Program, Eleutherian Mills-Hagley Foundation, Greenville, Delaware. Dr. Gibson has been managing editor of Delaware History from 1964-77 and is the general editor of the Marguerite du Pont de Villiers Boden Documents Series, publishing activities of the Historical Society of Delaware, Wilmington, Delaware.

Dr. Gibson has published previously in the field of U.S. history. He edited the Collected Essays of Richard S. Rodney on Early Delaware and the Diary of William P. Brobson. His articles have appeared in Proceedings of the Unitarian Historical Society, North Carolina Historical Review, Virginia Magazine of History and Biography, Georgia Historical Quarterly, Delaware History, Journal of Southern History, Labor History, Textile History Review, Furman Studies, and Sea Frontiers.

Dr. Gibson holds a B.A. from Furman University, Greenville, South Carolina, and an M.A. and Ph.D. from the University of North Carolina at Chapel Hill, where he was a Danforth Fellow.

*THE FUTURE OF PUBLIC BROADCASTING
edited by Douglass Cater
Michael J. Nathan

*MASS MEDIA SYSTEMS AND EFFECTS
W. Phillips Davison
James Boylan
Frederick T.C. Yu

*THE MEDIA AND THE LAW
edited by Howard Simons
Joseph A. Califano

POLITICS IN PUBLIC SERVICE ADVERTISING
ON TELEVISION
David L. Paletz
Roberta E. Pearson
Donald L. Willis

THE SUPREME COURT IN THE MEDIA:
A Theoretical and Empirical Analysis
David W. Leslie
D. Brock Hornby

*Also available in paperback as a PSS Student Edition